5-

CUISINE RAPIDE

Clarkson N. Potter, Inc./Publishers

NEW YORK

DISTRIBUTED BY CROWN PUBLISHERS, INC.

CUISINE

230 DELECTABLE
RECIPES
FOR COOKS
IN A HURRY

Carol Cutler

RAPIDE

Published by Clarkson N. Potter, Inc., One Park Aveune, New York, New York 10016, and simultaneously in Canada by General Publishing Company Limited

Previously published as The Six-minute Soufflé

Manufactured in the United States of America

Library of Congress Cataloging in Publication Data
Cutler, Carol.
   Cuisine rapide.

   Previously published as: Six-minute soufflé and other culinary delights. c1976.
   Includes index.
   1. Cookery, French. I. Title.
TX719.C87 1983   641.5'55   82-16566
ISBN: 0-517-54901-8
10 9 8 7 6 5 4 3 2 1
First Paperback Edition

CONTENTS

INTRODUCTION

With so many cookbooks on the market, one should have a very good reason to write still another one. Here, along with some autobiographical explanation, is my reason:

I fell in love with good food during the twelve years I lived in Paris. Given the glory of French cuisine and the splendid fresh products available in that country, it was easy to be seduced by the joys of the table. With my husband, I traveled throughout France and much of Europe, eating in good restaurants and, whenever possible, talking to chefs about how and why they did certain things. I took cooking lessons at the Cordon Bleu and from Simone Beck and Louisette Bertholle, two estimable French ladies who wrote *Mastering the Art of French Cooking* along with our own Julia Child. Over a period of time, I became an accomplished cook, and I now realize that I enjoyed showing off my skill at dinner parties. I would put in long hours and much work in the kitchen preparing classic and difficult dishes and would glow with pride when they were extravagantly praised, especially by my French guests. Toward the end of my stay in Paris, I began to wonder if I was putting in too much time on things culinary, but in the food-oriented society in which I lived, I put that heretic thought out of my mind.

Back in the United States, my attitude changed in a hurry. For one thing, I took a full-time job, and it was obviously impractical to devote as much time to cooking as I had in Paris. Also, I became mildly affected by the climate of women's liberation and began thinking, "What the devil am I doing struggling with this recalcitrant puff paste when he [my husband] is lolling about reading the sports page?" Finally, the city where we live had a lot to do with changing my habits. Washington is an intensely political place, filled with conversation that is informed, valuable, interesting, and catty. I determined that I wouldn't be filleting duck breasts in the kitchen when the current scandal concerning the White House or the State Department was being discussed in my living room.

So I began to search for a style of cooking that would satisfy my liking for fine food and my need for more time. I looked over cookbooks that promised good cooking in a hurry and found none that met my requirements. In some the recipes took too long to do. Others suggested that you stir dried onion soup into sour cream and call it a gourmet dish. No thanks. Then I buckled down to finding out whether new techniques and shortcuts would permit excellent dishes, menus, and dinner parties to be put together in reasonably short amounts of time. It worked, and this book is the result of my experiments.

The luckiest break I got was discovering that, in many classic recipes that I love, certain traditional steps could be eliminated without affecting the results noticeably. Let us take a couple of examples: When I was taught to make champagne sauce, one step was mincing the shallot; another step was straining the shallot bits out of the sauce. Now I peel and halve a shallot and stick each piece on a toothpick in the sauce. After the sauce has simmered, I retrieve the shallots cum toothpicks. It's quicker and the sauce tastes the same. I also have ceased browning meat (Escoffier, forgive me!) before putting it into stews and similar dishes. I realize this is the rankest kind of culinary heresy, but try it; you will save time, dirty one fewer frying pan, and no one will notice the difference. (Incidentally, throughout the book I try to hold down the number of pots and pans used. I not only left my heart in Paris; I left my maid there.)

Truth-in-packaging is a consumer demand these days, and I do not want to claim too much for this book. I am not, and I cannot promise "instant haute cuisine" or "gastronomy without effort." Many classic French dishes require time-consuming steps, meticulous attention to detail, and considerable labor. Therefore they are not within the scope of this book. The classics that I could streamline, though, are here, and I think they will please you. In addition, appropriate recipes that I devised and that were given to me by friends are included.

If speeding up preparation time is my main theme, cooking in advance is the next one. A working wife or busy host cannot remain calm while putting together a dinner party under the gun; and guests aren't comfortable when the hostess is harassed. Doing things hours before or the day before makes life easier for both cook and guests. So, toward the end of each recipe, there are instructions on how the dish can be done ahead of time. Happily, many dishes are better for having matured a day in the refrigerator, which makes a virtue out of necessity. Not all the do-ahead recipes are for casseroles and stews. There is, for example, a cold *Boeuf à la Mode en Gelée* (Braised Beef in Aspic) that is a beautiful looking and tasting party dish.

There are times when a person has not prepared anything in advance, comes home after a day's work, and wants to put together a good, fast meal. One answer is to use convenience or frozen foods, which I am not high on. For people who want another solution, a number of complete meals that can be prepared at the end of a working day are in the chapter on menus. Other last-minute recipes can be found throughout the book.

I am a fancier of cold main courses, and not just in the summertime. A cold main course is an ace in the hole all year round. It usually must be made the day before, so there is less last minute flurry. Knowing that the main dish is made builds a busy cook's confidence. What is more, cold main courses are not banal at dinner parties, so they are appreciated and remembered. I like to precede a cold main dish with a hot first course and follow it with a hot vegetable as a separate course. If the vegetable course is omitted, it is a good idea to serve a hot dessert, producing a nice sequence of hot, cold, and then hot dishes. The menu chapter contains a number of meals planned around cold main courses. Try them; they unfrazzle a cook's nerves.

Every recipe in the book is timed. The amount of time one spends preparing a dish is the first figure given: Working Time. Then come marinating, baking, broiling, cooking, chilling, or freezing time. This is done to avoid the false impression that, say, because Baked Ratatouille requires only 12 minutes of work, one can come home at the end of the day and still have it ready for dinner. In fact it takes 4 to 5 hours of baking time in a slow oven, but that isn't time you have to put in; nobody stands around watching things bake.

The Working Times are as accurate as I could make them. Every recipe was timed more than once, without the cook racing at breakneck speed. Of course it is assumed that persons using this book have some proficiency in the kitchen. If someone spends five minutes peeling a potato, he'll take more time than is listed. My timing started the moment work began after all the required ingredients were on the counter. Getting everything together first is a good work habit that most experienced chefs practice, even when not trying to save time. Since a recipe may call for thawed spinach or butter at room temperature, it is most important to read through a recipe before starting so that the ingredients will be at the right temperature.

If a recipe is entirely new to a reader (let's say he's never seen a paté), it should take him some extra time to prepare the dish on the first try. The next time he'll know which baking dish to use, how to handle the meat, and what the end product is supposed to look like.

As often as possible, the recipes have been written to help one plan one's working time. When onions are to simmer for 15 minutes, the directions proceed to the next step. No one should watch onions simmer; it's boring. Simmering time or baking time is a great time to go off and set the table, make a phone call, or sit down with a glass of wine.

Although this book was written mainly to help readers cook well and quickly and is by no means a "diet book," I did not want to ignore good nutrition, food safety, and good heart health. Let us take them up one by one.

I admit to a strong bias in favor of fresh foods. Even though prepared foods are famous as time-savers, I used them as little as possible in recipes. (An exception is canned chicken and beef broth, which come in very handy.) Fresh foods almost always taste better and often they are safer, not containing additives that can be dangerous. Many prepared foods have been liberally "helped" with sugar in unconscionable amounts (which is fattening, a cause of tooth decay, and possibly connected with heart attacks); during processing, most manufacturers lace food with walloping amounts of salt, one of the chief causes of high blood pressure in this country; Red #2 food coloring, nitrates and nitrites (which are suspected of having links to cancer); and assorted artificial colors and flavors, preservatives and chemicals, which may turn out to do the Lord only knows what.

So the recipes call for no packaged mixes. Not a single sliver of bacon or frankfurter is used, since they are laced with nitrates. Only six frozen foods are recommended, for times when their fresh equivalents have short seasons, such as raspberries, peas, and lima beans. Elsewhere, recipes are given for fresh products, with notes on how to make adjustments if frozen food must be substituted. Actually one doesn't give up much by eschewing so-called convenience foods. They cost more than the real thing; they don't taste nearly so good, and sometimes they don't even save you any time.

A word about good heart health: Over 90 percent of the recipes on these pages come with low-cholesterol variations. Recipes that normally contain saturated animal fats have been reworked to eliminate those products, which most heart specialists now believe contribute to today's epidemic of heart attacks, especially among men. The theories used in altering the recipes were based on research done for my earlier book, *Haute Cuisine for Your Heart's Delight—A Low-Cholesterol Cookbook for Gourmets*. I strongly advise that you cut down on the use of salt or eliminate it entirely wherever possible. You can perk up food flavors with a squeeze or two of lemon juice, a good grinding of pepper, or herbs and spices to taste.

And a final note about good food: Now we come back to square one, because this is what the book is basically all about—good food without having to spend too much of your life in the kitchen preparing it. More and more in this country, if you want to dine extremely well, you will have to do so at home. There are some exceptions which each reader knows, but most restaurants are simply not worth eating in. By and large, restaurant cooking is poor, service inept or surly, and the quality of ingredients dubious. And all that was before spiraling costs caused many restaurant owners to boost prices and cut corners on quality. In many posh places—unknown to the patrons—the skill of the "chef" lies in removing the cellophane from fancy frozen dishes, like *Chicken à la Kiev* or *Quenelles de Brochet*, and reheating them. These "gourmet specialties" come from huge factory kitchens, often half a continent away from the restaurant. Again with some exceptions, such is the future of dining out in America. Soon good cooking will be found almost exclusively in private homes. This book is aimed at helping you get ready. Bon appétit.

CUISINE RAPIDE

MENUS

The following menus were planned from recipes in this book. A few dishes, marked by brackets, are not in the book, since hardly anyone needs a recipe for (salad) and will most likely buy (vanilla ice cream). The menus are made up of colors, textures, and flavors that I think follow each other logically and well. I must stress that the suggestions are merely that and are not meant to be unchangeable. So if oysters are not for you, forget Oysters in Champagne Sauce and try, perhaps, Hot Mushroom Canapés before the Escalope Colonnade. Another example: Peppers and Anchovies, Italian Style, may be too Italian for some tastes before going on to the Tuna-Macaroni Salad. If so, Sunday Night Soup (Spinach and Beef Broth) would fill the bill. The menus were designed to allow you to pick and choose at will. They will be better, though, if in substituting, an effort is made to keep their balance of colors, textures, and flavors.

With each menu I have suggested wines that I think go well with particular dishes or the entire meal. Any similar wine, or any wine you like with a certain food, should be freely substituted. In this vein, I remember a bit of advice given some years ago by André Soltner, owner of the Lutèce restaurant, which was then considered New York's finest, "The best fish dish we make," he said, "is just as good with a Riesling as with a Bâtard Montrachet." Since Lutèce charged three times more for the Montrachet than for the Riesling, his point is worth remembering.

When the budget is tight, you can serve California jug wines at dinner parties. They are outstanding values and better than some French country wines now being sold here. I have had good luck with, among the reds, Louis Martini Mountain Claret, Gallo Hearty Burgundy, the Christian Brothers Burgundy, and C. K. Mondavi Zinfandel. Among the whites, Inglenook Vintage Chablis, Gallo Chablis Blanc, the Christian Brothers Rhine Wine, Korbel Mountain White, and Almadén Mountain Chablis have worked out well. With a little trial and error, you can find your own favorite jug wines. If you serve them from crystal decanters, wine snobs will be intimidated into silence.

As for the temperature to serve wine, the old rules are collapsing under the desire to be different. Once the only reds that would be chilled were Beaujolais, Côtes-du-Rhône, country wines, and Italy's Lambrusco. Now Parisians who are more chic than knowledgeable are refrigerating all reds, even fine Bordeaux. Better not to be chic, chilling kills the aroma and flavor of a good red wine. Of course white wines and rosés should be served well chilled. The splendid sweet dessert wines from Sauternes and Barsac should be served very cold. They are underrated and underpriced these days, and I like to end a formal dinner with them. Even if you aren't serving a sweet, letting guests sip a small glass of chilled Sauternes as dessert is a memorable end to a meal.

Brunch

Grapefruit Jaipur

Scrambled eggs with onions
Corn pudding

[**Fresh Fruit**]

Whatever white wine you like, say a dry Vouvray, Muscadet, or Riesling from Alsace or California.

Aspèrges à la normande *(Asparagus with cream sauce on toast)*
Apple compote

Peach butter on [**thin slice of sponge cake**]

A white Burgundy or Burgundy style from California.

Cheddar cheese soufflé
Céleri gratin niçois *(Baked celery in tomato sauce)*

Honey mousse

A rosé would complement this brunch.

[**Bloody Marys**]
Deep-fried eggs
Sunny rice

Pear compote

No wine needed after Bloody Marys.

[**Sliced cold Virginia ham**]
Cold tomatoes with hot curry sauce
[**Sliced cucumbers, sprinkled with salt and dillweed**]

Mincemeat squares

Because of the hot curry sauce, an ice-cold wine is most welcome—a California Chablis or a rosé from Provence.

Luncheon or after-the-theater supper

Scallop soup

Emerald cream *(Cold herb custard)*

Tomato bake, as a separate course

Pear compote

A white from the Loire, such as Sancerre, a Riesling from Alsace or California, an Italian Soave.

Superquick borscht

Marinated fish Piraeus
[**Salad**]

Jamaican squares

Marinades are not the best friends to wine. So a simple white—a Muscadet, Macon Blanc, California Pinot Blanc, or better jug wine.

Provençal fish salad

Radis au beurre *(Sautéed radishes)* **as a separate course**

Frozen maple mousse

Any light, dry white, say a Muscadet, Macon, California Riesling, Pinot Blanc, or Chablis.

Brioches aveyronnaises *(Hot Roquefort-filled rolls)*
Baked cucumbers

Oatmeal cake

A chilled Beaujolais with the hot cheese rolls—quite a combination.

Country cheese pie
Haricots verts Provençal *(Provençal string beans)*

Orange-mincemeat squares

The cheese pie seems to ask for a chilled Pinot Chardonnay from Burgundy or California—or your favorite rosé.

Clams florentine

[Salad]

[Cheese and crackers]

An Italian Soave, a German Moselle, a Riesling from Alsace or California. Red wine with the cheese only if your guests aren't going back to work.

Greek eggplant soup

Cold herb omelet
Hot Dijon-style mushrooms

Peanut-buttered bread and [Fresh fruit]

A light white Burgundy, like a Pouilly-Fuissé, would enhance the omelet. Or that most versatile luncheon wine, a crisp rosé from France or California.

Peppers and anchovies, Italian style

Tuna-macaroni salad with black olives and potato chips

Six-minute chocolate cake

No fine wine here—an inexpensive white, say an Italian Frascati or California Chablis.

Informal dinners

Avgolemono (Greek egg and lemon soup)

Marinated turkey drumsticks
Mashed potatoes in red wine
Lettuce in cream

Blueberry clafouti

The turkey imitates game, so try a big red, a Burgundy, Châteauneuf-du-Pape, California Pinot Noir, or Barolo from northern Italy.

Country bean-and-cabbage soup with [French bread]

[Cheese and crackers]

[Fruit] or Coffee granita

Wine isn't needed with soup, but a cool Beaujolais or Zinfandel will go from the hearty soup right through the cheese.

Eggplant caviar

Cassoulet (Baked beans with meats in tomato sauce)

[Fresh fruit] and/or Frozen banana morsels

With Cassoulet the French like a Corbières or Cahors from the countryside where the dish originated. A sturdy Côtes-du-Rhône does just as well.

[Prosciutto or other cured pork]

Shrimp steamed in beer

Stir-fried bean sprouts

Blueberried cake

A well-chilled Muscadet, Chablis, Riesling from Alsace or California, or Pinot Blanc would suit the shrimp.

[Prosciutto or other cured pork]

Swiss fondue

[Salad]

[Fresh fruit]

The Swiss have a legend that cold white wine or beer with fondue causes a lump in the stomach. It's never happened to me. I think their legend is merely an excuse to drink Kirsch with fondue. That is good too.

Hot mushroom canapés with cocktails

Pumpkin supper
Golden grilled tomatoes

Baked bananas

A rosé from the Rhone, Provence, or California would bridge these courses very well.

Dinners for entertaining

Crevettes en aspic (Shrimp in aspic)

Daube de mouton (Lamb Stew with red wine)

[Salad]

Crème aux poires (Pear cream)

A Muscadet or other dry white wine. Then,
with the lamb, a Bordeaux, Côtes-du-Rhône,
or California Zinfandel.

Ramequin d'oeuf Provençal (Egg ramekins)

Pâté de poulet et jambon (Chicken and ham
pâté)

Chinese asparagus

Frozen maple mousse

A perfect one-wine meal. Perhaps a white
Burgundy, such as Meursault, or a Pinot
Chardonnay from California.

Roquefort soufflé (Hot cheese soufflé)

Boeuf à la mode en gelée (Braised beef in
aspic)

Baked ratatouille

Champagne snow

With the hot cheese and cold beef, try a light
red wine —a Beaujolais, Zinfandel, small
Bordeaux, or California Gamay.

Cold pumpkin soup

Saumon au vin rouge (Salmon in red wine)

Spinach gratin, as a separate course

Pears with ginger

Red wine with fish? Sure, especially since the
salmon is cooked with it. A cool small Burgundy, say a Savigny, a Zinfandel, or one of
the bigger Beaujolais wines.

Huitres aux champagne (Oysters with champagne sauce)

Escalope colonnade (Veal or pork scallop
with artichokes and tomato garnish)

Kidney bean purée

Alsatian pears (Poached pears with raspberry
sauce)

If any champagne is left from the sauce, serve
it. Otherwise a Riesling from Alsace. The
same wine with the escalope or a good rosé or
cool light red.

Grapefruit Jaipur

Pâté panaché en aspic (Mixed pâté in aspic)

[Black olives and potato chips]
Gratin parisien (Mushroom gratin)

Baked strawberries

A dry rosé from Provence, the Rhône, or
California. A dry white Graves or Burgundy
also would do well.

Cold tomatoes with hot curry sauce

Langue de boeuf Lucullus (Stuffed beef
tongue in aspic)

Laitues braisées (Braised lettuce)

Apple cake mousse

A good rosé, good white, or small red Burgundy, chilled Beaujolais or California Zinfandel.

Hot asparagus soup

Vitello tonnato (Veal with tuna sauce)

Mousse aux concombres (Cucumber mousse)

Pêches caramelisées (Caramelized peaches)

This veal dish warrants your best white Bur-
gundy, a Chassagne-Montrachet, or a good
Chablis. Or, if you like, a fine Bordeaux or
Chianti Classico.

Courgettes à la Grecque (*Marinated zucchini*)

Hot baked lamb curry
Baked cranberries
Fried chick-peas

Pear gratin

The curry flavor says save your best wines. A rosé, Beaujolais, Zinfandel, or young Spanish Rioja will do fine.

Danish cauliflower

Boeuf à l'estouffade des mariniers du Rhône (*Beef braised in piquant sauce*)

Baked gnocchi

Tropical sherbet

Would you believe a cold Châteauneuf-du-Pape? That's what they serve with estouffade in Avignon. Or try a cold red Côtes-du-Rhône or California Pinot Noir.

Cold cucumber soup

Coq au vin (*Chicken in red wine*)
New potatoes sautéed in butter
[**Salad**]

Cobbled peach bake

Coq au Vin wants a big wine to talk back to it —a red Burgundy, St. Émilion, Châteauneuf-du-Pape, Italian Barolo, or California Pinot Noir.

Bean-sprout salad

Terrine de foies de volaille (*Chicken-liver pâté*)
[**Potato chips**]

Baked celery with herb sauce, as a separate course

Champagne fruit cup

It's easy to match this terrine with a red wine: a Burgundy, Bordeaux, California Cabernet, or other good wine.

Baked oysters or marinated oysters

Poulet Yvonne
Corn pudding

[**Sherbet**] **and thin slices of honey cake**

A white from Alsace, such as Riesling or Sylvaner, a white Burgundy, say Pouilly-Fuissé, or a California Riesling right through the meal.

Crevettes en aspic (*Shrimp in aspic*)

Lemon chicken
Chick-pea purée
Baked onions

Crème aux poires (*Pear cream*)

A one-wine dinner. Use a Tavel, Provence, or California rosé or a dry white from Burgundy, Alsace, or California. Or break the rules and serve a chilled young Beaujolais (if authentic).

Virginia's Chinese mushrooms

Filets de sole Neva (*Fillets of sole with smoked salmon or salmon eggs*)

Pain d'épinards (*Spinach loaf*)**, as a separate course**

Frozen maple mousse

For the sole, your best white —a Burgundy, Graves, Rhine, or California Pinot Chardonnay.

Hot or cold buffet
(serves 18 to 20)

Wine-marinated mushrooms
Italian artichokes
Terrine de foies de volaille *(Chicken liver pâté)*
Cold baked lamb curry
Meat loaf à la pâté
Candied tomatoes
Bean-sprout salad
Dijon-style mushrooms
Lentil salad
Texas sheet cake and [Fresh fruit]

This buffet calls for a rosé or chilled Beaujolais or Zinfandel. But have some white jug wine for guests who disagree.

One-fish bouillabaisse
[French bread or hot rolls]

[Cheese and crackers]

[Fresh fruit] and thin slices of honey cake

A light white wine, such as Muscadet, dry Vouvray, Italian Soave, California Pinot Blanc or, if you like, a rosé.

Potage velours *(Tomato-tapioca soup)*

Quick pepper steak
Potato pudding
[Salad]

Coffee cream custard

A sturdy red —Côtes-du-Rhône, St. Émilion, Hermitage, California Pinot Noir—but not too fine because of the pepper.

Cheese mousse slice on lettuce

Leg of lamb steak
Baked caraway potatoes
Peas with mint

Tarte alhambra

The mousse and lamb are worth a good Bordeaux or Cabernet Sauvignon. However, no laws will be broken by a Burgundy from the Côtes de Beaune.

Peppers and anchovies, Italian style

Baked chicken cacciatore
Baked gnocchi
[Salad]

Lemon sherbet

Stay with the Italian flavor and serve a young Chianti.

Marinated fish Piraeus

Sautéed chicken livers
Polenta [or rice]
[Salad]

Banana cream

Until the dessert the flavors have strong personalities. Make it white or rosé all the way through, especially a dry rosé from Provence.

Crème de crevettes *(Cream of shrimp soup)*

Lapin à la diable *(Mustard rabbit)*
Spinach gratin

Marrakesh-orange fruit plate

The pungent mustard coating on the rabbit rules out fine wine. A cool Côtes-du-Rhône or California Zinfandel would fill the bill.

Fast menus for after a working day

Grapefruit Jaipur

Shrimp in beer
Tomato bake

Poires en chemise (Pears baked in foil)

Beer with Shrimp in Beer, or a French Chablis, Macon, Riesling or Muscadet. Any dry white California, including your favorite jug wine, well chilled.

Potage à la chinoise

Pork chops with Italian garnish
Lima-bean purée
[Salad]

Apricot sherbet

This garnish on pork calls for a coolish light red wine—other possibilities would be a Beaujolais or an Italian Valpolicella or Bardolino, a Zinfandel or Gamay Beaujolais from California.

Bean-sprout salad
Clams florentine
Fried chick-peas

Baked strawberries

Any white wine that isn't too sweet. A Chablis or an American Chablis-type, for instance. A dry jug white.

Chinese asparagus

Oven-fried fish fillets
Corn pudding

Six-minute chocolate cake

To reach from the Chinese asparagus to the chocolate cake, a nice white. Say a Burgundy like Pouilly-Fuissé or Meursault or a California Pinot Chardonnay.

Roquefort soufflé

Sautéed soft-shelled crabs

Cauliflower gratin

Blueberry clafouti

The delicate soft-shelled crabs want a fine white—a Chassagne-Montrachet, a good French Chablis, a Pouilly-Fumé from the Loire or a better Pinot Chardonnay from California.

Wilted salad

Leg-of-lamb steak
Baked caraway potatoes

Cobbled peach bake

The French say Bordeaux with lamb, but lamb is treated here like red meat and I say a red Burgundy like Savigny or other Beaune; a good California Pinot Noir or Zinfandel. And for Francophiles a Médoc, of course.

Hot mushroom toasts

Milky-way chicken
[Salad]

[Vanilla ice cream] with Hot chocolate sauce

Chicken made this way would be enhanced by a white Burgundy, an Alsatian Riesling or a Pinot Chardonnay from France or California. For those who prefer red, a Beaujolais, small Bordeaux, or California Gamay Beaujolais.

[Hot beef broth with crackers]

Baked chicken cacciatore
Baked corn on the cob
[Salad]

Pear gratin

No problem: this chicken cacciatore gets along with white, rosé, and light red wine.

Brioches aveyronnaises (Hot Roquefort-filled rolls)

Potato supper
Peas with mint

Lemon sherbet

The hot potato and cold sour cream taste best with a white. A Sylvaner from Alsace or California would do nicely.

Crème de crevettes (Cream of shrimp soup)

Ham steak with sherry sauce
Stir-fried bean sprouts
[Salad]

[Cheese and crackers; fresh fruit]

A dry rosé from start to finish, or a light red say a fruity Zinfandel.

Italian artichokes

Croque neptune (Hot open clam sandwiches)
Golden grilled tomato
[Salad]

Jamaican squares

This simple supper calls for a dryish white wine—anything from your favorite jug white to a Riesling from Alsace or California, to a Macon or Pinot Chardonnay.

[Thinly sliced prosciutto]

Swiss fondue
[Salad]

[Fresh fruit]

Beer or white wine. A California Folle Blanche or similar wine would be just right.

Sunday-night soup

Coquilles Saint-Jacques Georgettes (Scallops with mushrooms and boiled ham)

Creamed lettuce

Orange-mincemeat squares

The coquilles deserve a nice white, say a Burgundy or a Pinot Chardonnay or Johannesberg Riesling from California.

Baked oysters

Steak au poivre (Pepper steak)
Fried chick-peas
Radis au beurre (Sautéed radishes)

Bananes roties (Baked bananas)

A hearty red wine, but not too expensive a one. The pepper steak makes it hard to distinguish a great Burgundy from a lesser wine. Perhaps a chilled Beaujolais to put out the fire.

Wilted salad

Ham soufflé
Cauliflower gratin

Champagne fruit cup

No wine is served with the vinegary wilted salad; a small Bordeaux or California Zinfandel with the ham soufflé while waiting for the champagne—the important part of the dessert.

Baked oysters

Jambon à la crème (Ham with cream sauce)
Flemish noodles

[Salad]

Apple clafouti

Warm oysters and chilled white wine is a combination to remember. A Muscadet would be perfect, or a dry California Pinot Chardonnay. Serve the white throughout the meal.

Oysters with champagne sauce

Lamb sauté touteron
Baked corn on the cob

Banana soufflé

The oysters deserve champagne, what else? A sparkling Vouvray could also carry the meal from start to finish.

Low-cholesterol menus

Pumpkin soup

Country cheese pie
Provençal string beans

Pear gratin

Cheese pie calls for a white wine, a Macon or Burgundy Aligoté or a Chenin Blanc from California. Or your favorite jug white served from a carafe.

Grapefruit Jaipur

Tuna-stuffed peppers
Baked corn on the cob

Six-minute chocolate cake

This menu would be enhanced by a medium-dry white, a French Graves or California Riesling. A rosé would do well too.

One-fish bouillabaisse
[Salad]

Oranges confites *(Candied oranges)*

Bouillabaisse is a fine dish but would overpower a fine wine. Try a gutsy white, a Macon, Muscadet, or California Chablis. A rosé from Provence, the Rhône Valley, or Northern California would be near perfect.

Cold tomatoes with hot curry sauce

Agneau des alpes *(Lamb boiled in wine and herbs)*
[Salad]

Meringue des îles, Hot chocolate sauce
(Coffee-flavored meringue with hot chocolate sauce)

A big white or light red. Any good white Burgundy or a white Hermitage or California Pinot Chardonnay. A Médoc if red is preferred.

Cold cucumber soup

Estouffade des mariniers du Rhône *(Beef braised with capers and anchovies)*
Potato pudding
[Salad]

Coffee granita or Frozen banana morsels

The hearty estouffade wants a sturdy red. Suggestions: any Burgundy like Gevrey-Chambertin; a Châteauneuf-du-Pape, a California Pinot Noir or a better California jug Burgundy.

Baked oysters

Baked chicken cacciatore
Baked polenta
[Salad]

Tarte alhambra

Why not go Italian all the way? A Chianti from Tuscany or a Barbera from California. Chicken cacciatore likes a rosé also.

Gratin parisien *(Hot mushroom gratin)*

Cold marinated fish Piraeus

Baked celery with herb sauce

Marrakesh orange slices

With marinated fish, a nice white that isn't too costly: an Alsatian Riesling or a Macon. A rosé would also suit this menu from start to finish.

Courqettes à la Grecque *(Marinated zucchini)*

Tranche de boeuf au madère *(Beef braised in Madeira)*
Mashed potatoes with red wine

Banana cream

The beef needs a full red — small Burgundy, Bordeaux, or California Cabernet. The luscious Banana cream deserves the compliment of an icy-cold sweet Sauterne.

SOUPS

One might well ask if the busy modern cook should take the time to make soup when such an abundant choice of canned soups is available. Of course canned soups have their place, but I do not believe that place is at an important luncheon or dinner. No amount of "doctoring" up canned soups or combining them in exotic combinations will achieve the fresh, sparkling flavor of a good homemade soup. With an electric blender in almost every kitchen, the real chore has been taken out of soup making. Now one whizzes right through a recipe.

However, in many places in this book, including this chapter, canned chicken and beef broths are used in the braising of meat and chicken. In working out these recipes I used canned broths because they are fine for the purpose and because I know they would be used most often by readers. Adjustments have been made in the seasonings to bring out the best in these broths.

The soups that follow range from a Jellied Borscht to Cold Cucumber Soup, to Pumpkin Soup (served hot or cold) to a soup that's an entire meal in itself. Only with the latter (Country Bean-and-Cabbage Soup) would wine be served, and in this case a chilled Beaujolais or Côtes-du-Rhône would be perfect.

Potage, crème portugaise

Portugaise in French cuisine usually refers to a tomato dish —stuffed, garnished, sauced. Although there is tomato in this delicious soup, its contribution is delicate, not overpowering. The color is rose, the flavor smooth, and the cost only pennies per serving. Although either canned or fresh tomatoes are indicated, use fresh when tomatoes are at their best.

SERVES 10

WORKING TIME: 13 minutes

COOKING TIME: 30 to 35 minutes

INGREDIENTS

3	tablespoons butter
2	medium onions, sliced
2	garlic cloves
3	medium potatoes
1	1¼-pound can tomatoes, undrained, (or 2 or 3 fresh tomatoes)
1½	quarts (6 cups) hot water
1	tablespoon tomato paste
1	teaspoon sugar
1	bay leaf
1	tablespoon salt
1	teaspoon pepper

PREPARATION

1 Melt the butter in a 4-quart pot while peeling and cutting the onions in thick slices. Add the onions to the butter; peel the garlic cloves, cut them in thirds, and add them to the onions. Cover the pot and simmer the vegetables very slowly for 10 minutes. The onions must not brown.

2 While the onions are simmering, peel the potatoes and cut them into chunks. If fresh tomatoes are used, plunge them into a small pot of boiling water; remove with a skimmer after a few seconds and slip off the skins. Cut the tomatoes into chunks, discarding the stem ends.

3 Add to the pot the potatoes, tomatoes, water, tomato paste, sugar, bay leaf, salt, and pepper. Bring the water to a boil, reduce the heat, cover the pot, and simmer the soup for 20 to 25 minutes, or until the potatoes are soft. Discard the bay leaf.

4 Ladle some of the soup into a blender and purée it. Pour the puréed soup into a large mixing bowl and continue puréeing the rest of the soup. Return the soup to the pot.

5 Reheat the soup and taste for seasonings; correct if necessary.

TO SERVE

Please don't be tempted to dress up this pale soup with a sprinkling of paprika or chopped parsley. Serve it in individual bowls, pure as it is.

COOKING AHEAD

Like most soups, Crème Portugaise can be prepared a day or two in advance and refrigerated. Reheat at serving time.

LOW-CHOLESTEROL VERSION

Use polyunsaturated margarine instead of butter; no other changes in the recipe are necessary.

Potage velours

Cooked tapioca (or cream of wheat) gives a very nice texture to this soup, adding a smooth body to the hot broth. When tomatoes are at their best, use fresh ones; at other times the canned variety is better.

SERVES 8 TO 10

WORKING TIME: *8 minutes*

COOKING TIME: *35 minutes*

INGREDIENTS

1	14½-ounce can tomatoes, undrained, (3 or 4 ripe tomatoes)
6	cups strong beef consommé
1	thick onion slice
1	bay leaf
1½	teaspoons tomato paste
¼	cup tapioca or cream of wheat
1½	tablespoons butter
1	tablespoon chopped parsley

PREPARATION

1   Plunge fresh tomatoes into boiling water for a few seconds and slip off the skins. Heat the consommé in a 3-quart pot while cutting the tomatoes into chunks and discarding the stem ends. To the consommé add the tomatoes, onion, bay leaf, and tomato paste; bring to a boil. Cover pot loosely and simmer briskly for 15 minutes. (If canned tomatoes are used, use the entire contents of the can, first removing the sprig of basil.)

2   Remove the bay leaf and put the contents of the pot through the blender in 2 or 3 operations. Return the soup to the pot and bring it back to a boil. Stir in the tapioca or cream of wheat and stir for ½ minute to prevent the cereal from sticking to the bottom. Cover loosely and simmer briskly for 20 minutes more. Keep the soup at a boil or the cereal will clump together.

TO SERVE

Ladle the soup into individual soup bowls and place ½ teaspoon of butter in each one. Sprinkle with parsley.

COOKING AHEAD

Potage Velours can be prepared a day or two in advance and refrigerated. Reheat at serving time.

LOW-CHOLESTEROL VERSION

Substitute polyunsaturated margarine or low-fat yogurt for the butter.

Asparagus soup

Chilling time is given because I think this soup's flavor is more refined when cold —especially when fresh asparagus is used. Many people prefer the soup warm. Either way, it's a fine way to begin an important meal.

SERVES 6

WORKING TIME: *13 minutes*

COOKING TIME: *15 to 20 minutes*

CHILLING TIME: *3 hours*

INGREDIENTS

1   **pound frozen asparagus, or 1½ pounds fresh asparagus**

1   **medium onion, thinly sliced**

3   **cups chicken broth**

2   **tablespoons flour**

2   **teaspoons lemon juice**

¼   **teaspoon celery seeds**

   salt and pepper

   Optional: ½ to 1 cup additional chicken broth or milk

PREPARATION

1   Cut off the tips from 6 asparagus stalks and reserve. (If fresh asparagus is used, also snap off and discard the tough woody bottoms of the stalks. Rinse well.) Put asparagus in a flat skillet, add the onion and ½ cup of chicken broth. Bring to a boil, cover, and simmer for 7 minutes. (For fresh asparagus, add 1 cup of broth and simmer until tender, about 15 minutes.)

2   Meanwhile, poach the reserved tips in boiling salted water until just tender—about 2 minutes for frozen tips, 5 minutes for fresh tips. Drain at once, cool under cold water, and set aside.

3   Scoop the cooked asparagus and liquid into a blender and purée.

4   Pour 2¼ cups of chicken broth (or 1¾ cups for fresh asparagus) into a pot and heat. In a small bowl, stir the remaining ¼ cup of broth into the flour until smooth. When the stock begins to simmer, stir in the flour paste and whisk to keep smooth. Cover and simmer for 5 minutes.

5   Add the puréed asparagus to the stock, plus the lemon juice, celery seeds, and salt and pepper to taste. When tasting, remember that the flavor will be less strong if the soup is to be served chilled. This is a fairly thick soup; it can be thinned with more broth or milk, if desired.

TO SERVE

Ladle the soup into individual soup cups and garnish each one with an asparagus tip.

COOKING AHEAD

Asparagus soup can be prepared a day in advance and refrigerated.

LOW-CHOLESTEROL VERSION

No changes in the recipe are necessary.

Scallop soup

This scallop soup is a kissing cousin to a popular French mussel soup called Billy-Bi. Many different explanations are given for the mussel soup's odd name. Maxim's in Paris doesn't bother to explain it, just serves it hot or cold, as you like. I prefer it cold, since the delicate flavor comes through better that way. For the same reason, I suggest serving this scallop soup warm, not boiling hot. Its subtlety will be better appreciated at a lower temperature. You will also find this version not as unctuously rich as so many similar soups.

Economy note: since the scallops are puréed, size doesn't matter. Save a few pennies and buy the larger ones.

SERVES 6

WORKING TIME: 8 minutes

COOKING TIME: 20 minutes

INGREDIENTS

1	**quart water**
¾	**cup dry white wine**
1	**shallot or 1 tablespoon scallion, thinly sliced**
⅛	**teaspoon saffron**
⅛	**teaspoon curry**
¼	**teaspoon dry mustard**
1½	**teaspoons salt**
½	**teaspoon pepper**
½	**pound scallops**
¾	**cup cream**
2	**teaspoons chopped chives; or paprika**

PREPARATION

1 In a nonaluminum 2-quart pot put the water, wine, shallot, saffron, curry, mustard, salt, and pepper. Bring to a boil, cover, and simmer 15 minutes. Add scallops, cover, and simmer just 5 minutes more.

2 Purée contents in a blender, half at a time. The scallops do not purée completely, but remain in tiny pieces. Return soup to the pot and add cream; stir thoroughly. Reheat, but do not boil.

TO SERVE

When ladling soup from the pot make sure you stir up the bottom to include pieces of scallops which will have collected there. Pour into individual soup cups, and sprinkle with chives or paprika. Serve quite warm, but not hot.

COOKING AHEAD

The soup can be finished ahead and given the final reheating at dinnertime. It also freezes well.

LOW-CHOLESTEROL VERSION

Substitute 1 full cup of frozen polyunsaturated dairy substitute for the ¾ cup cream. When reheating the soup add 1 tablespoon polyunsaturated margarine and 1 teaspoon soy sauce.

Crème de crevettes

Shrimp doesn't figure much in this book because of the pesky time-consuming chore of peeling them when raw. I don't know why, but few fishmongers have stepped into the breach to provide that service. Unfortunately, for most recipes, the frozen, shelled shrimp just aren't good enough. But for this soup they fill the bill perfectly. The only thing better would be to find that rare fishman who does peel them, or perhaps an obliging offspring.

SERVES 6 TO 8

WORKING TIME: *11 minutes*

COOKING TIME: *23 minutes*

INGREDIENTS

¼   **cup oil**

1   **pound shrimp, peeled and deveined**

¼   **cup flour**

2   **cups milk**

2   **cups canned tomatoes, drained**

1   **cup dry white wine**

2   **teaspoons brandy**

1   **small onion**

1   **celery rib without leaves**

1   **small bay leaf**

     salt and pepper

1½   **cups cream**

     juice of ½ lemon

PREPARATION

1   Pour the oil into a deep nonaluminum pot. Heat the oil to medium hot, then add the shrimp and stir for about a half minute.

2   Sprinkle the flour over the shrimp and stir to distribute the flour. Pour in the milk, tomatoes, wine, and brandy. Peel and cut the onion into thick slices; slice the celery into ¼-inch pieces and add both vegetables to the soup. Add the bay leaf, salt and pepper. Bring the liquid to a simmer, cover and cook gently for 20 minutes.

3   Remove the bay leaf and discard; lift out 4 or 5 shrimp and reserve. Purée the remaining shrimp and liquid in an electric blender. Rinse the pot and return the soup to the pot. Stir in 1 cup of cream and lemon juice and reheat gently. If you prefer a thinner soup, stir in the remaining ½ cup of cream. Cut the reserved shrimp into several large pieces.

TO SERVE

Ladle the rose-colored soup into individual soup cups or a tureen and garnish with the shrimp pieces.

COOKING AHEAD

The soup can easily be made several days in advance and refrigerated, but do not add the cream and lemon juice until reheating it.

LOW-CHOLESTEROL VERSION

At this writing shrimp is not permitted on a low-cholesterol diet.

Avgolemono

One Greek soup that has achieved an international reputation is Avgolemono
. . . with good reason. It is a wonderfully light soup with a bit of a fillip that comes from the lemon. I'm partial to a pronounced lemon flavor, but there are those who prefer a milder taste. Decide for yourself. Begin with a quarter-cup, adding more later if you like. It is important that the eggs and lemon juice are at room temperature to prevent the eggs from curdling.

SERVES 8

WORKING TIME: 8 minutes

COOKING TIME: 5 or 25 minutes

INGREDIENTS

6   cups well-seasoned chicken stock

1   cup cooked rice, or 1/3 cup raw rice

3   eggs

½   cup lemon juice
    salt and pepper

PREPARATION

1   Heat the stock in a pot. Add the cooked rice and bring to a boil, simmer for 2 minutes. If raw rice is used, cover and simmer for 20 minutes.

2   Break the eggs into a bowl and beat with a whisk. Pour in ¼ cup of lemon juice and beat again.

3   Pour the egg-juice mixture very slowly into the simmering soup while whisking constantly and rapidly. Keep the liquid just under the boiling point. Taste for lemon flavor, adding the remaining ¼ cup if desired. Add salt and pepper to taste (the seasoning of the stock will determine the amount added).

TO SERVE

Serve while very hot, ladling the soup into individual soup cups, making certain that each serving of soup contains some rice.

COOKING AHEAD

Avgolemono can be prepared in advance and refrigerated. Reheat very slowly, without boiling.

LOW-CHOLESTEROL VERSION

For the egg, substitute 1 tablespoon of flour. Stir the lemon juice into the flour to a smooth paste and pour it into the soup. Add 1 tablespoon of polyunsaturated margarine after the lemon juice has been mixed into the soup.

Sunday-night soup

I think of this as Sunday-Night Soup because it can save your life when unexpected guests linger on for Sunday supper. All the necessary ingredients are usually on hand, and this delicious, country-style soup can be prepared in minutes. Of course, if you don't have to do it at the last minute, you'll find that it improves if left in the refrigerator for a day. Though a whole package of spinach is not used, it makes sense to cook the remainder for later use as a vegetable, or to make twice as much soup and freeze what is not needed. There should not be a mass of spinach in the broth, just some green leaves floating about.

SERVES 6

WORKING TIME: 4 minutes

COOKING TIME: 9 minutes

INGREDIENTS

3   tablespoons oil

1   medium onion, thinly sliced

1   teaspoon curry powder

2   cups cold water

3   cups beef broth

½   package frozen leaf spinach, thawed

1   tablespoon Madeira or Port
    grated Parmesan cheese

1 Heat the oil in a 2-quart pot while peeling and thinly slicing the onion. Add the onion to the pot, cover and simmer gently for 2 minutes. The onion must not brown.

2 Add the curry powder, stir, and simmer for 1 minute more while opening the cans of broth. Add the broth and cold water. Bring the liquid to a gentle boil, cover and simmer for 5 minutes.

3 Squeeze the spinach gently to remove the excess water and cut into 2 or 3 parts. Add the spinach to the soup and bring back to a fast boil. Remove the pot from the heat and add the Madeira.

TO SERVE

Ladle the soup into soup bowls and pass the Parmesan cheese.

COOKING AHEAD

As noted above, this soup improves if left to stand for a day in the refrigerator.

LOW-CHOLESTEROL VERSION

Use polyunsaturated oil for frying the onions; no other changes in the recipes are necessary. Pass low-fat grated cheese.

Greek eggplant soup

Just because it's served cold, don't limit this delicious soup to summertime menus. It is just as good in December as in July. There is a lot of full flavor from the eggplant and green pepper. The adjectives "subtle" and "exotic" seem poles apart, but this Greek soup somehow manages to bring them together.

SERVES 8

WORKING TIME: *8 minutes*
COOKING TIME: *16 minutes*
CHILLING TIME: *4 hours*

INGREDIENTS

6 tablespoons olive oil

1 pound eggplant, peeled and cut into 1-inch cubes

1 green pepper, seeded and cut into chunks

½ cup water

salt and pepper

1 garlic clove, sliced

½ teaspoon mint flakes

3 cups plain yogurt

Optional: ½ cup milk

2 tablespoons chopped chives

PREPARATION

1 Heat the olive oil in a pan while preparing the eggplant and green pepper. Add them to the hot oil and mix to coat all pieces thoroughly. Cover and simmer for a minute. Add the water, salt, pepper, and garlic, and simmer 15 minutes.

2 Purée the cooked vegetables and their liquid and the mint leaves and yogurt in a blender (or pass through a food mill). If you prefer a thinner soup, add the optional milk. Chill for at least 4 hours.

TO SERVE

Sprinkle each serving of the cold soup with chives.

COOKING AHEAD

The soup can be prepared a day or so before serving and kept refrigerated.

LOW-CHOLESTEROL VERSION

Substitute polyunsaturated oil for the olive oil; use low-fat yogurt and skimmed milk.

Jellied borscht

There is a jewellike color and shimmer to this Russian favorite. Although the beets themselves don't get used in the finished soup, they are necessary for the authentic, strong flavor. Save them to add to all kinds of salads.

SERVES 8

WORKING TIME: *10 minutes*
COOKING TIME: *16 minutes*
CHILLING TIME: *3 hours*

INGREDIENTS

4	**pounds canned beets, undrained**
4	**cabbage leaves**
3	**cups beef broth**
1	**teaspoon meat extract (like BV)**
3	**whole cloves**
1	**tablespoon wine vinegar**
	juice ½ lemon
½	**teaspoon salt**
½	**teaspoon pepper**
½	**chopped onion**
1	**celery stalk**
2½	**tablespoons gelatin**
¼	**cup cold water**
	Optional: 1 cup sour cream or plain yogurt

PREPARATION

1 Put all ingredients except the gelatin and cold water in a large pot. Bring to boil and simmer 15 minutes. Taste for seasonings. The flavor should be slightly tart. Add more lemon juice or vinegar if desired. Strain.

2 Soak the gelatin in the cold water, add to the hot soup, and return to the heat 1 more minute while stirring until gelatin dissolves. Cool; then chill until set, which takes about 3 hours.

TO SERVE

Spoon the ruby-colored jellied borscht into soup cups or tall wine glasses, add a dollop of the optional sour cream or yogurt on top. Pass the rest of the cream or yogurt separately.

COOKING AHEAD

Jellied borscht can be made a day or two before needed and kept in the refrigerator, closely covered.

LOW-CHOLESTEROL VERSION

No changes in the recipe are necessary, but use a low-fat yogurt, not sour cream, for optional topping.

Superquick borscht

Traditionally, borscht is a long-simmering combination of beef and beets, the meat slowly giving up its flavor to the broth. In this version, ready to put on the table in 15 minutes, stronger sausage is substituted for the beef. It flavors the broth quickly and pungently. Once the beets have accomplished their role of coloring and flavoring the soup, they are strained out. Refrigerate them and add to salads later. For a Russian touch, pass sour cream at the table to be dolloped on top. The amount of sausage served in the borscht varies according to the copiousness of the meal that follows.

SERVES 6

WORKING TIME: *5 minutes*
COOKING TIME: *15 minutes*

INGREDIENTS

6	**cups beef broth**
½	**pound sausage, Polish type or similar**
1	**small bay leaf**
⅛	**teaspoon thyme**
1	**½-pound can sliced beets, drained**
	pepper
½	**teaspoon Worcestershire sauce**
1	**tablespoon vinegar**
	Optional: sour cream

1   Pour the beef broth into a pot and bring to a slow simmer. While heating the broth, slice the sausage into ¼-inch rounds and add to broth. Add bay leaf and thyme. Cover and simmer for 10 minutes.

2   With a skimmer, remove the sausage slices to a soup tureen or to individual bowls. Add beets, pepper, and Worcestershire sauce to the soup. Cover and simmer for 5 minutes. Add the vinegar, give one boil and remove from heat. Strain out beets and bay leaf.

TO SERVE

Ladle the red borscht over the sausage and spoon in a tablespoon of sour cream. Serve while still quite hot. When stirred the sour cream will separate into small bits.

COOKING AHEAD

Prepare the soup and strain out the beet slices. Combine soup and sausage and refrigerate. Before reheating, remove layer of chilled fat from the surface.

LOW-CHOLESTEROL VERSION

For the sausage, substitute leftover roast beef cut into slivers and cook 20 minutes. Add 1 or 2 onion slices with the meat. Increase the Worcestershire sauce to 1 teaspoon, and add 1 tablespoon polyunsaturated margarine when the vinegar is added. Pass low-fat yogurt at the table instead of sour cream.

Cold cucumber soup

Many people find Vichyssoise too rich and too much of a cliché. I quite agree and prefer to start a meal with a lighter, more interesting kind of soup. When you would like to serve a chilled soup, try this one. It has a sparkling, delicate flavor that is not masked by the seasonings. It also looks good with flecks of dark green garnishes floating on the pale green liquid.

INGREDIENTS

2   **cucumbers, peeled and quartered**
2   **cups chicken broth**
2   **tablespoons chopped onion**
   salt and pepper
¼   **teaspoon curry**
1   **teaspoon dillweed**
2   **cups plain yogurt**
   Optional: milk

   Optional Garnishes: very thin slices of cucumber; chopped parsley; chopped fresh dill; or chopped fresh tarragon

PREPARATION

1   Peel and quarter cucumbers, and remove seeds. Put cucumbers in a pot with the broth, onion, salt, pepper, curry, and dillweed. Cover and cook for about 10 minutes until cucumbers are soft.

2   Pour half the cooked ingredients and half the broth into a blender, add 1 cup yogurt and purée. Pour the soup into a bowl. Treat the other half the same way.

3   Cool soup. Taste for seasoning and correct if necessary. If the soup is thicker than you would like, thin with a little milk. Chill thoroughly.

TO SERVE

Sprinkle any one of the garnishes over each cup of soup.

COOKING AHEAD

Since the soup is to be served chilled it must be prepared ahead, even a day or two, if you like.

LOW-CHOLESTEROL VERSION

Use low-fat yogurt; no other changes in the recipe are necessary.

Country bean-and-cabbage soup

The time count on this recipe is a bit longer than for most others in the book. But those few extra minutes give you almost a whole meal —for 14 people. In addition, the cooking can be interrupted at any point; even carried out over two days, if need be. This is not a soup that gets served in fancy little consommé cups. Use big bowls, since the thick and hearty soup is the main course. All things considered, Country Soup makes an inexpensive party meal, for nothing more than a cheese plate and some fresh fruit should follow.

I usually call this my "vat of soup" because that's about the quantity I make. And I always try to make it at least one or two days before it's needed, which makes the flavor stronger and better. Reheating any leftover soup only improves it. It also freezes perfectly. All this for just about ½ hour of your time. The dark roux added at the end is a small and unusual step, but a vital one, so please don't omit it. One other note before plunging in: The recipe is for a large quantity —about 2 gallons of soup. If your cupboard doesn't hold a pot that large, better make half.

14 MAIN-COURSE SERVINGS

WORKING TIME: 45 minutes

SOAKING TIME: Overnight

COOKING TIME: 3 hours

INGREDIENTS

2⅓	cups dry pea beans (or Northern or navy beans)
1	3-pound smoked picnic ham, bone in
1	stalk celery, sliced
2	carrots, quartered lengthwise and sliced
5	parsley sprigs and 2 bay leaves tied in an herb bouquet
3	onions, 2 of them sliced
2	whole cloves
4	garlic cloves, mashed
½	teaspoon thyme
½	teaspoon pepper
1	teaspoon salt
1	2-pound can tomatoes
2	tablespoons tomato paste
1	3-pound head cabbage
¼	cup lard
3	tablespoons flour

PREPARATION

1 Rinse the beans and place them in a large soup pot. Cover with 2 quarts cold water and let stand overnight. If pressed for time, bring the water to a boil, remove from fire, and soak for 1 hour.

2 Rinse the ham and add it to the pot. The water should cover at least half the ham, if not, add some. Bring water to a boil and simmer for 15 minutes, skimming off all foam that rises to the top.

3 Meanwhile, prepare the celery, carrots, herb bouquet, and onions (2 sliced, 1 whole with the cloves pressed into it). When foam stops rising, add prepared vegetables and herb bouquet, plus the garlic, thyme, pepper, and a little salt. (Ham is salty; correction can be made later if necessary.) Cover and simmer 1½ hours.

4 Add the tomatoes and tomato paste; simmer another ½ hour. From now on, when stirring the soup, mash the tomatoes against the side of the pot to break them into smaller pieces.

5 Remove the thick, coarse outer leaves of the cabbage. Cut into quarters, then cut out and discard the hard core from each section. Lay each section on a cutting board and cut across into ¼-to-½-inch slices. Add shredded cabbage to the soup and simmer another ½ hour.

6 Make a very dark roux by melting the lard in a skillet, adding the flour and stirring constantly with a wooden spoon until the flour is well browned. The heat should be moderately high so that the browning can be accomplished in about 15 minutes, but without burning the roux. The color should be almost that of light chocolate. Add a ladleful of soup to this roux and mix quickly and thoroughly. Be careful as a lot of steam will boil up as the hot liquid hits the hot skillet. Add a few more ladlefuls of soup to the skillet, mixing well after each addition. Then pour the contents of the skillet back into the soup pot. Simmer briskly for 15 minutes more.

7 Retrieve the whole onion and the herb bouquet with a long-handled slotted spoon and discard. Strip away all the fat and bone from the ham. Cut the meat into bite-sized pieces and return to the pot. Correct seasoning. Serve hot.

COOKING AHEAD

Before proceeding with step 7, cool the soup and chill it. (This requires a lot of refrigerator space, so if the weather is cold enough, cover the pot with some towels, weight the lid with bricks and chill outdoors.) The following day remove the fat that has congealed on top. Then proceed with step 7. When ready to serve, reheat and taste for salt; correct if necessary.

LOW-CHOLESTEROL VERSION

Use very lean pork hocks instead of ham; or strip all fat off the ham before cooking. Substitute polyunsaturated oil for the lard. The soup must be chilled and congealed fat removed.

Pumpkin soup

In Europe the colorful pumpkin is not restricted to desserts. It's prepared as a mellow vegetable; other times as a rich and creamy soup. Come to think of it, in many years of living abroad I never saw a pumpkin pie that wasn't made especially for Americans. Although this recipe is a whiz to do, its flavor is quite luxurious —hot or cold.

SERVES 6 TO 8

WORKING TIME: *9 minutes*

COOKING TIME: *17 minutes*

INGREDIENTS

1 small onion, sliced (about ½ cup)

3 cups chicken broth

1 1-pound can pumpkin

salt and pepper

1 cup heavy cream

1 tablespoon butter

PREPARATION

1 Slice the onion and put it in a pot with 1½ cups of chicken broth. Bring to a boil, cover, and simmer 10 minutes.

2 Stir in the pumpkin, then 1 cup more of the broth. Add salt and pepper to taste. Cover again and simmer for 5 minutes more.

3 Purée the pumpkin mixture in a blender and return the soup to the pot. Stir in the cream and butter. If you prefer a thinner soup, stir in the remaining ½ cup broth. The soup will still be fairly thick. Reheat slowly. Serve hot or cold.

COOKING AHEAD

Pumpkin soup can be made days in advance and refrigerated. It freezes quite well, but may have to be smoothed out.

LOW-CHOLESTEROL VERSION

Use a medium onion, making about ¾ cup when sliced. Substitute evaporated skimmed milk for cream and 2 tablespoons of polyunsaturated margarine for the butter.

Potage à la chinoise

This is a light, delicious soup made with just a few ingredients. There is one essential ingredient, though – the dried Chinese mushrooms which can be kept in the cupboard for months on end. You will find that the exotic flavor they add to many dishes will make them an invaluable addition to your pantry. Chinese mushrooms are dark and flat with a light speckling. In Japanese food shops they are called Japanese mushrooms. Both are the same.

SERVES 6

WORKING TIME: *3 minutes*

SOAKING TIME: *15 minutes*

COOKING TIME: *4 minutes*

INGREDIENTS

4	dried Chinese mushrooms, 3 if large
6	cups chicken broth
1	teaspoon soy sauce
2	eggs

PREPARATION

1 Rinse the mushrooms, put them in a small bowl, and cover them with boiling water, then cover the bowl. Let stand 15 minutes.

2 Bring the chicken broth to a slow boil, adding the soy sauce and 1 cup of water from the bowl containing the mushrooms. While the broth is heating slice the mushrooms into thin strips, discarding the hard stem centers. Add the mushroom slices to the broth, cover and simmer 2 minutes.

3 Taste the soup for salt and pepper; correct if necessary. Just before serving, beat the eggs well in a small bowl and very slowly pour them into the boiling soup, stirring all the time. Boil for 2 minutes. Serve at once.

COOKING AHEAD

This recipe will improve if made a day in advance, allowing the strong mushroom flavor to further enhance the soup. The beaten eggs, however, must be added at the last moment.

LOW-CHOLESTEROL VERSION

To the simmering broth add 2 tablespoons of cooked rice, or cook 1 tablespoon of raw rice in the broth for 20 minutes. Small pieces of spaghetti or a few cooked peas could be added instead. Do not add the eggs.

ENTREES

Before the curtain rises on an opera, the orchestral prelude whets our aural appetite for the drama and melodies to follow. In a way it's a bit of lighthearted teasing. I look upon the first course of a meal in much the same way, especially at dinner.

Egg Ramekins, Roquefort Soufflé, Danish Cauliflower, or Emerald Cream, for example, help set the stage for what follows. Entrées should be light and in sensibly sized portions. At other times, though, many of the recipes that follow can take on a starring role as the main course at a luncheon or late-night supper.

None of these entrées take much time to do. Even the Roquefort Soufflé can be put together in 6 minutes. All the recipes have been designed to look pretty on the plate, please the palate, and leave the diners anticipating what comes next. I believe that serving the right small first course can turn any meal into an occasion.

The wines to serve will depend on the rest of your menu. In most cases either red or white is suitable with these entrées. Light fruity wines from the Moselle region in Germany would complement Cold Tomatoes with Hot Curry Sauce, Croque Neptune or Egg Ramekins. The Roquefort Soufflé and Brioches Aveyronnaises would especially welcome a chilled Beaujolais or Gamay. Though rosé wines can bridge many serving problems, they do have a distinct identity of their own that is often overlooked. A chilled rosé would be perfect with Eggplant Caviar, Cold Herb Omelet, or Asperges à la Normande.

It is advisable not to serve wine with any dish that has a vinegar sauce, since the acid in vinegar distorts the taste of wine. That is why the French prefer to serve salad as a separate course and drink nothing with it. For this reason I would not serve wine with Wilted Salad, Bean-Sprout Salad, Courgettes à la Grecque, Peppers and Anchovies, or Grapefruit Jaipur, in the latter case because the fruit itself contains a lot of acid.

Shrimp in aspic

An aspic dish is always an attractive way to begin a meal. Here the pink shrimp and the green peas are caught in the shimmering aspic and create an appealing color contrast. Canned shrimp are indicated here to show the possibilities they have. Fresh cooked shrimp, of course, can also be used. In that case, cut the shrimp in halves except for one at the bottom of each mold.

SERVES 6

WORKING TIME: *10 minutes*

COOKING TIME: *3 minutes*

CHILLING TIME: *2 ½ hours*

INGREDIENTS

½   **cup dry vermouth**

1   **8- or 9-ounce can shrimp, or
    ¼ pound fresh cooked shrimp**

1   **shallot, or 3 scallions, chopped**

½   **teaspoon tarragon**

    pepper

1   **cup chicken broth**

2   **anchovy fillets, or 2 teaspoons anchovy paste**

2   **tablespoons gelatin**

    few drops Tabasco

¼   **cup canned tiny peas, drained
    lettuce for garnish**

    Basil Mayonnaise (page 227)

PREPARATION

1   Put the vermouth in a small pot and bring it to a boil. Meanwhile, drain the shrimp and place them in a bowl. Taste the shrimp for saltiness, this will dictate how much anchovy you use later. Chop the shallot and sprinkle it over the shrimp. Sprinkle on the tarragon and pepper. Pour the hot vermouth over the shrimp and mix them gently. Cover the bowl at once and put it aside for 30 minutes. (Canned shrimp are very fragile and break easily; handle them as little as possible.)

2   Put the chicken broth in a small pot and add 1 or 2 anchovy fillets, depending on the saltiness of the shrimp. Bring the broth to a boil. The anchovies will dissolve in it.

3   Put the gelatin in a small cup and drain the vermouth from the shrimp over it. While draining the vermouth, hold back the shrimp with your hands or a lid. Let the gelatin stand a few minutes to soften, then add it and the vermouth to the hot broth and stir for a few seconds to dissolve the gelatin. Add pepper and Tabasco to the broth and put it aside to cool.

4   Select six 1-cup custard cups. Place 1 whole shrimp on the bottom of each cup. Add the peas to the rest of the shrimp and mix lightly, preferably with your hands. Divide the shrimp and peas among the 6 cups. Place the cups on a baking sheet and put it in the refrigerator.

5   When the aspic is cool, pour it into the 6 cups with shrimp and return them to the refrigerator for at least 2 hours.

TO SERVE

Place a lettuce leaf on a salad plate. Run a knife around the aspic, giving a little pull with the tip of the knife as you reverse the mold onto the lettuce. Pass the Basil Mayonnaise separately.

COOKING AHEAD

Shrimp in Aspic can be prepared the day before serving.

LOW-CHOLESTEROL VERSION

At this writing shrimp is not permitted on a low-cholesterol diet. Poached fish fillets can be substituted. Once the fish is cool, flake it into pieces. No other changes in the recipe are necessary.

Asperges à la normande

Almost any dish is better if made with fresh vegetables instead of canned ones— including this recipe. But the season for fresh asparagus is not long, and most kitchen shelves always hold at least one can or jar of green asparagus spears. For this recipe canned asparagus seems better than frozen. I think you'll find that Asperges à la Normande makes something quite good out of the usual flat flavor of canned asparagus. Also, for relatively little cost, you have an easy and novel first course for dinner or a copious main course at luncheon.

SERVES 4

WORKING TIME: 12 minutes

COOKING TIME: 5 minutes

BROILING TIME: 3 minutes

INGREDIENTS

1	**14-to-16-ounce can green asparagus spears**
4	**slices white toast**
2	**tablespoons butter**
2	**tablespoons flour**
1	**teaspoon prepared mustard**
1	**cup milk**
	good pinch nutmeg
¼	**teaspoon Worcestershire sauce**
	salt and pepper
1	**tablespoon catsup**
4	**slices boiled ham**
1	**tablespoon grated Parmesan cheese**

PREPARATION

1 Let the asparagus drain while you prepare the sauce and toast the bread.

2 To make the sauce, melt the butter in a saucepan. When it is hot and foamy, add the flour and stir, thoroughly blending the two. Add the mustard and stir again. Remove the pan from the heat and add about ¼ cup of milk, stirring with a wire whisk to keep the sauce smooth. Return the pan to the heat and stir in the rest of the milk. Add nutmeg, Worcestershire sauce, salt, and pepper. Simmer gently for 3 or 4 minutes.

3 While the sauce is simmering, garnish the toasts. Spread each slice of toast with a generous teaspoon of catsup. Trim slices of boiled ham to fit the toast; reserve the extra ham. Lay a slice of ham on each piece of toast. Place the drained asparagus on the ham, 4 or 5 spears per serving depending on their size.

4 Chop the reserved ham and add it to the sauce. Remove the sauce from the heat and stir in the cheese. Spread the sauce over the asparagus toasts and place on a baking sheet.

5 Place the baking sheet under a hot broiler for about 3 minutes, or until the sauce has flecks of brown on it.

TO SERVE

Place asparagus toasts on individual plates and serve at once while still very hot.

COOKING AHEAD

The sauce can be prepared and the ham slices trimmed to size and refrigerated. The toasts, however, should not be assembled more than 15 minutes before broiling or the bread will become soggy.

LOW-CHOLESTEROL VERSION

Substitute polyunsaturated margarine for the butter; evaporated skimmed milk for the whole milk; low-fat grated cheese for the Parmesan cheese. Increase the mustard quantity to 2 teaspoons.

Croque neptune

There are delicious grilled sandwiches served in French cafes that come with chauvinist names. Croque Monsieur will get you grilled ham and Swiss cheese. But Croque Madame means white meat of chicken and Swiss cheese, clearly a more refined combination. Now I would like to offer a newcomer to the roster— Croque Neptune. The cheese used is Mozzarella, and clams provide the taste of the sea. This would be a novel first course at dinner, a luncheon main course or an after-theater supper.

SERVES 6

WORKING TIME: 12 minutes

COOKING TIME: 4 minutes

GRILLING TIME: 2 to 3 minutes

INGREDIENTS

6	slices white toast
2	tablespoons catsup
1	pound Mozzarella cheese
1	6-ounce can minced clams
2	anchovy fillets, or 2 teaspoons anchovy paste
2	tablespoons cornstarch
½	cup dry white wine
2	teaspoons soy sauce
2	teaspoons lemon juice
	pepper
2	tablespoons chopped parsley

PREPARATION

1 Toast the bread and spread a small teaspoon of catsup over each slice. Cut the cheese into slices and place on the toast. Trim the cheese to fit the toast.

2 To make the sauce, drain the liquor from the canned clams directly into a saucepot. Add the anchovy paste or fillets to the clam liquor and place the pot on heat. Bring the liquid to a simmer to melt the anchovies. Meanwhile, spoon the cornstarch into a small cup, then stir in the wine to achieve a smooth paste. Add this paste to the hot liquid and stir until the sauce thickens. Stir in the soy sauce, lemon juice, and pepper. (Salt is omitted because the clams contain it.) Add the minced clams and reduce the heat so the clams will not overcook and turn rubbery.

3 Place the bread slices under the broiler for 2 to 3 minutes, or until the cheese melts and begins to brown.

4 Remove the sauce from the fire and fold in the chopped parsley.

TO SERVE

Place the grilled cheese toasts on individual plates, spoon a tablespoon or so of the sauce over each slice and pass the rest of the sauce separately.

COOKING AHEAD

The sauce can be prepared and refrigerated. The bread can be toasted and the cheese sliced and wrapped in plastic. To prevent the toast from becoming soggy do not spread the catsup on the bread more than 15 minutes in advance. The grilling must be done just before serving, while reheating the sauce.

LOW-CHOLESTEROL VERSION

Use low-fat Mozzarella cheese. For restricted salt diets, omit the anchovies and increase the soy sauce to 1 tablespoon.

Brioches aveyronnaises

If you are lucky enough to know a bakery that makes brioches—that rich, funny-shaped French roll with a topknot—you are indeed lucky. They are perfect for this recipe. If not, select Parker House rolls or any soft, cupcake-shaped rolls. I have even used rectangular brown-and-serve sesame seed rolls. Aveyronnaise refers to the region in France where Roquefort cheese is produced. These hot brioches can be a new way to begin a dinner, or served in pairs for lunch.

SERVES 6

WORKING TIME: 10 minutes

BAKING TIME: 10 minutes

INGREDIENTS

  6   brioches (or any cupcake-shaped
      soft roll)
3½   ounces Roquefort cheese
  3   eggs
¼   cup heavy cream
      pepper
½   teaspoon brandy
½   teaspoon Worcestershire sauce
      few drops Tabasco
      Optional: ¼ to ½ cup milk

PREPARATION

Preheat oven to 325°.

1 Cut off the small puffed tops from the *brioches*, or cut through the other soft rolls ¼ of the way down from the top. Carefully pull out the bread from the inside of the main part of the rolls; reserve this bread. Do not break the shell of the rolls; it is better to leave a thicker shell than to puncture it. Replace caps on the rolls, place them on a baking sheet and put in the oven to warm.

2 While the rolls are warming, prepare the filling. Crumble the cheese into a small pot and mash with a fork. To the cheese add the eggs, cream, pepper, brandy, Worcestershire sauce, Tabasco, and the reserved bread. Stir well and put the pot on low heat for 5 minutes or until the mixture bubbles and thickens. This filling will be quite thick; some milk may be added if you prefer a thinner consistency.

3 Remove the rolls from the oven and increase the heat to 375°. Fill the rolls, replace caps, put the filled rolls on the baking sheet, and place it in the hot oven for 10 minutes. The rolls should be crisp and the filling quite hot. Serve at once.

COOKING AHEAD

Prepare the rolls and keep them in a plastic bag or container. Make the filling and refrigerate it. At serving time proceed with the warming of the rolls, reheat the filling, fill the rolls and bake. Although prebaked filled rolls can be reheated in a 350° oven, the crisp texture of the bread is lost.

Roquefort soufflé

In French the word soffler means to blow and has given the name to that culinary delight, the hot soufflé, a baked mixture that puffs up above the rim of its mold. The traditional way to make a soufflé is to start with a thick cooked sauce and then to carefully fold in firmly beaten egg whites. These days it can all be done quickly and easily in the blender. No other preparation is necessary; no sauce pot is used and the egg whites are not beaten. Still this streamlined soufflé puffs impressively and has none of the notoriously temperamental characteristics of the classic soufflé. It can wait, it can't fail, and it can be held for several hours before going into the oven. And even when baked, it won't collapse if kept in the oven.

The secret of all this is to use cream cheese in the batter. Cream cheese gives the consistency and body needed to support the batter as it mounts in the oven. Several variations follow this recipe, but many others are possible; just keep in mind that the basic flavoring ingredient must have some firmness of its own. Spinach, for example, is too watery, while peas or corn are just fine.

How long the soufflé should be baked depends on its role at dinner. If it is to serve as a first or main course, the batter should remain soft in the center. This approximates the presentation of classic soufflés where the undercooked center serves as a sauce. An unusual way to use the Roquefort Soufflé, particularly, is as a hot cheese course at an important dinner. In this case the batter should be completely baked, leaving no soft center. Either way, this family of delicious soufflés appears at the table as if by sleight of hand, and also disappears like magic.

SERVES 6 AS FIRST OR MAIN COURSE;

8 AS CHEESE COURSE

WORKING TIME: *6 minutes*

BAKING TIME: *40 to 50 minutes*

INGREDIENTS

6   eggs

½   cup heavy cream

1   teaspoon Worcestershire sauce

     dash Tabasco

¼   teaspoon pepper

     pinch of salt

½   pound Roquefort cheese

11   ounces cream cheese

1   tablespoon butter

PREPARATION

Preheat oven to 375°.

1 In a 6-cup blender container place the eggs, cream, Worcestershire sauce, Tabasco, pepper, and salt. (The Roquefort is salty, so very little salt is added.) Blend until smooth.

2 With blender running, break off pieces of the Roquefort and add to the container. Next break off chunks of the cream cheese and add it to the blender. After all the cheese is incorporated, blend the batter at high speed for 5 seconds.

3 Smear the butter in a 6-cup soufflé dish or other deep baking dish, or use individual 1-cup baking dishes. Pour in the batter and place in the hot oven.

4 If served as a first or main course, bake the soufflé for 40 to 45 minutes, depending on

the type of dish used (for individual soufflés, bake 15 to 20 minutes). The top should be nicely browned and when the dish is shaken the center should jiggle just a bit. If served as a hot cheese course, or if you prefer a firm soufflé, bake the soufflé until the batter is completely set. This will take 45 to 50 minutes and the surface will have cracked. Serve at once while still hot. If the dish must be held, turn off the oven and open the door a crack so the soufflé won't overbake.

TO SERVE

Serve from the baking dish, using two large spoons to lift out the soufflé.

COOKING AHEAD

As noted above, Roquefort Soufflé can be completely prepared in advance, poured into the buttered baking dish, covered and put aside for 1 or 2 hours at room temperature. If it must be prepared even longer in advance, refrigerate the mixture in the baking dish. Bring it back to room temperature before baking, or allow an extra 5 to 10 minutes of baking time.

Cheddar cheese soufflé

SERVES 6 AS FIRST OR MAIN COURSE;

8 AS CHEESE COURSE

WORKING TIME: *6 minutes*

BAKING TIME: *40 to 50 minutes*

INGREDIENTS

6   eggs

½   cup heavy cream

¼   cup grated Parmesan cheese

½   teaspoon prepared mustard

½   teaspoon salt

¼   teaspoon pepper

½   pound sharp cheddar cheese

11   ounces cream cheese

1   tablespoon butter

Follow directions for Roquefort Soufflé.

Ham soufflé

Although included in the Entrée chapter, this hot puffy soufflé could easily be served as a main course at either luncheon or dinner. It would prove an economical main course since only a half pound of ham serves six. The flavor of the ham, of course, will determine the final flavor of this soufflé. I like a mild hickory-smoked ham, but stronger hams might suit other tastes.

SERVES 6

WORKING TIME: *8 minutes*

BAKING TIME: *45 to 50 minutes*

INGREDIENTS

1   **tablespoon soft butter**

6   **eggs**

½   **cup heavy cream**

1   **teaspoon Worcestershire sauce**

    dash Tabasco

1   **teaspoon prepared mustard**

4   **teaspoons tomato paste**

    large pinch of salt

¼   **teaspoon pepper**

½   **pound mild smoked ham**

11   **ounces cream cheese**

PREPARATION

Preheat oven to 375°

1   Select a 6-cup soufflé dish or other deep baking dish and grease it liberally with the butter.

2   Put in an electric blender the eggs, cream, Worcestershire sauce, Tabasco, mustard, tomato paste, salt, and pepper. Blend until the batter is smooth.

3   While the blender is running cut the ham into ½-inch cubes, removing any fat. With the blender still running, add the ham, a few cubes at a time. Next add the cream cheese in pieces and blend until the ham and cheese are completely incorporated into the batter. Blend at high speed for a few seconds.

4   Pour the batter into the prepared dish and place it in the hot oven. When the top is brown and puffy, shake the dish a little. If the center is still soft it will jiggle. The soufflé can be served this way, or baked a few minutes longer until the center is firm. Serve at once.

COOKING AHEAD

This soufflé can be prepared and placed in its mold several hours in advance and kept in a cool spot. If the kitchen is hot put it in the refrigerator, but allow an extra 5 minutes for baking.

Hot potato soufflé

Here is another variation on the hot souf-flé theme. Served as a vegetable with steaks and roasts, this impressive potato soufflé would come as a culinary sur-prise to the most blasé guests. If served as a vegetable it should be baked until the center is completely cooked; as a first course, I prefer a soft center which serves as a kind of sauce.

SERVES 6 AS FIRST COURSE;

8 AS VEGETABLE COURSE

WORKING TIME: 7 minutes

BAKING TIME: 45 to 50 minutes

INGREDIENTS

1   tablespoon soft butter

6   eggs

½   cup heavy cream

2   teaspoons Worcestershire sauce

¼   teaspoon celery seed

½   teaspoon salt

¼   teaspoon pepper

1   medium-to-large potato

11   ounces cream cheese

PREPARATION

Preheat oven to 375°.

1   Select a 6-cup soufflé dish or other deep baking dish and grease it liberally with the butter.

2   Put in an electric blender all remaining ingredients except the potato and the cream cheese. Blend until the batter is smooth.

3   While the blender is running, peel the potato and cut it into ½-inch cubes. With the blender still running, add the potato, a few cubes at a time. Next add the cream cheese in pieces and blend until the potato and cream cheese are completely incorporated into the batter. Blend the batter at high speed for a few seconds.

4   Pour the batter into the prepared dish and place it in the hot oven. When the top is brown and puffy, shake the dish a little. If the center is soft it will jiggle. The soufflé can be served this way or baked a few minutes longer until the center is firm. Serve at once.

COOKING AHEAD

See notes for preceding soufflés.

Salmon soufflé

SERVES 6

WORKING TIME: 6 minutes

BAKING TIME: 40 to 50 minutes

INGREDIENTS

6   eggs

½   cup sour or heavy cream

1   teaspoon Worcestershire sauce
    dash Tabasco

1   teaspoon anchovy paste
    salt and pepper

1   8-ounce can salmon, drained

11   ounces cream cheese

1   tablespoon butter

PREPARATION

Follow above preparation steps. Remove the skin and bones from the salmon when placing it in the blender. Use a 5-cup baking dish.

Flossy cottage cheese

Why flossy? Because this is plain old cottage cheese dressed up with whipped cream, herbs, and a few other pungent tastes. When fresh herbs are available in the garden, the results will be flossier still. This improvement of cottage cheese is good any time of the day—at breakfast, as a luncheon salad, for snacks and—as here—an unusual first course at dinner. Also try it as a new cocktail hors d'oeuvre: fill mushroom caps with Flossy Cottage Cheese and sprinkle with paprika; half a recipe will fill 26 caps.

SERVES 6

WORKING TIME: *13 minutes*

STANDING TIME: *at least 2 hours*

INGREDIENTS

1 **cup heavy cream**

1 **teaspoon salt**

1 **pound small soft-curd creamed cottage cheese**

½ **teaspoon freshly ground pepper**

1 **tablespoon minced tarragon**

1 **tablespoon minced parsley**

1 **tablespoon minced chives**

1 **shallot, minced (or 1 tablespoon chopped scallion)**

3 **tablespoons oil**

4 **tablespoons white wine vinegar**

Garnish: lettuce leaves, tomato wedges or cherry tomatoes

PREPARATION

1   Beat the cream until very stiff, adding the salt once the cream is thick.

2   Beat ⅓ of the cottage cheese into the whipped cream with a wire whisk. Repeat with remaining cottage cheese.

3   Beat in the remaining ingredients, adding only 3 tablespoons of vinegar at first; then taste, and if you prefer a sharper flavor add the other tablespoon.

4   Line a sieve or colander with cheesecloth and place it over a deep bowl. Scoop the seasoned cottage cheese into the cheesecloth and press on it lightly. Fold the ends of the cheesecloth over the cottage cheese and refrigerate it with the bowl. Allow at least 2 hours for the liquid to drip out. Drain off the liquid once or twice if a lot collects.

TO SERVE

Unfold the top layer of cheesecloth and either reverse the entire dome of Flossy Cottage Cheese onto a serving dish or spoon individual portions onto salad plates. In either case, line the dish with lettuce leaves and garnish with tomato wedges or cherry tomatoes.

COOKING AHEAD

Flossy Cottage Cheese may be made as much as a day before using, leaving it in the cheesecloth suspended over the bowl.

Emerald cream

A sweet custard dessert is nothing out of the ordinary. But a cold herb custard at the beginning of a meal is an unexpected pleasure. The flavor of this one is delicious and delicate. The smooth custard arrives hidden under an emerald green coating of herbs. Emerald Cream can also be an elegant innovation as a main course for a summer luncheon.

SERVES 6

WORKING TIME: 14 minutes

BAKING TIME: 1 to 1¼ hours

CHILLING TIME: 3 hours

INGREDIENTS

1   **quart milk**

2   **teaspoons salt**

½   **teaspoon pepper**

1   **teaspoon dry tarragon**

½   **teaspoon dillweed**

6   **eggs plus 2 yolks**

1   **tablespoon flour**

¼   **cup warm water**

1   **tablespoon minced parsley**

¼   **cup minced watercress***

¼   **cup minced scallion greens***

2   **teaspoons Worcestershire sauce**

　 few drops Tabasco

2   **tablespoons Bourbon or Scotch whiskey**

2   **teaspoons oil**

*Lacking watercress or scallions, increase the amount of parsley and tarragon to compensate for the green and the flavor.

PREPARATION

Preheat oven to 350°

1   In a nonaluminum pot heat the milk with the salt and pepper. Meanwhile, put the dried tarragon and dillweed in a 2-quart mixing bowl and crush between the fingers until they are fine and powdery.

2   Add the eggs and egg yolks in the mixing bowl and beat until light. When the milk almost reaches the boiling point, slowly pour it into the beaten eggs while beating rapidly. Return the eggs, herbs, and milk to the pot.

3   Put the flour in a small cup and slowly stir in the water. Mix until smooth, then add to the hot milk. Return the pot to low heat for about 1 minute while adding parsley, watercress, scallions, Worcestershire sauce, and Tabasco. Remove from the heat and add whiskey.

4   Lightly oil a 6-cup soufflé dish (or any ovenproof mold). Pour the liquid into the mold and place it in a pan containing enough hot water to cover ⅓ of the mold. Bake for about 1 to 1¼ hours. The timing will vary according to the size of the egg yolks and the depth of the dish.

5   The Emerald Cream is done when it puffs slightly, has a small crack in the top and begins pulling away from the sides of the dish. A knife plunged into the center should come out clean. The herbs will have floated to the surface and been baked into a green topping. Let cool, then chill well.

TO SERVE

Serve from the mold, using two large spoons.

COOKING AHEAD

Since the Emerald Cream must be chilled, it can be baked a day in advance. It should not stand longer than that since it will lose some of its delicacy.

Cold herb omelet

This is not the usual puffy rolled omelet, but really a flat flourless pancake, the kind so popular in the south of France and Spain. It is a captivating introduction to a meal, but would be equally appreciated as a main course at lunch. To be really effective, it must be well chilled.

SERVES 6 AS FIRST COURSE; 4 AS MAIN COURSE

WORKING TIME: *10 minutes*

COOKING TIME: *6 minutes*

CHILLING TIME: *2 hours*

INGREDIENTS

8	**eggs**
2	**tablespoons heavy cream**
¾	**cup cooked green peas**
1	**tablespoon each: tarragon, chives, chervil (chopped if fresh, crushed fine if dried)**
2	**tablespoons chopped parsley**
	salt and pepper
2	**tablespoons butter**

PREPARATION

1 Put the eggs and cream in a bowl and beat together thoroughly. Add the peas, all the herbs, salt, and pepper. Put the bowl aside for 10 minutes, 20 minutes if the herbs are dried.

2 Preheat the broiler. Heat the butter in a heavy skillet or omelet pan until it is hot, but not smoking hot as for a rolled omelet. Pour in the egg mixture and lower the flame a little. Stir the eggs with a fork, lifting the edges to let the liquid run underneath. This will take 3 or 4 minutes.

3 While there is still some liquid on top, place the pan under the broiler to finish cooking the top. Put the pan aside to cool.

4 Run a knife around the outside of the omelet to loosen it. Reverse the omelet onto a serving dish—the bottom is now the top and should be a nice brown color. Chill for at least 2 hours.

TO SERVE

Cut in wedges at the table. Serve with crusty French bread.

COOKING AHEAD

Cold Herb Omelet must be prepared in advance, but cook it the day it is to be served.

Egg ramekins

There is something quite festive about this elegant first course. Perhaps the element of surprise helps, since guests rarely guess what is nestling inside the little cups. Ceramic cups that can go into the oven are most effective, but even in plain ovenproof custard cups this is a meal opener with flourish. No one would believe that it costs pennies a serving.

SERVES 6

WORKING TIME: *8 minutes*

BAKING TIME: *approximately 20 minutes (Lacking leftover cooked rice or tomato sauce, add 10 minutes to working time.)*

INGREDIENTS

2	**teaspoons oil**
½	**cup cooked rice**
½	**cup heavy cream**
6	**medium eggs**
	salt and pepper
½	**cup Quick Tomato Coulis (page 225)**
3	**tablespoons grated Parmesan cheese**

PREPARATION

Preheat oven to 375°

1   Select six 1-cup baking dishes and grease them with the oil. Spoon into each cup 1 well-rounded tablespoon of cooked rice. With the tip of the spoon, make a slight depression in the center of the rice. (This helps center the egg.) Spoon 2 teaspoons of cream over the rice.

2   Break an egg into each cup, spoon on another 2 teaspoons of cream and sprinkle with salt and pepper.

3   Carefully add 1 tablespoon of tomato sauce over each egg. Sprinkle the top with 2 teaspoons of cheese.

4   Place the baking cups in a roasting pan and place it in the oven for about 20 minutes. The eggs should not be baked until firm; they are best when still somewhat runny in the center. Check the degree of doneness by shaking one of the cups: the less its contents jiggle, the firmer the egg. (If you are timid about that test, poke at an egg with a toothpick and reserve this one for yourself.)

TO SERVE

Place the cups on saucers and serve with teaspoons. Pass French bread or toast.

COOKING AHEAD

The ramekins can be assembled and refrigerated an hour or two ahead of time. Either bring them back to room temperature before baking, or allow an extra 10 minutes in the oven. I find it most convenient to have all the ingredients ready and to assemble the ramekins during the cocktail hour.

Scrambled eggs with onions

Strange as it may seem to some people, pungent onions do marry beautifully with delicate eggs. The secret is in the very, very slow cooking of the chopped onions—in the process they turn quite sweet. The onions can be done days in advance and kept refrigerated. Scrambled Eggs with Onions makes a perfect after-the-theater supper dish; the final scrambling can easily be done while guests are having a cocktail. I also find this a lovely luncheon dish as well as first course at dinner. In the latter case, these quantities will serve 8 amply. To make the dish still more substantial, a slice of warmed boiled ham can be placed under the eggs. A grilled tomato looks pretty beside the yellow mound. For a festive occasion Eggs with Onions can be served in warmed patty shells.

SERVES 6 TO 8

WORKING TIME: *13 minutes*

COOKING TIME: *35 to 50 minutes*

INGREDIENTS

7	**tablespoons butter**
1½	**cups chopped onion**
6-8	**slices white toast, or patty shells**
1	**teaspoon salt**
14	**eggs**
5	**tablespoons heavy cream**
¼	**teaspoon pepper**

PREPARATION

1   In a heavy nonaluminum pan slowly melt 4 tablespoons of butter while peeling and chopping the onions. The onions should be cut rather fine. Add the onions and ½ teaspoon salt to the butter. Stir, cover closely, and reduce the heat to the lowest position possible (a heat-deflecting pad can be placed under the pan). Sauté the onions 30 to 45 minutes without browning.

2   While the onions are cooking, prepare the toast and spread each slice with ½ teaspoon of butter and keep warm.

3   Add the remaining 2 tablespoons of butter to the pan with the onions and turn the heat to medium. Break the eggs into a bowl; add 3 tablespoons of cream, ½ teaspoon salt, and the pepper. Beat the eggs gently then pour them into the pan; stir to mix the eggs completely with the onions. Keep stirring eggs, scraping from the sides and bottom where the eggs set first. The eggs cannot be left unattended. They should be almost set in 5 or 6 minutes, depending on the size of pan used. Do not cook until dry. Remove the pan from the fire and stir in the remaining 2 tablespoons of cream.

TO SERVE

Place a slice of warm toast on each plate and heap with the scrambled eggs. Serve at once.

COOKING AHEAD

As mentioned above, the onions can be cooked even days ahead and kept tightly covered in the refrigerator. Reheat with the remaining butter when ready to scramble the eggs. The eggs cannot be cooked in advance.

LOW-CHOLESTEROL VERSION

Since the basic ingredient in the master recipe is fresh eggs, obviously the low-cholesterol version will not be a substitute, but it can be an approximation. The onion flavor will make something special of liquid egg substitutes now on the market. Use 24 ounces of the egg substitute. Use polyunsaturated margarine for frying and at the end stir in evaporated skimmed milk or frozen polyunsaturated dairy substitute.

Eggplant caviar

Almost every country in Europe and the Middle East with an abundant supply of eggplant has its own version of Eggplant Caviar, often called Poor Man's Caviar. From Greece, Russia, Turkey, and Italy come some of the better-known variations. This recipe is basically Russian, the wine being my own addition to a classic dish. As an hors d'oeuvre, serve the "caviar" with thinly sliced dark bread. It also makes a lovely first course at dinner, mounded on crisp lettuce and garnished with black olives.

MAKES 2 CUPS—

SERVES 12 AS HORS D'OEUVRES;

4 AS FIRST COURSE

WORKING TIME: *10 minutes*

BAKING TIME: *1 to 1½ hours*

COOLING TIME: *30 minutes*

MATURING TIME: *1 day*

INGREDIENTS

1 **2-pound eggplant**
   juice of 1 lemon
1 **tablespoon dry white wine**
2 **tablespoons olive oil**
1 **garlic clove, mashed, or to taste**
   salt and pepper
   Optional: 2 teaspoons Texas green chili peppers (makes a spicy version)
2 **tablespoons chopped parsley**

PREPARATION

Preheat oven to 325°

1   Bake the eggplant for about 1 to 1½ hours, or until the skin is dark and shriveled and the pulp is soft. If several smaller eggplants are used, 1 hour of baking should be sufficient. Cool.

2   Peel off the skin and gently squeeze out the excess moisture—don't force it out. Put the pulp through a food mill or mash well in a bowl, but do not use a blender which would make the texture too smooth. There should be some distinct pieces in the purée. The soft seeds which remain enhance the caviar look.

3   Stir in the lemon juice, wine, olive oil, mashed garlic, salt, and pepper. Add the optional chili peppers. Taste and correct seasoning if necessary. Stir in the parsley.

4   Refrigerate for at least a day so that the flavors can mellow and blend together. Remove from refrigerator at least 1 hour before serving.

TO SERVE

As an hors d'oeuvre, mound the caviar in a bowl and place on a platter with thin slices of dark bread. Use a teaspoon or butter knife for spreading. As a first course: place a lettuce leaf on a salad plate, heap with "caviar" and decorate with a few black olives.

COOKING AHEAD

Eggplant Caviar must be prepared in advance. It will keep in the refrigerator for up to 4 days.

LOW-CHOLESTEROL VERSION

Substitute polyunsaturated oil for the olive oil; no other changes in the recipe are necessary.

Danish cauliflower

Usually when cauliflower is served cold, it is also raw, having become America's favorite dipping vehicle. But to cook it, then chill it while enveloped in a mildly piquant sauce is to elevate the snow-white morsels from the cocktail hour to the dinner hour. Danish Cauliflower offers an interesting blending of flavors. This, plus the purity of its looks, makes it a favorite way to begin a meal for me. The white cauliflower lies under a cream-colored sauce, with just a few flecks of parsley sprinkled about. The obvious thing would be to add sliced tomatoes to "give it some color." I'd rather not. Danish Cauliflower can stand by itself on the strength of its own delicious flavor. It can also brighten any cold meat platter or buffet table.

SERVES 4

WORKING TIME: 8 minutes

COOKING TIME: about 6 minutes

CHILLING TIME: 3 hours

INGREDIENTS

1   **large head cauliflower**

1   **teaspoon salt**

1   **cup mayonnaise (p. 226)**

½   **cup plain yogurt**

1½   **tablespoons prepared mustard**

    juice ½ lemon

    salt and pepper

2   **teaspoons chopped parsley**

PREPARATION

1   Bring a large quantity of water to a boil while preparing the cauliflower. Trim away all the green leaves and break the cauliflower into flowerets. Add salt and cauliflower to the water and cook for about 5 minutes once the water returns to a boil, or just until the cauliflower is tender but still slightly crisp. Do not overcook. Drain at once. Plunge into cold water and drain again very well.

2   While the cauliflower is cooking, prepare the sauce by beating together the mayonnaise, yogurt, mustard, lemon juice, salt, and pepper.

3   Put the cauliflower in a deep serving bowl and pour sauce over. Carefully turn to coat all surfaces with the sauce. Wipe the sauce off the edges with a paper towel. Chill for about 3 hours.

TO SERVE

Serve from the bowl or on individual plates, sprinkled lightly with parsley.

COOKING AHEAD

Danish Cauliflower can easily be prepared the day before.

LOW-CHOLESTEROL VERSION

Substitute low-fat yogurt for full-fat yogurt. No other changes are necessary.

Courgettes à la grecque

Here is a light, inexpensive first course that one rarely sees, even in restaurants. Still, it's elementary cooking, but with a dashing flavor. The zucchini are not peeled, which speeds up the timing greatly. For zucchini, you can substitute unpeeled mushrooms or eggplant, even cauliflower broken into flowerets. Save the leftover marinade to perk up salads.

SERVES 4 TO 6

WORKING TIME: 10 minutes

COOKING TIME: 7 to 10 minutes

CHILLING TIME: 3 hours or more

INGREDIENTS

¼ cup olive oil

1 medium onion, sliced

1½ cups dry white wine

juice of 1 lemon

2 teaspoons coriander seeds, or 1½ teaspoons ground coriander

salt and pepper

1½ pounds zucchini

PREPARATION

1 Heat the oil in a large flat skillet while peeling and slicing the onion. Add the onion, cover and simmer for 3 minutes.

2 Add the wine, lemon juice, coriander, salt, and pepper. Bring this court bouillon to a simmer, cover, and cook while preparing the zucchini.

3 Trim the ends off the zucchini, then scrub and slice them. First cut the zucchini in halves or quarters, lengthwise, depending on thickness. Now cut these slices in half crosswise. The sliced zucchini pieces should be no more than 3 to 4 inches long and ½ inch wide.

4 Add the zucchini to the court bouillon. Bring the liquid back to a boil, cover and simmer gently for 7 to 10 minutes or until the zucchini is almost tender. The zucchini will cool in the hot liquid and continue softening, so do not overcook.

5 Cool and transfer the cooked vegetables to a serving dish. Chill at least 3 hours and serve very cold.

COOKING AHEAD

Courgettes à la Grecque must be prepared in advance so it can chill. It may even be prepared 2 days before serving.

LOW-CHOLESTEROL VERSION

Substitute polyunsaturated oil for the olive oil and add ¼ teaspoon basil.

Wine-marinated mushrooms

Cold mushrooms make a nice addition to buffets and picnic baskets. Or serve them as a first course, heaped on a bed of lettuce and topped with a slice of tomato sprinkled with freshly chopped herbs.

SERVES 6

WORKING TIME: 10 minutes

MARINATING TIME: at least 6 hours

INGREDIENTS

1 pound fresh mushrooms, preferably small size

Dressing

¼ cup chopped pimento

¾ cup oil

½ cup red wine

¼ cup red wine vinegar

2 teaspoons horseradish

1 teaspoon garlic salt

½ teaspoon pepper

2 teaspoons lemon juice

1 teaspoon oregano

PREPARATION

1 Rinse the mushrooms under running water. If they are large, cut in halves or quarters. Place in a bowl.

2 Put all the ingredients for the dressing in a jar and shake well. Pour over the mushrooms and mix well. Cover.

3 Leave at room temperature for ½ hour, then refrigerate for at least 6 hours, preferably overnight.

COOKING AHEAD

The dish can be prepared a day or two in advance and allowed to marinate.

LOW-CHOLESTEROL VERSION

Substitute polyunsaturated oil for regular oil; no other changes are necessary.

Italian artichoke hearts

This is the kind of artichoke you would not be surprised to find on the antipasto cart of a fine Italian restaurant. The warm cooked artichokes are tossed with a few carefully balanced flavorings. The final subtle result has no relationship to the oily, vinegary version that comes in little jars.

SERVES 6

WORKING TIME: 5 minutes

COOKING TIME: 4 minutes

MARINATING TIME: 30 minutes

INGREDIENTS

2   **9- or 10-ounce packages frozen artichoke hearts**

¼   **cup olive oil**

¼   **cup vermouth**

   juice of 1 lemon

½   **teaspoon oregano**

2   **tablespoons chopped pimento**

   salt and pepper

6   **lettuce leaves**

   Optional: 6 tomato slices

PREPARATION

1   Place artichokes in a small quantity of boiling salted water. Once the water comes back to a boil, cook for 4 minutes. Drain at once and place artichokes in mixing bowl.

2   Work quickly while artichokes are still hot. Sprinkle over them the oil, vermouth, lemon juice, oregano, pimento, salt, and pepper. Toss well to coat all the hearts with the dressing. Cover and put aside for about 30 minutes. Stir occasionally.

TO SERVE

If used as a first course, place a lettuce leaf on each plate and garnish with a portion of the marinated artichokes and an optional tomato slice. For the cocktail hour spear each artichoke with a toothpick.

COOKING AHEAD

Although Italian Artichoke Hearts are at their optimum when prepared just a little before serving, they can easily be made hours earlier and kept in a cool spot in the kitchen. If they must be prepared a day or two before, marinate them at room temperature for 15 minutes, then refrigerate. Remove from refrigerator at least 1 hour before serving.

LOW-CHOLESTEROL VERSION

The only substitution necessary is polyunsaturated oil for the olive oil. I would recommend, though, adding an extra pinch of oregano.

Peppers and anchovies, italian style

Both French and Italians like the combination of peppers and anchovies. They do, however, have two very different ways of serving them. In France, this simple first course consists just of large, mild pimentos and a generous portion of anchovies served on the same plate. One eats both of them together. It's an intriguing marriage of wildly differing flavors and textures. Italians, on the other hand, cook the two together and produce an equally unusual and delicious combination. I particularly like to cook the peppers in the early fall when both red and green varieties are available. But this dish is good even without that artistic touch.

SERVES 6

WORKING TIME: *12 minutes*

FRYING TIME: *10 minutes*

INGREDIENTS

2	**tablespoons olive oil**
2	**pounds peppers (5 or 6), green and red, if possible**
2	**tablespoons capers, drained**
2	**garlic cloves, mashed**
2	**teaspoons oregano**
2	**tablespoons tomato paste**
2	**tablespoons red wine vinegar**
1½	**cups tomato juice or water**
1	**2-ounce can anchovies**
2	**tablespoons chopped parsley**
6	**lemon wedges**
	Optional garnish: lettuce and black olives

PREPARATION

1 Heat the oil in a large skillet while cutting the peppers in half and removing the core and seeds. Cut into strips, about ½-inch wide. Add the peppers to the hot oil and stir to coat all pieces with the oil. Cook on high heat, stirring from time to time.

2 While the peppers are frying, drain and chop the capers and peel the garlic. Add the capers to the peppers and mash the garlic directly into the skillet. Add oregano and stir.

3 Put the tomato paste in a small bowl and stir in the vinegar and tomato juice. Pour this over the peppers and mix thoroughly. Cover and simmer slowly.

4 Drain the oil from the anchovies by holding the opened can lid in place and pressing against the contents. Chop the anchovies coarsely.

5 Remove the skillet from the heat and immediately add the anchovies. Stir will to distribute them. The anchovies will melt in the heat. Cover and put aside.

Note: Do not wait between steps. As soon as you are ready, proceed with the additions. The frying should be kept to a minimum. The peppers are better if still slightly crunchy.

TO SERVE

The peppers can be served hot or cold. Either way, stir in the parsley just before serving and garnish each plate with a lemon wedge. If the peppers are a cold first course, make a bed of lettuce for them and garnish with a few black olives.

COOKING AHEAD

To serve as a hot dish, complete the entire recipe and refrigerate. When reheating, put on low fire and bring just to simmer. Do not overcook. It can be made several days in advance.

LOW-CHOLESTEROL VERSION

Substitute polyunsaturated oil for the olive oil and rinse the anchovies in cold water. If a low-sodium diet is also being followed, the anchovies should be omitted.

Wilted salad

This zesty first course is related to German hot salad, but easier and faster to make. With the addition of some diced sausage or leftover roast, Wilted Salad can serve nicely as a main course at lunch or late supper.

A word about the lettuce: There is confusion in this country about what is endive or chicory. Imported Belgian endive is a compact, white root vegetable. But there is also a dark green curly lettuce sometimes called endive, and sometimes chicory (in Europe it is known as chicory). Whatever the name tagged to it, the green curly variety of lettuce is what you want for this recipe. The whole problem could be avoided if dandelion greens were readily available. They have no nickname and are the best for this salad.

SERVES 4

WORKING TIME: 10 minutes

COOKING TIME: 15 to 20 minutes

INGREDIENTS

1	medium head chicory or curly endive lettuce
5	tablespoons oil
2	garlic cloves
4	slices white bread cut into ¼-inch cubes
¼	cup thinly sliced onion
⅓	cup vinegar
¼	cup water
¼	cup white wine
1½	teaspoons sugar
2	tablespoons chopped pimento
¼	teaspoon Worcestershire sauce
	good dash of Tabasco

PREPARATION

1 Wash the endive leaves well and let them dry thoroughly. Refrigerate to keep crisp. At serving time, put the lettuce in a deep bowl, leaving at least 2 inches of space above the lettuce level.

2 Put 4 tablespoons oil in a skillet. Peel garlic cloves and add to oil. Heat oil very, very slowly for 10 to 15 minutes until garlic is a dark brown. This step needs no attention if the heat is low enough. Remove garlic.

3 While the garlic is browning, dice the bread slices and peel and slice the onion. Turn up the heat and add the bread croutons to the oil. Fry until they turn a nut brown color. Remove with skimmer.

4 Add the remaining tablespoon of oil to the skillet along with the onions. Simmer for 2 or 3 minutes without allowing the onion to brown. Add the vinegar, water, wine, sugar, pimento, Worcestershire sauce, and Tabasco. Bring to a boil and pour over lettuce. Toss well. Add the fried croutons and toss again. Serve at once.

COOKING AHEAD

The croutons can be fried and the vinegar dressing prepared well ahead of time, even the day before, and put aside until needed. At serving time, bring the dressing back to a boil and proceed as above.

LOW-CHOLESTEROL VERSION

Use polyunsaturated oil; no other changes in the recipe are necessary.

Cold tomatoes with hot curry sauce

This dish is one way to let guests know that dinner is going to be something special. Nevertheless, it's easy to do and costs very little. The success of the recipe depends entirely on the contrast between the cold, cold tomato and the superhot spicy sauce. Although this recipe works best when good tomatoes are in season, it can give even pale winter tomatoes some semblance of glamour. This is a good luncheon dish or a lively kickoff for dinner.

SERVES 6

WORKING TIME: *10 minutes*

CHILLING TIME: *at least 3 hours*

COOKING TIME: *5 minutes*

INGREDIENTS

6   **small-to-medium ripe tomatoes**
3   **tablespoons butter**
3   **tablespoons flour**
4   **teaspoons curry, or to taste**
2   **cups light cream**
3   **tablespoons finely chopped chutney**
    salt and pepper
6   **slices white bread, crusts removed**

PREPARATION

1   Plunge the tomatoes into boiling water for a few seconds and remove with a skimmer, then slip off the tomato skins and cut out the stem ends. Chill tomatoes in the refrigerator for at least 3 hours.

2   Meanwhile, prepare the sauce: Melt the butter in a saucepan, add the flour and curry powder and stir until smooth, making certain that none of the roux (flour and butter) clings to the edges of the pan. Cook for a minute or 2, stirring constantly. Remove the pan from the heat and slowly stir in the cream, beating constantly with a wire whisk. Once the sauce is smooth, return it to the fire. Chop the chutney on a small chopping board or dish so that you lose none of its liquid. Scrape the chutney and liquid into the sauce and sprinkle on salt and pepper. Simmer the sauce for 2 minutes.

3   At serving time, toast the bread and place the slices on individual plates. Place a tomato on each slice and spoon a tablespoon of the hot sauce over it. Pass the rest of the sauce separately to keep it as hot as possible. (The sauce cools quickly once it is on the cold tomato.) Serve at once.

COOKING AHEAD

The tomatoes must be skinned in advance and chilled. The sauce can be cooked and refrigerated. All that remains to be done at serving time is to reheat the sauce and toast the bread. The final assembly takes a minute.

LOW-CHOLESTEROL VERSION

Substitute polyunsaturated margarine for the butter and evaporated skimmed milk for the cream. Use more curry powder and add 1 teaspoon of lemon juice to the sauce.

Grapefruit jaipur

You can count on the tangy flavor of grapefruit to snap taste buds to attention. That's one reason it's so good on the breakfast table. The unadorned grapefruit half also makes an occasional appearance at the dinner table, either as a beginning course, or with sugar, as dessert. But watch what happens when grapefruit's crispness is married with the heady flavor of chutney. In a few minutes, a plain old predictable fruit becomes an exotic creation.

SERVES 6

WORKING TIME: *10 minutes*

BROILING TIME: *5 minutes*

INGREDIENTS

3   grapefruit

6   tablespoons chutney

¼   cup brandy

PREPARATION

1   Cut grapefruit in half and remove the center membrane and any seeds. Loosen each section with a grapefruit knife. Place halves in a baking pan with a rim, not a baking sheet.

2   Spread 1 tablespoon of chutney over each grapefruit half, then sprinkle each with 2 teaspoons of brandy. Some brandy will dribble into the pan, but it doesn't matter.

3   Just before serving, place the grapefruit under hot broiler for 5 minutes.

TO SERVE

Place each grapefruit half on an individual dish and spoon over it some of the juices that have collected in the pan.

COOKING AHEAD

The grapefruit can be cut, spread with chutney and sprinkled with brandy well in advance. Refrigerate if kept more than 2 or 3 hours. Broil at serving time, allowing an extra 2 minutes if the grapefruit has not been brought back to room temperature.

LOW-CHOLESTEROL VERSION

No changes in the recipe are necessary.

Bean-sprout salad

The boom in Chinese cooking in this country has many good side effects. Even those of us who don't like to chop food all day appreciate the lightness (and low calories) of Chinese cuisine. With so many people cooking with woks today, Chinese produce is more easily available. Many supermarkets now carry fresh ginger, Chinese cabbage, and fresh bean sprouts.

The sprouts are among the easiest of all vegetables to handle, since absolutely nothing except a fast rinsing need be done to them. In the vegetable section of this book bean sprouts are suggested as a hot vegetable (page 139). This recipe makes a pretty and crunchy salad of them. There are several colors to admire —white, tan, red, and green. The textures vary from the crispness of sprouts to the crunch of green peppers, with the mushroom slices somewhere in between. This is a first course (or salad course) at dinner that is unusual, exotic looking, and as low-budget as it is low-cal.

SERVES 6

WORKING TIME: *8 minutes*

INGREDIENTS

1   **pound fresh bean sprouts, soy or mungo**
¼   **pound fresh mushrooms (5 to 8, depending on size)**
½   **cup oil**
2   **tablespoons vinegar**
     juice of 1 lemon
2   **tablespoons soy sauce**
1   **teaspoon prepared mustard**
½   **teaspoon paprika**
2   **tablespoons chopped pimento**
1   **teaspoon salt**
½   **teaspoon pepper**
½   **green pepper, chopped (about ½ cup)**

PREPARATION

1   Dump the sprouts into a colander, rinse them under cold running water and put aside to drain. Rinse the mushrooms and let stand to dry.

2   Put the ingredients for the dressing in a jar with a lid: oil, vinegar, lemon juice, soy sauce, mustard, paprika, chopped pimento, salt, and pepper. Shake well.

3   At serving time, chop the green pepper and slice the mushrooms and put them in a large salad or mixing bowl. Dump the sprouts into the bowl; shake the dressing again and pour it over the vegetables. Mix very well to distribute the dressing evenly. (I find that turning the vegetables with my hands is the easiest method; the sprouts can slip out from between a salad spoon and fork.)

TO SERVE

Present the salad at the table in the bowl and serve individual portions heaped on salad plates.

COOKING AHEAD

The salad dressing can be made well in advance. The sprouts can be rinsed, drained, placed in a tightly sealed plastic bag and refrigerated. The slicing of the mushrooms and the final mixing should be done just before serving to preserve the salad's crispness. If need be, the salad can be mixed 30 minutes before serving, but no longer.

LOW-CHOLESTEROL VERSION

Use polyunsaturated oil; no other changes in the recipe are necessary.

Virginia's chinese mushrooms

Although this is a true Chinese recipe, I have never seen it served in a Chinese restaurant. Cost may be a factor. Dried Chinese (or Japanese) mushrooms — essential to the success of this dish — have become rather expensive. Usually, one finds only slivers of the mushroom mixed into other ingredients. But even these thin pieces are enough to work their perfumed magic.

An elegant Chinese friend served these beautiful whole mushrooms as a first course. Their great purity of flavor is a rare taste experience. Either as a smashing way to begin a meal or served with cold meats, Virginia's Chinese Mushrooms are a treasure from behind the Great Wall. Besides, many a banal first course can cost much more than this dish. Save the cooking liquid to add an exotic flavor to many foods; rice especially. The liquid can be frozen for use later.

SERVES 6

WORKING TIME: *3 minutes*
SOAKING TIME: *1 hour*
COOKING TIME: *30 minutes*
CHILLING TIME: *2 hours*

INGREDIENTS

2   **ounces dried Chinese (or Japanese Shitake) mushrooms**
2   **teaspoons soy sauce**
     soy sauce to pass at table

PREPARATION

1   Rinse the mushrooms in cold water. Put them in a pot and cover with boiling water. Cover and let stand for at least 1 hour.

2   Remove mushrooms, reserving water. With a small sharp knife cut off and discard the stem ends. They are very tough and won't soften with any amount of cooking.

3   Return mushrooms to the soaking water, put on heat, cover and bring to a boil. Simmer for 15 minutes.

4   Add 2 teaspoons of soy sauce, re-cover, and simmer for 15 minutes more.

5   Cool mushrooms in cooking liquid, then chill.

TO SERVE

On each plate put 1, 2, or 3 mushrooms, depending on size. Spoon 2 tablespoons of the cooking liquid over the mushrooms. Pass with soy sauce, which should be sprinkled on quite liberally.

COOKING AHEAD

This dish is better if done the day before.

LOW-CHOLESTEROL VERSION

No changes in the recipe are necessary.

BRUNCH & LUNCH

Brunch and lunch dishes (not to mention supper) need not be limited to the few in this chapter. Many recipes in the chapter on entrées would be excellent choices at any of those meals, especially Croque Neptune, Cold Herb Omelet, Scrambled Eggs with Onions, Asperges à la Normande, Flossy Cottage Cheese, or Emerald Cream. A light fish dish is another good choice.

Two recipes found here are particularly appropriate when a crowd is expected for supper. Swiss Fondue and Pumpkin Supper are convivial conversation makers, easy to do and delicious.

Red, white, or rosé wine could be served with any of the following dishes, except fondue. Despite firm rules to the contrary, I like white wine, a Riesling preferably, with fondue.

Pumpkin supper

A whole supper baked in a pumpkin? Not only is it a novel idea but a delicious one. This can be a hearty feast after a football game, a one-dish Sunday night supper, or a warming reward ready for young ones back from trick-or-treating. The long, slow baking produces a rich and unctuous filling that is scooped out along with the soft pumpkin pulp.

The amount of time you spend on scraping out the pumpkin fibers and seeds will dictate the final preparation time. My 17 minutes includes the cleaning of a particularly pesky specimen. Here at last is a grand dish that requires little attention and does not use a single pot or pan.

A whole pumpkin makes a dramatic table presentation, but unfortunately shops sell them for a relatively short period. Acorn squash, on the other hand, enjoys a long market season. They work just as well, and are far easier to clean.

SERVES 6 TO 8

WORKING TIME: *17 minutes*

BAKING TIME: *about 2 hours*

INGREDIENTS

- 4 **slices white bread**
- 1 **3-to-4-pound pumpkin, preferably with stem intact, or 6 1-pound acorn squashes**
- 1 **tablespoon oil**
- 4 **ounces Swiss cheese, grated**
- 3½ **cups half-and-half cream**
- **scant 1 teaspoon salt**
- ½ **teaspoon pepper**
- ¼ **teaspoon nutmeg**

PREPARATION

Preheat oven to 350°

1   Cut the bread into about ½-inch pieces; precision doesn't matter at all. Put on baking sheet or foil pan and toast in oven until golden brown, about 7 minutes.

2   Meanwhile wash and dry the pumpkin. Using a strong serrated knife, cut off a cap about ¼ down from top. Pull out as many of the fibers and seeds as possible, then scrape out the rest of fibers with a spoon. Rub outside of the pumpkin and cap with the oil.

3   Grate the cheese. Beat together in a bowl 2½ cups of the cream and the salt, pepper, and nutmeg.

4   Place the pumpkin on a pie dish or strong baking sheet. Layer into the pumpkin the bread cubes and cheese, finishing with a layer of cheese. Fill ¾ of the space in the pumpkin. Pour in enough cream to just cover the filling, using the remaining cream if necessary. Place cap back on pumpkin.

5   Place in oven and bake for about 2 hours. Stir from time to time. Pumpkin Supper is done when the pulp is tender when pierced with a small sharp knife and the skin turns a rust-orange.

TO SERVE

At the table remove the cap from the pumpkin and ladle out the thickened custard and pumpkin pulp into soup dishes.

COOKING AHEAD

This dish cannot be baked ahead. The soft pulp would collapse and be most unattractive. A slower baking is possible, about 3 hours at 325°, but no lower. In this case, raise the heat to 350° for the last 15 or 20 minutes. The pumpkin can be completely prepared, filled, and refrigerated for up to 6 hours before baking.

LOW-CHOLESTEROL VERSION

Use low-fat cheese (Saint Otho or any of the low-fat filled cheeses); skimmed milk instead of half-and-half; add 1 tablespoon polyunsaturated oil and ½ cup liquid egg substitute.

Country cheese pie

This delicious cheese pie is to country cooking what Quiche Lorraine is to more sophisticated cuisine. It is also far less rich, which means it's better suited to today's more restrained eating habits. It comes to the table hot and puffy, looking every bit the taste treat it is. I've used it as a first course at dinner, also as a main course at both dinner and lunch. Nutritionally, it's loaded: high in protein, calcium, Vitamin A, iron, thiamine, riboflavin, and niacin. Not bad for a dish that costs so little. With Country Cheese Pie one can sip well-chilled white wine or rosé, or even a light red, like Beaujolais, that has been cooled a little in the refrigerator.

SERVES 8 AS FIRST COURSE

WORKING TIME: 6 minutes

(plus pie crust)

BAKING TIME: 45 minutes

INGREDIENTS

1 **9-inch partially baked pie shell (see page 220)**

1 **pound farmer cheese**

6 **tablespoons yogurt**

½ **teaspoon ground coriander**

¼ **teaspoon freshly grated nutmeg**

1 **tablespoon minced chives or scallion**

1 **teaspoon sugar**

   salt and pepper

3 **eggs, well beaten**

¼ **cup Parmesan Cheese**

PREPARATION

Preheat oven to 375°

1 Prick bottom of pie shell and bake for 10 minutes. Meanwhile mix together in a bowl the farmer cheese, yogurt, coriander, nutmeg, chives, sugar, salt, and pepper. (Taste cheese for salt before adding any; some brands are rather salty.) Beat with a wooden spoon until smooth. Add eggs and beat thoroughly again.

2 Pour batter into the pie shell and smooth the top with a spatula. Sprinkle with the Parmesan cheese. Bake for 45 minutes or until top is nicely browned and puffy. Serve immediately.

TO SERVE

Place pie dish on a round platter and cut in wedges at the table.

COOKING AHEAD

The pie shell can be baked for 10 minutes any time during the day. The batter can be mixed ahead and refrigerated; remove from refrigerator 30 minutes before baking, or increase baking time by 5 to 8 minutes.

LOW-CHOLESTEROL VERSION

Substitute the following ingredients for those listed above: skimmed milk farmer cheese; low-fat yogurt; 4 egg whites (½ cup) instead of 3 whole eggs, or ½ cup liquid egg substitute; plus 3 tablespoons polyunsaturated oil. Use recipe for Low-Cholesterol Piecrust (page 221).

REMARKS

For serious weight watchers, bake the cheese batter in baking cups without any crust.

Provençal fish salad

A really good fish salad is a welcome addition to summertime menus. It shouldn't be a bland or mundane affair if flagging hot-weather appetites are to be stimulated. Here is a remarkably easy fish salad to prepare, and also one that doesn't strain the budget. One-and-a-half pounds of fish fillets will serve six hearty appetites since a piquant sauce and cooked rice stretch the salad nicely. See remarks below for how to prepare rice if you have none left over.

SERVES 6

WORKING TIME: *12 minutes*

COOKING TIME: *10 to 13 minutes*

CHILLING TIME: *at least 2 hours*

INGREDIENTS

1½	**pounds fillets of flounder, turbot, cod, or halibut**
2½	**cups milk**
½	**small onion, sliced**
1	**small bay leaf**
	salt and pepper
3	**cups cooked rice, chilled**
½	**cup chopped parsley**
	lettuce leaves

Sauce

2	**cups mayonnaise (p. 226)**
¼	**cup lemon juice**
2	**garlic cloves**
6	**anchovy fillets, plus 1 tablespoon anchovy oil**
1	**tablespoon capers**
1	**tablespoon basil**
½	**teaspoon brandy or whiskey**
1	**teaspoon soy sauce**
	salt and pepper
	Optional garnish: black olives, cherry tomatoes, 2 anchovy fillets

PREPARATION

1 Lay the fish fillets in a nonaluminum pan and pour in enough milk to just cover. Separate the onion slices into rings and scatter them over the fish. Break the bay leaf in half and add to the milk, then sprinkle with salt and pepper. Cover and put the pan on medium heat. Slowly bring the milk to a simmer, reduce the heat and simmer very slowly for 10 minutes, or until the fish is firm and white and flakes when pierced with a fork. Remove the pan from the fire and let the fillets cool in the milk. Lift the fillets out of the milk and flake them into a bowl, then chill.

2 Put all the ingredients for the sauce into a blender and purée.

3 Once the fish is chilled, add the chilled rice and toss together gently. Pour on the sauce, add the chopped parsley and mix thoroughly, but gently.

TO SERVE

Arrange Provençal Fish Salad in a mound on lettuce leaves and decorate with optional garnishings, crisscrossing the two anchovy fillets on top.

COOKING AHEAD

The fish can be poached and flaked, the sauce prepared, and the rice cooked and all kept chilled in the refrigerator until needed. Mix together just before serving.

LOW-CHOLESTEROL VERSION

No changes in the recipe are necessary, though mayonnaise made at home with polyunsaturated oil is preferable to prepared mayonnaise.

REMARKS

If you have no leftover cooked rice, prepare it ahead. Heat 2 tablespoons of oil in a small heavy pot, stir in ¾ cup rice and mix until the grains turn white and opaque, in about 2 minutes. Add 1½ cups of hot water, and sprinkle with salt and pepper; cover and simmer slowly for 20 minutes. Scrape into a mixing bowl and chill. Allow 3 minutes' additional working time.

Swiss fondue

Any cold day when friends are coming, think of fondue and turn their visit into a party. No single dish guarantees so much conviviality. How can one be standoffish when eating from a communal pot?

Four to six participants is the perfect number at the table. Many more can enjoy the same bubbly concoction at a cocktail party. For dinner, little else need be served since fondue is a rich and filling dish. So the working time indicated above is for practically the whole meal. This time is for grating by hand; any mechanical grater will reduce the working time considerably. Although cheese fondue is very easy to do, there are a few tricks to insure its success. It can easily separate, or melt into a hard mass. Follow the simple directions below to avoid disappointment.

SERVES 6

WORKING TIME: 18 minutes

COOKING TIME: about 8 minutes

EQUIPMENT

1   **earthenware casserole with handle (the Swiss call it a** *calcon***), or chafing dish, or enameled iron casserole**

1   **alcohol stove with adjustable flame; or electric hot plate with a heat-deflecting pad**

INGREDIENTS

1   **garlic clove cut in half**

2½   **cups dry white wine**

1½   **pounds cheese, preferably half domestic Swiss mixed with half imported Emmenthaler, Gruyère, Fribourg, Vacherin, or Appenzeller**

⅓   **cup flour**

1   **loaf white bread with hard crust (not presliced type)**

2   **tablespoons kirsch**

¼   **teaspoon nutmeg**

salt and pepper

PREPARATION

1   Rub the *calcon* with the cut side of the garlic clove. Pour in the wine and add the garlic pieces. If possible let this steep for at least ½ hour.

2   Grate the cheese into a bowl. Sprinkle flour over the cheese and toss with your hands to coat all pieces. (The flour prevents the separation of the cheese and wine.)

3   When ready to prepare the fondue, heat the wine slowly until air bubbles rise to the surface (do not let it boil), remove the garlic and add a handful of cheese. Stir with a wooden spoon until the cheese melts. Keep adding handfuls of cheese, one after the other as each addition melts.

4   While the cheese is melting cut or break the bread into bite-sized pieces and place them in a bread basket.

5   When all the cheese is melted add the kirsch, nutmeg, salt, and pepper. Add an extra ¼ teaspoon nutmeg if desired. Stir the fondue until it bubbles, then remove the pot to the alcohol burner on the dining table. Your cooking is now finished; the guests take over.

TO SERVE

Each guest should be provided with a plate and, if possible, a long-handled fork. Firmly spear a piece of bread with the fork and dip it into the fondue. Lift and twirl the fork to hold all the fondue clinging to it. I recommend holding it over your own plate for a few seconds to allow the fiery hot mixture to cool enough to be eaten comfortably. It is important that all guests stir as they dip into the fondue to help maintain the proper consistency. Adjust flame to keep the fondue bubbling slowly.

ETIQUETTE

What to do when someone loses a piece of bread in the fondue: There are many penalties; among them, the guilty party buys another bottle of white wine; he buys everyone at the table a drink of kirsch; he or she kisses all members of the opposite sex (remember, this is an old European custom, pre-Fem Lib). Set the ground rules before beginning.

REMARKS

When all the fondue is gone there will be a crisp crust on the bottom—a special delicacy. Loosen this with a knife and cut it into portions for all at the table. The *dentelle* (lace) that clings to the side of the pot is equally delicious, but less crisp.

BEVERAGES

There are many theories. Some say drink nothing cold with fondue during the meal. A small glass of kirsch, or other brandy, is permitted. Hot coffee or tea would then follow. That's the classic way. Nevertheless, I like cold white wine with fondue.

Potato supper

Potato Supper is for the family and good friends on Sunday night. It's nothing more than a few boiled potatoes and some sour cream. The contrast between hot and cold is intriguing, as is the difference between the starchy potato and smooth, smooth cream. In Central Europe, where this is a popular country dish, yogurt or buttermilk is often used instead of sour cream. Sometimes fried onions are sprinkled over the potatoes. There are many variations that can be tried, but this is the way it began.

SERVES 4

WORKING TIME: *10 minutes*
BOILING TIME: *about 20 minutes*

INGREDIENTS

8   **potatoes**
2   **teaspoons salt**
3   **cups sour cream**
    Garnish: paprika or chopped chives

PREPARATION

1   Bring a large quantity of water to a boil while peeling the potatoes. Add the salt and the potatoes to the water, partially cover and boil for about 20 minutes or until the potatoes are soft.

2   Meanwhile, divide the sour cream among 4 individual bowls.

TO SERVE

On a dinner plate, place 1 bowl of sour cream and 2 potatoes, sprinkled with paprika or chives. Pieces of potato are cut with a tablespoon, dipped into the cream and eaten at once before the potato cools.

COOKING AHEAD

The potatoes can be peeled hours in advance, placed in a bowl, and covered with cold water. For best results, however, they should be boiled just before serving.

LOW-CHOLESTEROL VERSION

Instead of sour cream use low-fat yogurt or buttermilk. This is no compromise since they are both used in Potato Supper in many Central European countries.

Tuna-stuffed peppers

Here is an imaginative combination that turns a few easily available ingredients into an admirable main course. These peppers, served with a wedge of lemon, are equally good cold.

SERVES 6

WORKING TIME: *12 minutes*

BAKING TIME: *40 to 45 minutes*

INGREDIENTS

6	green peppers
1	1-pound can tuna in oil
½	cup chopped black olives
⅓	cup chopped parsley
¾	cup bread crumbs
¾	cup oil
	juice of 1 lemon
	salt and pepper
	oil for baking

PREPARATION

Preheat oven to 350°.

1 Cut the tops off the peppers and reserve; pull out the membranes and seeds from inside the peppers and rinse the peppers. The running water will wash away any clinging seeds.

2 In a bowl mash together all the remaining ingredients, including the tuna oil, but use only ½ cup of vegetable oil. If the mixture seems a little dry, add the remaining ¼ cup oil.

3 Stuff the peppers with the mixture, replace the caps, and stand the peppers up in a baking dish. Dribble a little oil over each pepper. Pour water in the dish to a depth of about ¼ inch. Bake for 40 to 45 minutes, or until the peppers are tender when pierced with a sharp knife. Do not bake until they are mushy.

COOKING AHEAD

The peppers can be stuffed and refrigerated for several hours before baking. If they must be baked ahead, cook them only partially, for about 30 minutes. Before serving the peppers, reheat them in a 375° oven for 10 to 15 minutes.

LOW-CHOLESTEROL VERSION

Use polyunsaturated oil. For very strict diets, drain the oil from the can of tuna and add extra polyunsaturated oil to compensate for it.

Tuna-macaroni salad

Here is an economical, easy-to-do salad that gets its out-of-the-ordinary flavor from the lively sauce. No unusual ingredients are called for, so it can be prepared on a moment's notice.

SERVES 6

WORKING TIME: *13 minutes*

COOKING TIME: *about 10 minutes*

INGREDIENTS

5	ounces elbow macaroni
	salt
1	pound canned tuna in oil
½	cup chopped green pepper
3	tablespoons chopped pimento
½	cup diced celery

Sauce:

1	cup sour cream
¼	cup lemon juice
1	teaspoon sugar
1	tablespoon soy sauce
¼	cup white wine
1	tablespoon dillweed
1	tablespoon prepared mustard
	Garnish: lettuce leaves, 2 tomatoes, 2 hard-cooked eggs

PREPARATION

1 Cook the macaroni in a large quantity of boiling salted water. Do not overcook the macaroni but keep it *al dente*; this should take about 10 minutes.

2   While the macaroni is cooking, combine all the sauce ingredients in a jar and shake well. Drain the tuna and flake it directly into a mixing bowl. Add the chopped green pepper, pimento, and celery to the tuna.

3   Drain the macaroni as soon as it is cooked, rinse under cold running water and drain again thoroughly. Add the macaroni to the mixing bowl. Pour the sauce over the ingredients in the bowl and mix well. Chill.

TO SERVE

Spoon the salad into a mound shape on a bed of lettuce leaves. Garnish with alternating quarters of tomato and hard-cooked egg.

COOKING AHEAD

Tuna-Macaroni Salad should be prepared and chilled at least 1 hour ahead, but can stand a full day in the refrigerator.

LOW-CHOLESTEROL VERSION

Substitute low-fat yogurt for the sour cream in the sauce. Increase the quantity of soy sauce to 2 tablespoons and mustard to 1½ tablespoons.

Deep-fried eggs

Fried eggs, sunny-side up, have been a long-established breakfast staple. Now, as people tend to eat more lightly, eggs, in many forms, are increasingly popular at lunch and even dinner. The nutritious egg is an extremely versatile food which we panfry, scramble, poach, bake, and turn into omelets. But the accommodating egg can be treated in still another manner: deep fried. Cooked this way the egg becomes a golden brown oval puff that is as intriguing in looks as it is in taste. In a simple presentation, it crowns a slice of toast. For a more glamorous setting, it can perch on a lightly sautéed artichoke bottom or tomato half. Here is a superquick, last-minute dish that will surprise and delight drop-in guests.

SERVES 4

WORKING TIME: *5 minutes*
FRYING TIME: *2 to 3 minutes*

INGREDIENTS

oil for deep frying
4   **slices white bread**
4   **eggs**
    salt and pepper

PREPARATION

1   Pour the oil in a large skillet to a depth of at least 1 inch. Heat the oil while toasting the bread. Keep the toast warm in a slow oven.

2   When the oil is hot, but not smoking, break an egg into a small cup and slip the egg quickly into the oil. At once, using two wooden spoons, pull the egg white over the yolk.

3   Keep turning the egg, continuing to wrap the white around the yolk. In less than a minute, the egg will be a crisp golden color and a puffy oval shape. Remove the fried egg to drain on absorbent paper and sprinkle with salt and pepper. (Until you've done Deep-fried Eggs once or twice, it is best not to work with more than 2 eggs at a time in the pan. Four is the maximum to fry at one time.)

4   The 1-minute frying will produce a lightly cooked, runny interior. If you prefer a firmer yolk, cook until you feel a slight resistance when pressing the yolk.

TO SERVE

Place a slice of toast on a warm individual plate and garnish it with a deep-fried egg. Serve at once.

COOKING AHEAD

Cook the eggs to just the runny stage and do not season. To reheat the eggs, lightly oil a baking sheet and carefully place the eggs on it and warm in a 350° oven for about 7 or 8 minutes. Sprinkle with salt and pepper.

Grilled sardine toasts

These tasty little hot open sandwiches are offered as a fast, last-minute snack when you want to serve something that looks and tastes a bit special. Sardine Toasts can also serve as the opening course at an informal dinner.

SERVES 4

WORKING TIME: *7 minutes*

BROILING TIME: *about 1 minute*

INGREDIENTS

2	**4½-ounce cans skinless, boneless sardines, or mackerel fillets**
4	**slices white toast**
3	**tablespoons tartar sauce**
	juice of ½ lemon
	Garnish: black olives

PREPARATION

1 Preheat the broiler. Open the sardine cans by completely removing the lids. (The easiest way is to turn the cans upside down and use a manual can opener that can grip the bottom ledge.)

2 Spread about 2 teaspoons of tartar sauce over the entire surface of each slice of toast, reaching to the corners. Open the sardines flat and place them, flat side down, on the toast. Squeeze lemon juice over the fish.

3 Arrange the sardine toasts on a baking sheet and place it under the broiler for about 1 minute or until the tops of the sardines just begin turning brown.

TO SERVE

Place the hot sardine toasts on individual plates and garnish with a few black olives. Serve immediately.

COOKING AHEAD

Grilled Sardine Toasts can be prepared 30 to 45 minutes in advance of broiling, but no longer. The toast will become soggy if it stands too long with the tartar sauce and sardines on it.

LOW-CHOLESTEROL VERSION

No changes in the recipe are necessary, but you might like to drain the sardines on paper towels to remove excess oil.

FISH

Here are fish dishes, made in simple and fancy ways: as soups for the first or main course; cooked in beer or smothered in champagne sauce; in aspic, broiled, grilled, fried, poached, baked. Not one takes more than twenty minutes to do, and that is for a complete main course for eight people. For instance, tender, spicy Marinated Oysters need only one and one-half minutes of working time.

I suppose it's evident that I'm extremely fond of fish of every persuasion and presentation. In Spain I once unknowingly ordered gray fish gills swimming in a thick green sauce. The waiter, who was used to seeing Americans turn as green as the sauce, stood by ready to whisk the plate away, but retreated at my obvious delight.

In addition to being delicious and low in calories, fish used to be an economy food. No more, except for a few local varieties and smelts, or whiting as they are sometimes called. A recipe that capitalizes on tíny, low-cost smelts is included. When pricing fish, one should keep in mind that there is little waste, so the cost per serving is lower than it appears.

White wines, clearly, are best with most fish dishes. Sautéed Scallops, Baked Salmon, or Oven-Fried Fish Fillets would go well with a white Burgundy such as Meursault, a Soave, an Alsatian or a California Riesling, or Pinot Chardonnay. That contrary recipe Saumon au Vin Rouge (Salmon in Red Wine Sauce) can be enhanced by a cooled Zinfandel, light red Burgundy or good Beaujolais. And what would be better with Shrimps Steamed in Beer than beer?

Marinated oysters

What a surprise it is to bite into what looks like a raw oyster, only to find that it's been poached with complementary seasonings. There are other reasons to serve Marinated Oysters besides their originality. Shucked oysters can be used instead of oysters on the half shell, meaning a much smaller bill from the fish store. Also, many people today shy away from raw oysters because of fear of hepatitis. Cooking the oysters eliminates that danger. But above all, marinated oysters are offered because they are so good.

SERVES 6 AS FIRST COURSE;

12 AS HORS D'OEUVRES

WORKING TIME: *1½ minutes*

COOKING TIME: *about 5 minutes*

MARINATING TIME: *1 hour*

CHILLING TIME: *2 hours*

INGREDIENTS

1   **pint shucked oysters with their liquor**

1   **cup dry white wine**

½   **cup salad oil combined with ¼ cup olive oil**

1   **tablespoon wine vinegar**

¼   **cup dry vermouth**

   juice of 2 lemons

2   **bay leaves**

⅓   **teaspoon Tabasco**

2   **teaspoons peppercorns**

   lettuce leaves

   chopped parsley

6   **lemon wedges**

   Optional: buttered bread squares for serving with cocktails

PREPARATION

1   Put the oysters and their liquor in a small pot. Pour in the wine, oil, wine vinegar, vermouth, and lemon juice. Add the bay leaves, Tabasco, and peppercorns. Stir to blend the marinade.

2   Put the pot on medium heat and bring the marinade to the boiling point. As soon as the liquid begins to boil, remove the pot from the fire. Cover and let marinate for at least 1 hour. Refrigerate about 2 hours to chill.

TO SERVE

As first course: line 6 small bowls with lettuce leaves. Lift 5 or 6 oysters from the marinade and arrange on the lettuce. Spoon a tablespoon of marinade over the oysters, then sprinkle with parsley. Add a lemon wedge. As cocktail hors d'oeuvre: put the oysters and some of the marinade in a deep bowl and sprinkle with the chopped parsley. Surround the bowl with 1½-inch squares of buttered bread. Whole wheat bread is especially good with these oysters.

COOKING AHEAD

Marinated Oysters must be made at least 3 hours in advance, but could very well be made the day before serving and kept refrigerated.

LOW-CHOLESTEROL VERSION

Use polyunsaturated oil in the marinade; no other changes in the recipe are necessary.

Oysters with champagne sauce

If oysters are considered somewhat of a luxury, then covering them with an unctuous champagne sauce is really gilding the lily. But what could be a more attractive or better dish? Only a handful of superstar restaurants in France serve this impressive first course. They use oysters on the half shell, a lavish presentation, but one that raises several practical problems for home service: most private dining rooms don't have dishes large enough to accommodate neatly 5 or 6 large oyster shells nor broiler space to grill a large quantity of oysters at a time; also, oysters on the half shell cost much more than shucked ones.

Those are the practical reasons for using fresh shucked oysters to make Oysters with Champagne Sauce and cooking them in scallop shells. However, the most important one is that while the recipe is amazingly simple to prepare, it gives oysters an indescribably subtle and delicious taste. There is a little trick used in this recipe that can easily be used to save time in other dishes. I am referring to the chopping of shallots, which is not necessary for sauces. My way, described below, gives you all of the perfume, none of the fuss. If you are lucky enough to have some leftover champagne sauce, use it (hot or cold) to glorify other foods: chicken salad, crab salad, hot asparagus, poached salmon (hot or cold), poached eggs, or spread on tomato halves and broiled.

SERVES 6 OR 7

WORKING TIME: *12 minutes*
COOKING TIME: *13 minutes*
BROILING TIME: *2 to 3 minutes*

INGREDIENTS

1	**tablespoon cornstarch**
¾	**cup heavy cream**
1	**cup dry inexpensive champagne, chilled**
1 or 2	**shallots**
	dash Tabasco
	salt and pepper
4	**egg yolks**
1	**pint shucked oysters**
6 or 7	**scallop shells**

PREPARATION

1 Measure the cornstarch into a small mixing bowl and stir in the cream. Pour this sauce base into a small heavy nonaluminum pot and add the champagne. Spear each shallot on a toothpick and add to the sauce with the Tabasco, salt, and pepper. Bring to a simmer and cook gently for 10 minutes, uncovered.

2 Put the yolks in the same bowl used for the cream and beat them well. Remove the shallots from the sauce and, while whisking, slowly pour the hot liquid into the beaten yolks. Return the sauce to the pot and taste for salt and pepper. Cook over very low heat for a minute or less, whisking constantly and not allowing the sauce to boil. The sauce is finished when it will easily coat a spoon and is quite thick.

3 While the sauce is simmering place 4 or 5 oysters in each scallop shell depending on size. Spoon about 2 tablespoons of hot champagne sauce over the oysters; the oysters must be completely covered by the sauce.

TO SERVE

Place the scallop shells under the broiler for 2 or 3 minutes or until the sauce bubbles. Place the shells on luncheon-size dishes and serve at once with an oyster fork and a teaspoon.

The champagne sauce can be made in advance and refrigerated, but do not add the egg yolks at this time. When reheating, finish the sauce with the egg yolk addition described in step 2. The oysters can be placed in the shells and kept refrigerated. The broiling must be done just before serving.

REMARKS

Even though it is to be used in cooking, chilled champagne is specified to reduce the risk of the cork shooting out of the bottle at a high velocity.

Baked oysters

Something very good happens to oysters when they are baked. Their fat little bodies plump up into moist, succulent morsels. So baking is another way to enjoy oysters and one that is simplicity itself. But the timing is crucial. If the oysters are overbaked they dry out. Perhaps that bit of extra attention in the kitchen explains why more restaurants don't serve baked oysters. Given the high cost of oysters today, the recipe below is given for four good friends. Double it for eight.

SERVES 4

WORKING TIME: *12 minutes*

BAKING TIME: *10 to 15 minutes*

INGREDIENTS

4	**cups rock salt (or aluminum foil)**
16	**oysters in their shells**
4	**tablespoons butter**
1	**teaspoon dry white wine**
2	**teaspoons lemon juice**
	salt and pepper

PREPARATION

Preheat oven to 450°.

1   Pour the rock salt into a jelly-roll pan or any baking sheet with sides. Smooth the salt to an even layer. (The salt helps keep the oysters from tipping over and the juice that escapes from burning the pan. Lacking rock salt, place a sheet of aluminum foil in the pan.)

2   Scrub the shells under cold running water and arrange the oysters flat side up on the salt, firmly imbedding them into the salt. Place the baking sheet in the oven for 10 to 15 minutes or just until the oyster shells begin to pop open. Any that don't open can be easily pried open with a knife.

3   While the oysters are baking, prepare the sauce. In a small pot melt the butter with the wine, lemon juice, salt, and pepper. Bring the sauce just to a boil and remove at once from the heat. Pour it into 4 individual custard cups.

TO SERVE

Bring the baking sheet with the oysters to the table. Each diner serves himself, one oyster at a time. The hot salt helps the oysters retain their heat. The top shell of the oyster is pulled off, the oyster speared by a fork and dipped into the hot butter sauce.

COOKING AHEAD

Hours before baking, the oysters can be scrubbed and imbedded in the salt on the baking sheet and refrigerated. The baking must be done just before serving. If they are cold when baked, add a few minutes oven time.

LOW-CHOLESTEROL VERSION

Substitute polyunsaturated margarine for the butter, and dry vermouth for the white wine.

Filets de sole neva

To spare the hostess last-minute flutters, this cookbook features recipes that can be done in advance. Fillets of Sole Neva is a bit different. While the fish can be partially prepared ahead, the final steps are unabashedly last-minute. But what a triumph it is. Despite its dramatic appearance, this fish dish is really very easy to do, since complicated techniques and sauces have been avoided. It gives a streamlined idea of what great French cooking is all about, and it can make one's reputation.

I usually serve only one sole fillet per person, since this is a very rich dish when it is part of a complete dinner. But if you are worried about not having enough, prepare a few extra fillets for friends with large appetites.

By the way, the "Neva" part of the title refers to the river that runs by Leningrad, a city that enjoys its share of salmon eggs and smoked salmon.

SERVES 6

WORKING TIME: 13 minutes

BAKING TIME: 15 to 20 minutes

SAUCE TIME: 5 minutes

INGREDIENTS

6	fillets of sole or flounder (if flounder is large, cut in half, lengthwise)
½	lemon
4	tablespoons butter (½ stick), room temperature
	white pepper
2	ounces smoked salmon, or 3 tablespoons red salmon eggs
	toothpicks
1½	cups dry white wine
2	egg yolks
1½	cups heavy cream

PREPARATION

Preheat oven to 375°.

1   Place the fish on a counter top and rub both sides of each fillet with the cut lemon half. (Do not discard the lemon.) Now arrange the fillets with the skin side up, that is, the darker side up and the white flesh against the counter.

2   Smear each fillet with 2 teaspoons of butter and sprinkle with pepper. If smoked salmon is used, slice it up coarsely and sprinkle it over the fillets, covering only about ⅓ of the fish. (If red salmon eggs are used, carefully spread 2 teaspoons of the eggs over each fillet; try not to mash the delicate eggs.) Whichever garnish is used, reserve about 1½ tablespoons of it for the sauce and garnish. Beginning with the small end, roll each fillet and secure the end with a toothpick. Place these rolled turbans upright in a baking dish that will hold them snugly.

3   Pour in the white wine, first about 1 tablespoon in the center of each turban and the rest in the dish. Cover the dish tightly and place in the oven. Bake for 15 to 20 minutes, depending on the thickness of the fillets. The fish is cooked when the flesh turns opaque white and flakes easily when pierced with a small sharp knife.

4   Lift the turbans onto a warm serving platter and pour the liquid from the dish into a saucepan and place on high heat to reduce it quickly to about half. Meanwhile, remove the toothpicks from the turbans and place the dish in a slow oven.

5   Beat the egg yolks in a small bowl and slowly stir in the cream. Remove the saucepan from the heat and lower the heat. Stir the cream mixture into the wine reduction and return to the heat. Add a few drops of lemon juice from the lemon half used previously. Taste for seasonings and correct if necessary. Simmer until the sauce thickens a little; it should have the consistency of very heavy cream. Stir in 1 tablespoon of the reserved chopped smoked salmon or salmon eggs, reserving the rest for the final garnish. Be careful not to mash the eggs when stirring the sauce.

TO SERVE

Remove the platter with the fish from the oven and pour into the sauce any juices that may have collected in the dish. Spoon 2 to 3 tablespoons of sauce over each fish turban and add a dab of smoked salmon or red caviar on top. Serve at once.

COOKING AHEAD

As much as 3 or 4 hours before baking, the fish fillets can be prepared, rolled, and placed on the baking dish. Cover and refrigerate, but do not add the wine at this point. Twenty-five minutes before serving time proceed with the recipe.

LOW-CHOLESTEROL VERSION

Use polyunsaturated margarine instead of butter and squeeze a few drops of lemon juice over each fillet before it is rolled. In the sauce, use either polyunsaturated frozen dairy substitute or evaporated skimmed milk. Stir ¼ cup of the milk into 2 tablespoons of cornstarch in a small cup and add this to the hot sauce as a thickening agent instead of the egg yolks. Add ½ teaspoon of vermouth to the sauce and a few drops of Tabasco.

Oven-fried fish fillets

This is an excellent way of "frying" fish while using a minimum amount of fat. Thus it is far lower in calories than deep-fried fish. There are other advantages, too—the fish dries out less than in deep frying; the final result has more flavor of the fish, rather than of the oil; and it needs far less of the cook's attention. Another plus—a baking dish is easier to wash than a skillet or deep fryer.

SERVES 6

WORKING TIME: *13 minutes*

BAKING TIME: *10 to 12 minutes*

DRYING TIME: *15 minutes*

INGREDIENTS

2½ tablespoons butter
6 fish fillets: sole, baby halibut, or flounder
1 cup bread crumbs
¼ teaspoon pepper
2 tablespoons chopped parsley
½ cup milk
½ teaspoon salt
paprika
6 lemon wedges
Optional: ⅛ teaspoon powdered thyme

PREPARATION

Preheat oven to 450°.

1 Smear 1 tablespoon of butter in a baking dish that will hold the fillets flat. Rinse the fillets and dry them on paper towels. Spread the crumbs on a large piece of waxed paper. Add the pepper and parsley (also thyme if frozen fish is used) and toss to mix well.

2 Pour the milk in a dish and add the salt. Stir for a second or two. Dip the fillets on both sides in the milk, shake off the excess, then dip the fillets in the bread crumbs. Pat the crumbs well onto both sides of the fish and place them in a baking dish. Let stand for at least 15 minutes.

3 Just before placing the dish in a hot oven, melt 1½ tablespoons of butter and sprinkle it over the fillets. Place the dish in the oven for 10 to 12 minutes; exact timing will depend on thickness of the fillets. Test by piercing with a toothpick: the flesh should be white and firm. Sprinkle with paprika for the last minute of baking.

TO SERVE

Serve directly from the baking dish with lemon wedges.

COOKING AHEAD

The fish can be completely prepared and placed in the baking dish. Keep refrigerated until ½ hour before baking time. If taken directly from the refrigerator and baked, add an extra 2 to 3 minutes of cooking time.

LOW-CHOLESTEROL VERSION

Add the ⅛ teaspoon thyme to the bread crumbs. Substitute polyunsaturated margarine for the butter and skimmed milk for whole milk. Also add a few drops of lemon juice to the melted margarine that is sprinkled on top.

Sautéed scallops

Fresh scallops, especially the tiny bay scallops, make a delicious treat. I see no reason to smother their natural sweet flavor with a lot of garlic and herbs. Those are devices to use when working with less good specimens, like frozen scallops. When quickly sautéed, these white morsels come to the table lightly browned and quite tender. Overcooking, as with most fish, will turn them into rubber.

SERVES 6 AS MAIN COURSE;

8 AS FIRST COURSE

WORKING TIME: *7 minutes*

FRYING TIME: *3 minutes*

INGREDIENTS

2   **pounds bay scallops, or sea scallops, quartered**
8   **tablespoons butter (1 stick)**
⅓   **cup oil**
    salt and pepper
    flour
2   **tablespoons chopped parsley**
6   **lemon wedges**

PREPARATION

1   Rinse the scallops under cold water and place them on paper towels to dry.

2   Select a large skillet that will hold the scallops in a single layer; otherwise use 2 skillets. Heat the butter and oil in the skillet until very hot. There should be almost ½ inch of melted fat.

3   While the fat is heating, sprinkle the scallops with salt and pepper. Spread flour in a large platter or on a sheet of waxed paper. Add the scallops to the flour and toss with your hands to coat all surfaces.

4   Shake off the excess flour and add the scallops to the hot fat. Keep the flame high while cooking. Turn the scallops a few times with a spatula to brown all surfaces.

5   While the scallops are frying, chop the parsley.

TO SERVE

Remove the sautéed scallops to a warm serving dish, sprinkle lightly with salt, pepper, and parsley. Pass with the lemon wedges.

LOW-CHOLESTEROL VERSION

Instead of butter, use polyunsaturated margarine and oil. Squeeze the juice of ½ lemon over the scallops while they are frying. Pass extra lemon.

Scallops with gin

Scallops and gin seem like an improbable combination, but it really works. What the gin does is cut through some of the richness of the cream sauce without interfering in any way with the delicacy of the scallop flavor. This is an easy dish to do that looks and tastes like much more time and work.

SERVES 4 TO 5

WORKING TIME: *8 minutes*

COOKING TIME: *6 minutes*

INGREDIENTS

4   **tablespoons butter (½ stick)**
1   **tablespoon oil**
¾   **cup flour, approximately**
1   **pound (1 pint) scallops**
¾   **cup gin**
1   **cup cream**
    juice of ½ lemon
    salt and pepper
1   **teaspoon chopped tarragon**
1   **tablespoon chopped parsley**

PREPARATION

1   Heat the butter and oil together in a large frying pan; use 2 frying pans if necessary to keep the scallops in a single layer. While the butter is heating, spread the flour on a dish or a large piece of waxed paper. Lift the scallops out of the container with your hands and add them to the flour. (Do not dump the scallops from the container into the flour; the liquid must be left behind.) Toss to coat the scallops thoroughly with flour, shake off the excess flour, and add the scallops to the frying pan when the butter is hot and foamy.

2 Cook the scallops just long enough to give them a nice light brown coating; this should take no more than 1 or 2 minutes. Keep turning them with a wide spatula. Pour in the gin, cream, lemon juice and sprinkle with salt and pepper. Reduce the heat to medium, cover the pan, and simmer for 2 minutes for tiny bay scallops, or 3 to 4 minutes for larger scallops.

TO SERVE

Spoon the hot scallops with the cream sauce into warm scallop shells. Sprinkle lightly with the chopped parsley and tarragon. In addition to a fork, each diner should have a teaspoon for the delicious sauce.

LOW-CHOLESTEROL VERSION

Substitute polyunsaturated margarine for the butter and frozen dairy substitute for the cream. Reduce gin to ½ cup. Add ½ teaspoon chopped tarragon to the cream while cooking the scallops.

Scallops seviche

Tender scallops don't have to be cooked with heat to be delicious. In this exotic recipe they are "cooked" by the marinade, turning just as opaque and white as they do when prepared over a flame. I like to buy the tiny bay or cape scallops and serve them on toothpicks as a light cocktail snack. Heaped into a lettuce-lined scallop shell this seviche is a reputation-making first course. There also is an apocryphal reason for enjoying this dish often—in Peru, where marinated fish is popular, the claim is made that in large quantities the phosphorus in fish seviche will sharpen one's intelligence.

SERVES 6 AS FIRST COURSE;

12 AS HORS D'OEUVRES

WORKING TIME: *9 minutes*

MARINATING TIME: *6 hours to overnight*

INGREDIENTS

1   **pound bay or cape scallops, or sea scallops, quartered**

½   **cup minced onion**

¾   **cup lime juice, some lemon juice may be mixed in, but it's not as good**

3   **tablespoons olive oil**

2   **tablespoons white wine**

½   **teaspoon ground coriander**

dash Tabasco sauce

1   **tablespoon chopped green chili peppers**

1   **teaspoon salt**

½   **teaspoon freshly ground black pepper**

Optional: sprig of fresh basil

¼   **cup chopped parsley**

PREPARATION

1 Drain off any liquid from the scallops and put them in a small bowl that will hold them and the marinade snugly. Sprinkle the onions over the scallops and mix well.

2 Into a jar pour the lime juice, oil, wine, coriander, Tabasco, chili peppers, salt, and pepper. Close the jar tightly and shake well. Pour this marinade over the scallops, which must be completely covered by the liquid. If not, add more lime juice and oil. Tuck in the optional basil. Cover and refrigerate for at least 6 hours, or overnight. Stir occasionally.

TO SERVE

Drain the scallops well, remove basil, and sprinkle with the parsley. If served as hors d'oeuvres, pass with toothpicks. If served as first course, place a lettuce leaf in a scallop shell or small dish and heap with the scallops.

COOKING AHEAD

This dish can be prepared a day ahead.

LOW-CHOLESTEROL VERSION

Substitute polyunsaturated oil for the olive oil; no other changes are necessary.

Coquilles chambrette

I've named this recipe after Chef Chambrette because it is in his tradition of inspired simplicity. Until recently, this remarkable man performed culinary magic at his restaurant, La Boule d'Or (The Golden Ball), in Paris. His working credo is to use the best-quality food with great care and to make no effort at self-promotion and publicity seeking. Yet he created some of the most glorious food in that capital of gastronomy.

SERVES 4 OR 5

WORKING TIME: *8 minutes*

SAUTÉING TIME: *5 minutes*

INGREDIENTS

8	**tablespoons butter (1 stick)**
2	**tablespoons chopped shallots, or scallions**
	flour
1½	**pounds bay scallops, or sea scallops, quartered**
	salt and pepper
	juice of 1 lemon
2	**tablespoons brandy**
½	**cup dry white wine**
½	**teaspoon Worcestershire sauce**
2	**tablespoons chopped parsley**

PREPARATION

1   While peeling and chopping the shallot, melt the butter in a heavy straight-sided skillet that will hold the scallops in a single layer, or use two skillets. Add the shallot to the butter, cover, and simmer gently for 2 or 3 minutes.

2   While the shallots are simmering, spread the flour on a large piece of waxed paper. Lift the scallops out of their container and add them to the flour. Toss the scallops with both hands to coat them lightly with the flour.

3   Turn up the heat under the skillet and add the scallops, shaking off the excess flour as you do. Mix and turn the scallops with a wooden spoon for 3 or 4 minutes, or until they have achieved a light brown coating.

4   Sprinkle salt and pepper over the scallops and squeeze in the lemon juice. Pour in the brandy, and simmer on high heat for half a minute. Lift the scallops out of the skillet with a skimmer and onto a warm serving dish.

5   Pour the wine and Worcestershire sauce into the skillet and boil briskly for 1 minute while stirring the bottom of the skillet to collect all the coagulated juices. Remove the skillet from the heat and add the parsley. Stir the sauce and pour it over the scallops.

TO SERVE

The scallops must be served at once, preferably on warmed dinner plates. Only rice or steamed potatoes should be put on the same plate; any other vegetable is best placed on a side plate, or passed as a separate course.

LOW-CHOLESTEROL VERSION

Use polyunsaturated margarine instead of butter. Use the juice of 2 lemons instead of 1 and increase the Worcestershire to 1 teaspoon.

Coquilles saint-jacques georgettes

I'm a firm believer in capitalizing on the sweet, fresh flavor of scallops. Heavy, rich sauces, to my way of thinking, detract from the luxurious taste of this gem from the sea. This recipe adds just a few hints of harmonious flavors that add a lot of eye appeal while pleasing the taste buds. Despite its easy 1-2-3 preparation, this is a subtle, show-off dish for your knowledgeable friends. It definitely is not to be served after three double martinis.

SERVES 6

WORKING TIME: 9 minutes

MARINATING TIME: 1 hour or more

BROILING TIME: 5 minutes

INGREDIENTS

2   **pounds bay, or sea scallops, quartered**

2   **shallots, minced, or 2 teaspoons chopped scallions**

    salt and pepper

2   **tablespoons brandy**

½   **cup dry white wine**

2   **parsley sprigs**

1   **bay leaf, broken in half**

18 **mushroom caps**

2   **slices boiled ham**

6   **tablespoons butter (¾ stick)**

3   **lemons, cut in half**

PREPARATION

1   Place the scallops in a flat dish. Chop the shallots and sprinkle them over the scallops along with the salt and pepper. Pour on the brandy and white wine. The liquid should not completely cover the scallops; they are meant to marinate, not swim in the wines. Turn the scallops a few times with your hands. Tuck in the parsley and bay leaf pieces. Cover the dish and let it stand at room temperature for at least 1 hour; 2 or 3 are even better. (The scallops can marinate overnight in the refrigerator, but add 2 tablespoons of oil to the marinade.) Turn occasionally.

2   Rinse the mushroom caps and let them stand to dry. If they are large, cut them in halves or quarters; the mushrooms should not be larger than the scallops. Dice the ham into ¼-inch or slightly smaller squares. Melt the butter.

3   Preheat the broiler for 5 minutes. Discard the parsley and bay leaf pieces and lift the scallops out of the marinade, shaking off the excess liquid. Place the scallops in a gratin dish. Add the ham and mushroom caps and mix all together with your hands. Sprinkle lightly with salt and pepper. Pour over the scallops ¾ of the melted butter and place the dish under the broiler. Broil for 3 minutes.

4   Toss the scallops and mushrooms with a spatula and sprinkle with the remaining melted butter. Broil for 2 minutes longer. If scallops are very large, broil for 3 minutes.

TO SERVE

Take the gratin dish to the table and serve directly from it onto individual plates. Place ½ lemon on each plate.

COOKING AHEAD

As noted above, the marinating must be done in advance. The scallops can be prepared in the gratin dish an hour before broiling, and kept covered. The 5 minutes of broiling must be done just before serving.

LOW-CHOLESTEROL VERSION

Substitute polyunsaturated margarine for the butter, but before melting it add 1 teaspoon lemon juice, ¼ teaspoon soy sauce, salt, and pepper. Proceed as above.

Saumon au vin rouge

In recent years French chefs have been breaking many hallowed cooking rules. First there was a craze for the seemingly bizarre combination of trout, raisins, and bananas (if you can believe it) in an attempt to disguise the inferior flavor of pond-raised trout. The latest infatuation is for fish cooked in red wine, with red wine in the glasses too. Naturally not all fish can stand up to this aggressive treatment, but salmon, a very rich fish, certainly can. This is one of the easiest ways I know to prepare this stunning dish, which just could become a fad in this country too. Serve with steamed potatoes.

SERVES 6

WORKING TIME: 6 minutes

COOKING TIME: 35 to 40 minutes

INGREDIENTS

3	**cups red wine**
⅓	**cup sliced shallots, or scallions**
1	**large bay leaf**
¼	**teaspoon thyme**
4	**parsley sprigs**
½	**teaspoon salt**
	freshly ground pepper
6	**salmon steaks, 1 inch thick**
6	**tablespoons butter**

PREPARATION

Preheat oven to 375°

1 Put the wine, shallots, bay leaf, thyme, parsley, salt, and pepper in a small heavy saucepan. Bring the wine to a boil, reduce the heat, cover the pan and simmer for 20 minutes. Strain the sauce into a bowl. Rinse out the pan, but do not wash it.

2 Put the salmon steaks in a baking dish that will hold them snugly. Lightly salt and pepper the salmon and pour about ¾ cup of the wine sauce over them. Cover the baking dish and bake the salmon for 10 to 15 minutes, or until the fish flakes easily. Do not overcook.

3 While the salmon is baking, return the remaining wine sauce to the saucepan and boil it rapidly, uncovered, to reduce it to a thick syrup. Remove the pan from the fire and stir in the butter. Then keep warm, on very low heat (or use a heat deflector pad), and do not allow the sauce to boil again.

TO SERVE

Lift the salmon out of the wine to a warm serving platter. If the sauce seems a little thick, spoon a tablespoon of wine from the baking dish into it to thin it a bit. Spoon the sauce over each salmon steak and serve at once.

COOKING AHEAD

The sauce can be cooked several hours in advance, but the salmon must be baked at serving time. It would dry out if reheated.

LOW-CHOLESTEROL VERSION

Substitute polyunsaturated margarine for the butter and add ½ teaspoon of brandy to the sauce for the final 5 minutes of cooking.

Baked salmon

This is not the usual baked salmon, but a method devised by the grande dame *who is president of the prestigious Cercle des Gourmettes in Paris. It also just happens to be wondrously simple. No fish stock is required, nor simmering of vegetables, nor a complicated sauce.*

Good fresh salmon is bathed in butter (remember this is a French invention), sprinkled with salt and pepper, and baked, covered. The lid is Madame's new twist to a time-honored formula, and it accomplishes magic. The salmon stays deliciously moist and succulent. You will find also that cold leftover salmon will be better because of that guaranteed moistness. Naturally, the recipe works best with fresh salmon, but even frozen fish is vastly improved when handled this way. Try it with any fish that can be bought in large pieces.

SERVES 6

WORKING TIME: 4 minutes

BAKING TIME: *approximately 40 minutes*

INGREDIENTS

3	**pounds salmon in 1 piece**
14	**tablespoons butter (1¾ sticks), room temperature**
	salt and pepper
	juice of 1 lemon
1½	**tablespoons dry white wine**
⅛	**teaspoon soy sauce**
½	**teaspoon tarragon**
3	**lemons cut in half**
	parsley for garnish

PREPARATION

Preheat oven to 425°.

1 Rinse the salmon and dry it on paper towels. Select a deep, covered baking dish that will hold the salmon snugly. Place the salmon in the dish and smear the fish all over, inside and out, with 8 to 10 tablespoons of butter. Sprinkle it with salt and pepper. Squeeze on lemon juice.

2 Measure the thickness of the fish at its thickest point. That is the distance from one side of the fish to the other, not the width or the length. Heat penetrates the flesh according to depth, not other dimensions. Cover and bake 10 minutes per inch of thickness. A 3-pound piece measuring 4 inches would require 40 minutes of baking time. Baste once or twice during baking.

3 While the salmon is baking prepare the sauce. In a small pot melt the remaining 4 tablespoons of butter with the wine, soy sauce, tarragon, salt, and pepper. Bring just to the boiling point and remove the pot from the heat. Let the sauce steep while the salmon is baking.

TO SERVE

Remove the salmon to a heated serving platter. Spoon 4 tablespoons of the butter from the baking dish into the sauce and reheat the sauce. Spoon some sauce over the fish. Decorate the platter with the lemon halves and parsley. Serve the salmon at the table, cutting through the fish straight down to the bones, loosening the flesh and lifting it off the bones onto warm dinner plates. Place a lemon half on each plate. Pass the sauce separately.

COOKING AHEAD

It is best not to bake the salmon in advance. It can be prepared and buttered and kept waiting in the baking dish in the refrigerator. Since it needs almost no attention once it is in the oven, it can easily be prepared even when entertaining. The sauce can be prepared ahead and refrigerated; reheat at serving time.

LOW-CHOLESTEROL VERSION

Substitute polyunsaturated margarine for the butter. Sprinkle 2 tablespoons dry vermouth over the salmon as well as the lemon juice. In the sauce, increase the soy sauce to ¼ teaspoon and the wine to 2 tablespoons.

Broiled salmon steaks with maître d'hôtel butter

Cooking salmon can be almost foolproof. Its high fat content helps prevent dryness, if overcooking is avoided. The timing must be watched carefully. The maître d'hôtel butter that finishes off this dish has a light flavor that accents, rather than masks, the delicacy of the salmon.

SERVES 6

WORKING TIME: *5 minutes*

STANDING TIME: *30 minutes*

BROILING TIME: *6 to 7 minutes*

INGREDIENTS

6	salmon steaks, about ½ inch thick
¼	cup oil
9	tablespoons butter (1 stick plus 1 tablespoon)
1½	teaspoons tarragon
1½	teaspoons prepared mustard
½	teaspoon lemon juice
	salt and pepper
6	lemon wedges

PREPARATION

1 Place the fish in a shallow oven dish. Sprinkle a scant tablespoon of oil over each steak and rub it into both sides. Let stand for 30 minutes.

2 Meanwhile, melt 3 tablespoons of butter and preheat the broiler. Prepare the *maître d'hôtel* butter by creaming together 6 tablespoons of butter with the tarragon, mustard, lemon juice, salt, and pepper.

3 Brush about ½ tablespoon of melted butter over each salmon steak and sprinkle with salt and pepper. Broil for 3 minutes. Turn and brush the other side with butter. Broil for another 3 or 4 minutes.

TO SERVE

Remove the fish to warm dishes, either individual plates or a large serving platter. Place 1 tablespoon of *maître d'hôtel* butter on each salmon steak. Garnish with lemon wedges. Serve at once.

COOKING AHEAD

The *maître d'hôtel* butter can be prepared anytime and kept handy in the refrigerator. (It can also be used on steaks, egg dishes, or with vegetables.) The salmon steaks can be oiled and left to stand for as much as 2 hours. The broiling, however, must be done at serving time.

LOW-CHOLESTEROL VERSION

Use polyunsaturated oil and polyunsaturated margarine in the preparation. Increase quantity of lemon juice to 1 teaspoon in the seasoned margarine.

Saumon au concombre

Though cucumber is quite good raw in a salad, I like to use it in other guises too. In other chapters I suggest it as a base for a delicate cold mousse (page 147) and as a cooked hot vegetable (pages 146 and 148). Here is still another way to take advantage of this hardy vegetable that fortunately is available the year round.

Cucumber sauce makes a very happy marriage with poached salmon. The sauce has a soft flavor that does not overpower the salmon, but does add a slight piquancy to the rich fish. Serve it just with plain rice. If a vegetable is to be included in the menu, I suggest offering it as a separate course after the salmon, though Golden Grilled Tomatoes (p. 172) on the platter make a pretty and edible decoration.

WORKING TIME: *12 minutes*

COOLING TIME: *30 minutes*

BAKING TIME: *15 to 20 minutes*

INGREDIENTS

Court Bouillon

2 **cups water**

½ **cup dry white wine**

1 **teaspoon salt**

2 **parsley sprigs**

½ **carrot, sliced**

½ **small onion, sliced**

6 **salmon steaks about 1 inch thick**

Sauce

2 **tablespoons butter**

1 **cup chopped cucumber**

3 **tablespoons flour**

2 **cups milk**

   dash Tabasco

3 **tablespoons dry Vermouth**

   salt and pepper (preferably white pepper)

¼ to ½ **cup heavy cream**

PREPARATION

Preheat oven to 375°.

1 Place all the ingredients for the court bouillon in a small pot, cover, and simmer briskly for 15 minutes. Put aside to cool.

Note: If there isn't enough time to allow the court bouillon to cool a little, just poach the fish in the court-bouillon ingredients and allow the cooked salmon to stand in this poaching liquid for 5 minutes before removing.

2 Place the salmon steaks in a baking dish that will hold them snugly. Strain the court bouillon over the salmon; it should just cover the fish. Cover the dish and place it in the oven for 15 to 20 minutes, or until the salmon flesh flakes slightly when pierced. (The salmon can also be poached on the stove in a skillet or flameproof dish, preferably with a flame-deflecting pad under the dish.)

3 While the salmon is poaching, prepare the sauce. Melt the butter in a saucepan while preparing the cucumber. Peel the cucumber, cut it in quarters and remove the seeds. Chop the flesh coarsely. Add the cucumber to the butter, cover, and simmer slowly for 5 minutes. Sprinkle in the flour and stir to mix well. Stir in the milk and cook over medium heat. Add the Tabasco, Vermouth, salt, and pepper. When the sauce has thickened, remove the saucepan from the heat and stir in the cream. The sauce should be about the consistency of heavy cream.

TO SERVE

While the sauce is cooking, remove the salmon to a warm serving platter or individual dishes and remove the skin. Drain off any water that might collect in the dish. Spoon about 3 tablespoons of sauce over each salmon steak and pass the rest of the sauce separately.

COOKING AHEAD

The court bouillon can be prepared even a day or two in advance and kept refrigerated. It should be brought back to room temperature before pouring over the salmon. The sauce can be prepared in advance and refrigerated. Do not add the cream at this time, but when reheating the sauce add ⅓ cup of cream. The salmon must be poached at serving time.

LOW-CHOLESTEROL VERSION

In the sauce substitute polyunsaturated margarine for the butter. Instead of milk use 2 cups of evaporated skimmed milk or polyunsaturated dairy substitute and ½ cup white wine. In addition to the other seasonings, add ½ teaspoon tarragon to the sauce.

Friture d'éperlans

*Tiny fried smelts are a treat regularly
served in French bistros, where they are
known as Friture d'Eperlans. The root of
the name éperlan is perle, which accu-
rately describes the pearly shine of the
tiny creatures. Small size smelts are the
key to success with this dish. Luckily
many fish shops and supermarkets now
carry smelts at low prices. Also, these
2- to 3-inch slithery spikes come already
cleaned, a service no fishmonger in
France provides.*

*Smelts are a freshwater fish, coming for
the most part from northern lakes. The
supply is almost constant, except when
winters are severe enough to freeze over
the lakes. There are only a few rules to
follow to ensure the success of the dish.*

SERVES 4

WORKING TIME: *12 minutes*

STANDING TIME: *15 minutes*

FRYING TIME: *about 3 minutes*

INGREDIENTS

1½	**pounds smelts**
2	**cups flour**
	salt and pepper
	oil for deep frying
2	**lemons cut in half**

PREPARATION

1   Rinse the smelts and roll them in a towel to
dry. Spread them on a large plate or piece of
waxed paper and sprinkle liberally with salt
and pepper. Pour on about ¾ cup of flour, and
using both hands, toss the fish with the flour
to coat them thoroughly. Let stand for at least
15 minutes.

2   Meanwhile, in a deep fryer or pan deep
enough to hold at least 3 inches of oil, heat the
oil until it shivers a little (375°) and is almost
smoking hot. (See Remarks.)

3   Just before frying, pour more flour on the
smelts. This second coating with flour is most
important. The previously applied flour will
have become damp and sticky. The second
coating will adhere to the first and present a
completely dry surface for frying.

4   Take a handful of smelts, shake off the
excess flour, and plunge them into hot oil,
scattering them throughout the pan with a
long fork or skimmer. Do not overcrowd;
overcrowding will greatly reduce the heat of
the oil, causing the smelts to clump together,
and the coating will not be crisp. Fast hot
frying is needed to seal the surface and prevent the absorption of fat into the fish itself.
The smelts will turn a dark golden color in just
a few minutes.

5   Remove fried smelts with a skimmer and
place on a baking dish lined with paper towels; keep warm in a slow oven while continuing to fry the remaining fish.

TO SERVE

Sprinkle the smelts with salt and heap them
onto a hot serving platter. Serve with lemon
halves. Tartar sauce may be passed, but
the fish have such a sweet delicate flavor
that they are better without it.

LOW-CHOLESTEROL VERSION

No changes in recipe are necessary as long as
polyunsaturated oil is used for frying.

REMARKS

Previously used oil produces the best results
for a golden coating. I learned this while living in Paris. I had been presenting at the
table mounds of fried smelts that were delicious to eat but a horror to look at. They re-
fused to brown properly and usually looked
more like cooked macaroni than fried fish.
I discussed the disaster with the owner of one
of our favorite bistros. We went through the
procedure step by step. Finally a light of com-
prehension flashed and he asked in an as-
tonished voice, "*Vous n'avez pas utilisé
l'huile vierge?*" (You didn't use virgin oil?)
There followed a lecture about fussy cooks
who insist on throwing out products that still
have life in them. The point was that used oil
is already dark colored and helps fry the fish
to an appetizing deep brown. So use well-
strained oil that has done previous service.

Once it's been used for fish, however, don't cook other foods in it. The fish taste will be passed on.

Larger smelts, 5 to 6 inches long, are not suitable for deep frying, but are very good pan-fried. They should be split to lie flat and fried on both sides in a mixture of butter and oil, then sprinkled with salt, pepper, and lemon juice. When eating these larger smelts, bones must be removed. In the smaller ones the bones are entirely edible.

Shrimp in beer

Having a champagne taste with a beer pocketbook sometimes can be an advantage in the kitchen. There, whatever beer may lack in glamour, it makes up in rich, velvety flavor. Cooking with beer is not a new idea. Probably more people around the world use beer in cooking than wine. Welsh Rabbit with beer is a classic; some Swiss substitute beer for the more usual white wine in making cheese fondue. Many chefs make frying batter with beer because its built-in leavening quality gives a crisper, lighter coating. My favorite use for beer is in steaming shrimp. Shrimp and beer go as well together in cooking as they do in a tavern.

SERVES 6

WORKING TIME: *4 minutes*

COOKING TIME: *4 to 5 minutes*

INGREDIENTS

2½	pounds fresh shrimp in their shells
	juice of 2 lemons
1	teaspoon celery seed
1	teaspoon paprika
2	bay leaves
¼	teaspoon Tabasco
	salt and pepper
1 to 3	cups beer
	For serving: 6 lemon halves, cocktail sauce

PREPARATION

1 Rinse the shrimp and put them in a regular pot. Squeeze in the lemon juice and add all the seasonings.

2 Pour in 3 cups of beer. Cover the pot tightly and bring the beer to a boil. Cook the shrimp for 3 to 5 minutes, depending on their size; stir once during the steaming.

TO SERVE

Heap the shrimp in a large bowl and place it in the center of the table along with plenty of paper napkins. Invite guests to help themselves and peel the shrimp with their fingers. Have a bowl handy for discarded shells. Pass the lemon halves and cocktail sauce. Leftover shrimp are excellent cold in shrimp cocktail.

COOKING AHEAD

The shrimp, seasonings, and beer can be put in the pot several hours before cooking, and refrigerated. The cooking must be done just before serving.

LOW-CHOLESTEROL VERSION

At this writing, shrimp is not permitted on a low-cholesterol diet.

REMARKS

This dish can be prepared in a pressure cooker, with excellent results. Use only 1 cup of beer, however. When the pressure cooker reaches 15 pounds of pressure, cook for 1½ minutes for medium shrimp, 2 to 2½ minutes for large shrimp.

Soft-shelled crabs

Fresh soft-shelled crabs are one of the glories of the American spring and early summer. The East coast is especially favored by their availability. For best results this is a dish to cook at the last minute because the crabs must come to the table piping hot and moist. Since only six minutes of sautéing time is needed, the cook can easily prepare them while others are finishing cocktails. If the crabs follow a first course, the frying can be done while dishes are being cleared from the table. Once in the pan they need little attention. I would serve them by themselves, to be followed by a vegetable or salad.

SERVES 6

WORKING TIME: 12 minutes

FRYING TIME: 6 minutes

INGREDIENTS

12	large or 18 medium soft-shelled crabs
8	tablespoons butter (1 stick)
	flour
	salt and pepper
	juice of 1 lemon
½	cup dry white wine
3	lemons cut in half

PREPARATION

1 Rinse the crabs under cold running water, shake off the excess water, and place them between paper towels. (This can be done ahead.)

2 At serving time, melt 2 tablespoons of butter in 1 or 2 skillets. (The crabs must fry in a single layer.) While the butter is melting, spread the flour on a sheet of waxed paper and lightly coat each crab on both sides; shake off the excess flour. (If the flouring is done in advance, the coating will become damp and prevent browning.) Place the crabs in the pan once the butter is hot and foamy. Cover.

3 After about 1 minute, sprinkle salt and pepper over the crabs; cover the skillet and sauté for 2 more minutes.

4 Turn the crabs, adding more butter as necessary. Sprinkle again with salt and pepper and squeeze lemon juice directly over the crabs. Cover and sauté for 1 minute.

5 Pour in the wine, basting some of the liquid over the crabs. Recover and sauté for 2 minutes more, basting once or twice. When done the crabs should be a vibrant red under a golden coating.

TO SERVE

Place the crabs on warmed individual plates and spoon some of the sauce over each one. Add ½ lemon to each plate.

LOW-CHOLESTEROL VERSION

Use polyunsaturated margarine for the frying and squeeze the juice of 2 lemons instead of 1 over the crabs.

Clams florentine

There's no use pretending that canned clams are as good as fresh ones. They can come fairly close, though, when mixed with a tangy sauce, as in this recipe. Whether canned or fresh, the cardinal rule in cooking clams is not to overcook. They will become quite rubbery if you do.

(In this recipe as in other parts of the book thawed but uncooked spinach is used. Most similar recipes call for precooking the spinach. I can't imagine why, since spinach cooks very quickly and gets more than enough time in the oven.)

Clams Florentine can begin a meal or be the main course for luncheon or supper.

SERVES 6 AS FIRST COURSE;

4 AS MAIN COURSE

WORKING TIME: 13 minutes

COOKING TIME: 20 minutes

INGREDIENTS

2   12-ounce packages frozen leaf spinach, thawed
1   6-ounce can minced clams
2   tablespoons butter
2   teaspoons minced onion
3   tablespoons flour
½   cup dry white wine
½   cup heavy cream
½   teaspoon anchovy paste
    juice ½ lemon
    few drops Tabasco
½   teaspoon oregano
1   teaspoon soy sauce
    pepper
3   tablespoons grated Parmesan cheese

PREPARATION

Preheat oven to 400°.

1   Put the thawed spinach in a sieve or colander to drain. Place a small sieve or strainer over a small mixing bowl and dump the clams into the strainer.

2   Heat the butter slowly in a small heavy pot while mincing the onion. Add the onion to the butter, cover and simmer slowly for 2 minutes. Add the flour to the onions and stir to blend the flour and butter. Measure the clam juice that has drained from the minced clams; there should be about 1 cup. If not, add water to make that amount.

3   Pour the clam juice slowly into the onion mixture while stirring with a wire whisk. Next pour in the wine and cream, whisking all the time to keep it smooth. Add the anchovy paste, lemon juice, Tabasco, oregano, soy sauce, and pepper. Taste for salt and add a little if necessary. Remove the pot from the heat and stir in the drained clams.

4   Select a 9-inch pie dish or similar oven-proof container. Take a handful of spinach at a time, squeeze the water out of it and put in the dish. Pat the spinach into a smooth layer.

5   Spoon the clam sauce over the spinach and sprinkle it with the cheese. Bake for 15 minutes or until the cheese has browned. If necessary slip the dish under the broiler for a few seconds to achieve the browning.

TO SERVE

Place the pie dish on a platter and serve at the table with a spatula and spoon. Pick up the spinach and clam sauce together.

COOKING AHEAD

Prepare the spinach in a pie dish, cover closely, and refrigerate. Prepare the sauce, cool it, then stir in the clams, cover, and refrigerate. At serving time, spoon the clam sauce over the spinach, sprinkle with cheese, and bake. Allow an extra 5 minutes of baking time if the ingredients are cold from the refrigerator.

LOW-CHOLESTEROL VERSION

Use polyunsaturated margarine instead of butter and polyunsaturated dairy substitute or evaporated skimmed milk for the cream. Increase the lemon juice to 1 lemon and the anchovy paste to 1 teaspoon. Use low-fat cheese, or eliminate it.

Florentine fish fillets

After seeing how much a good sauce can improve canned clams in the preceding recipe for Clams Florentine, I experimented to learn if the same principle could save frozen fish fillets, which tend to be tasteless. The result was surprisingly good. I don't pretend that frozen fish can hold a candle to good fresh fish, but for those times when you can't get to the fish store this recipe could prove helpful. Most of the ingredients called for are usually on hand in a well-stocked kitchen; combine them and give frozen fish a new look and taste.

SERVES 6

WORKING TIME: 13 minutes

BAKING TIME: 15 minutes

INGREDIENTS

2   **12-ounce packages frozen chopped spinach, thawed**

1   **pound frozen fish fillets (flounder, halibut, or cod), thawed**

2   **tablespoons butter**

2   **teaspoons minced onions**

3   **tablespoons flour**

1¼   **cups clam juice**

½   **cup dry white wine**

½   **cup heavy cream**

½   **teaspoon anchovy paste**

     juice ½ lemon

     few drops Tabasco

½   **teaspoon oregano**

1   **teaspoon soy sauce**

     pepper

½   **cup bread crumbs**

3   **tablespoons chopped parsley**

PREPARATION

Preheat oven to 400°.

1   Let the thawed spinach drain in a sieve or colander. Place the thawed fish fillets between paper towels.

2   Heat the butter slowly in a small heavy pot, while mincing the onion. Add the onion to the butter, cover, and simmer slowly for 2 minutes. Add the flour to the onions and stir to blend them together. Slowly stir in 1 cup of the clam juice, stirring with a wire whisk to keep the sauce smooth.

3   Next pour in the wine and cream, whisking all the time. Add the anchovy paste, lemon juice, Tabasco, oregano, soy sauce, and pepper. Simmer for about 2 minutes. If the sauce seems a little thick, stir in the remaining ¼ cup of clam juice.

4   Select a 9-inch pie dish or similar ovenproof dish. Take a handful of the spinach and squeeze the water out of it, then place the spinach in the pie dish. Repeat with the rest of the spinach and pat it into a smooth layer in the dish.

5   Lay the fish fillets on the bed of spinach and spoon the sauce over the fish. Sprinkle on a light layer of bread crumbs and bake for about 15 minutes, or until the fish flakes easily.

TO SERVE

Sprinkle the baked gratin with the chopped parsley. Serve at the table, using a spatula and a spoon to lift out individual portions of the sauce, fish, and spinach.

COOKING AHEAD

Prepare the spinach in the pie dish, cover closely, and refrigerate. Prepare the sauce, cool, cover, and refrigerate it. At serving time place the fish on the spinach and complete the recipe. Allow an extra 5 minutes of baking time if the ingredients are cold from the refrigerator.

LOW-CHOLESTEROL VERSION

Substitute polyunsaturated margarine for the butter and polyunsaturated dairy substitute or evaporated skimmed milk for the cream. Increase the lemon juice to 1 tablespoon and the anchovy paste to 1 teaspoon.

Marinated fish piraeus

A hot Greek sun and cold fresh fish from the Aegean made for a memorable lunch in Piraeus, the port serving Athens. The simple little restaurant from which this recipe comes served whole, small fish (which are awfully good). But for dinner-table presentation, filleted slices are easier to handle. It is essential to select a firm-fleshed fish that will not disintegrate when fried at high heat. For the same reason, fresh rather than frozen fish is recommended. Small portions can be served as a first course, but the dish is so good, most diners appreciate it as a hearty main course.

SERVES 6 AS MAIN COURSE;

8 TO 10 AS FIRST COURSE

WORKING TIME: 14 minutes

COOKING TIME: 20 minutes

CHILLING TIME: 24 hours

INGREDIENTS

Sauce:

1 **cup tomato sauce**

½ **cup vinegar**

½ **cup white wine**

¼ **cup olive or vegetable oil**

1 **teaspoon rosemary**

1 **teaspoon sugar**

pinch of saffron

3 **garlic cloves, mashed**

salt and pepper

oil for frying

3 **pounds halibut, haddock, or cod, cut into slices 1 to 1½ inches thick**

1 **cup flour, approximately**

PREPARATION

1 Put all sauce ingredients in a small pot, cover, and simmer for 20 minutes.

2 While sauce is simmering, pour oil in a skillet to a depth of about ½ inch and bring to almost hazy heat. Flour the fish slices and fry quickly in oil; turn to brown both sides. Fry the fish 1 to 2 minutes per side, depending on thickness. Remove fried fish to a deep dish large enough to hold the hot sauce. Sprinkle salt and pepper over the fish.

3 As soon as all the fish is fried, pour the boiling sauce over the slices. Cover at once and let cool at room temperature. Refrigerate for at least 24 hours.

TO SERVE

Lift a whole or part of a fillet onto individual dishes and cover liberally with the sauce. Pass crusty French bread to absorb the extra sauce.

COOKING AHEAD

Since the fish is marinated for at least 24 hours, it must be prepared in advance. These marinated fish slices will keep at least a week.

LOW-CHOLESTEROL VERSION

Use polyunsaturated oil for the sauce and the frying. No other changes necessary.

One-fish bouillabaisse

Eyebrows are sure to be raised at the thought of only one fish in a bouillabaisse. True, along the Mediterranean, cooks would not think of beginning this wonderful fish stew without at least 3 or 4 different species of fish—some that can be bought nowhere else. But go inland a bit into Provence, and you'll find that this hearty concoction is often served without some of the allegedly "essential" fish varieties and generally with the addition of a few potato slices. The Italians have their version as do the Spaniards, Portuguese, and Greeks.

In this recipe the one-fish limit streamlines the preparation and simplifies the serving. (Ever count how long it takes to bone 4 different cooked fish?) But while minutes have been gained, flavor has not been lost. The secret is the well-seasoned broth in which the fish is poached.

SERVES 8

WORKING TIME: *20 minutes*

COOKING TIME: *45 to 50 minutes*

INGREDIENTS

½   cup olive oil

2   onions, thinly sliced

3   potatoes, peeled, cut in half, and sliced ¼ inch thick

1   rib celery, sliced into ¼-inch pieces

4   garlic cloves, mashed

1   2-pound can plum tomatoes, mashed

2   cups white wine

2   cups clam juice

1   2-ounce can anchovy fillets

2   teaspoons fennel seeds

½   teaspoon each: oregano, thyme, basil

¼   teaspoon saffron
     Optional: 2 tablespoons anise-flavored liqueur (Ouzo, Pernod, and so on)

2   tablespoons tomato paste
     pepper

2   pounds fish in 1 piece—fresh, smoked, or frozen haddock, cod or other firm white fish.

PREPARATION

1   In a large heavy pot, heat the oil while preparing the onions. Add the onions, cover, and simmer while preparing the potatoes, celery, and garlic.

2   Add the vegetables to the onions along with the tomatoes, crushing the pulp with your hands as you put them in the pot. Next add all ingredients except the fish: the wine, clam juice, anchovy fillets, fennel seeds, oregano, thyme, basil, saffron, liqueur, tomato paste, and pepper. (Salt is omitted at this point since the anchovies are salty. Taste can be corrected later.) If using smoked haddock, reduce anchovy fillets to 1 ounce. Cover and simmer for 30 minutes or until the potatoes are soft.

3   Taste the broth for seasoning and correct if necessary. (If using smoked haddock, taste the broth for seasoning after having cooked the fish in it.) Add the fish, re-cover and simmer until the flesh turns white and separates easily. Allow 10 minutes per 1 inch of thickness.

4   Lift the fish out of the *bouillabaisse* stock, let cool slightly, then remove the skin and any bones. Flake the fish into good-sized chunks and return to the pot to reheat.

TO SERVE

Serve the fish stew in deep bowls along with lots of crusty French bread.

COOKING AHEAD

So much the better. The *bouillabaisse* will improve if it stands for a day. Any leftover soup may be frozen, but only if the fish and potatoes are removed.

LOW-CHOLESTEROL VERSION

No changes in the recipe are necessary as long as polyunsaturated oil is used.

REMARKS

For a new version with a vigorous taste, try smoked haddock. It needs no help from any other fish, Mediterranean or otherwise. Even frozen fish can be used with rather good results.

Matelote de cod

Matelote in French cooking refers to a hearty kind of fish stew. Rarely is a delicate fish used. It takes a firm-fleshed, robust species to stand up to the onions, seasonings, and whiskey. French recipes, of course, call for brandy, but in this particular combination I think whiskey provides a sharper note. As with most stews, the finished dish does not have a showy presentation, but the good hearty flavor will make it a family favorite.

SERVES 6

WORKING TIME: 9 minutes

COOKING TIME: 10 to 15 minutes

INGREDIENTS

3 **tablespoons butter**

1 **medium onion, minced**

2¼ **pounds of cod, halibut, or haddock**
   salt and pepper

¾ **pound mushrooms**

1 **cup dry white wine**

2 **teaspoons Scotch, Bourbon, or Canadian Whiskey**
   juice of 1 lemon

2 **teaspoons anchovy paste, or 1 anchovy fillet**

½ **cup sour cream**

2 **teaspoons soy sauce**

PREPARATION

1 Melt the butter slowly in a large heavy skillet while preparing the onion. Add the onion to the butter, stir, cover, and simmer slowly while preparing the fish.

2 Rinse the fish and cut into 1½-inch pieces. Add the fish to the skillet, sprinkle with salt and pepper and stir. Cover the skillet and simmer the fish while preparing the mushrooms.

3 Rinse the mushrooms and cut them in halves or quarters, depending on the size. Add the mushrooms to the fish with the wine, whiskey, lemon juice, and anchovy paste. Cover and simmer gently for 5 to 8 minutes, depending on the thickness of the fish.

4 With a skimmer remove the fish, mushrooms, and onions to a hot serving bowl; keep warm. Rapidly boil the juices in the pan to reduce by half. Remove the pan from the heat and stir in the sour cream and soy sauce. Pour the sauce over the fish and serve hot.

COOKING AHEAD

The matelote can be completed and refrigerated overnight and reheated at serving time. Care must be taken to reheat very gently, not allowing the sauce to boil.

LOW-CHOLESTEROL VERSION

Substitute polyunsaturated margarine for the butter and a combination of ¼ cup evaporated skimmed milk and ¼ cup low-fat yogurt for the sour cream. Increase anchovy paste by 1 teaspoon.

POULTRY

While many foods have soared in price, chicken fortunately has remained reasonably priced, which is one good reason to serve it often. This is easy to do because of chicken's great versatility. Among the recipes that follow are one that simmers chicken in milk, another that does it in red wine, and a third that uses a lemon sauce. Such additional flavors help improve even today's supermarket fowl, which isn't of top quality.

Most traditional recipes for cooking chicken in a sauce call for the pieces to be browned in hot oil first. In most cases I have found this an unnecessary and messy step. In my version of that classic, Coq au Vin (Chicken in Red Wine), no browning is needed—but marinating is. Marinating does more for the flavor than any amount of splattering oil. In another recipe, largely for aesthetic reasons, chicken pieces are broiled to a light golden color. Broiling is a far neater way than frying to do the browning. These changes save time and wash-up chores.

Ask the question "Should we serve white wine or red wine with chicken?" and you'll get strong opinions on both sides. White wine advocates follow the old rule (no one knows where it started) that white wine is served with white-fleshed meats like veal and chicken. People who are concerned with which body and flavor best go with chicken ignore that rule and serve red. A light Bordeaux, like a Medoc, often appears on French tables. Among American wines that go well with chicken are California Cabernet Sauvignon and Zinfandel.

Poulet à la marguerite

Poulet à la Marguerite *is refined and piquant at the same time, just like its namesake. In the French province of Normandy, chicken, cream, and Calvados (apple brandy) are staples in the kitchen. Calva, as the brandy is known familiarly, is used to flavor everything from an eye-opening cup of coffee to fruitcakes. Realizing that other liquors are more readily available in America, I've worked out the seasonings to go with whiskey. In this recipe the alcohol is present, but it has been softened to a hint, not an assault. Celery does wonderful things for the sauce.*

SERVES 6

WORKING TIME: *12 minutes*
COOKING TIME: *45 minutes*

INGREDIENTS

4	**tablespoons butter (½ stick)**
1	**large Spanish onion, or 2 regular onions, sliced**
3	**celery ribs (without leaves)**
¼	**cup plus 1 tablespoon Scotch, Bourbon, or Canadian Whiskey**
½	**cup white wine**
4	**parsley sprigs**
4	**pounds chicken, cut in pieces**
1½	**cups chicken broth**
	salt and pepper
4	**egg yolks**
½	**cup heavy cream**

PREPARATION

1 Select a large heavy casserole, preferably enameled cast iron. Melt the butter in the casserole slowly while peeling and slicing the onion. Scrub the celery and slice it in ¼-inch pieces. Add the onions and celery to the butter, cover the pot, and simmer the vegetables slowly for 5 minutes.

2 Add ¼ cup of whiskey, the white wine, and parsley to the simmering vegetables. Cover and simmer for another 5 minutes.

3 Add the chicken to the casserole and stir to distribute the vegetables among the chicken pieces. Pour in the chicken broth; it should cover almost three-fourths of the chicken. Sprinkle with salt and pepper, reduce the heat, and simmer slowly for about 30 minutes or until the chicken is tender. Turn the pieces once during the cooking.

4 Leaving the stock in the casserole on the heat, remove the chicken to a warm serving dish or platter and keep warm while finishing the sauce. Remove and discard the parsley. In a small mixing bowl beat the egg yolks with the remaining tablespoon of whiskey, then stir in the cream. Beat a ladleful of the hot stock into the egg-cream mixture. Remove the casserole from the heat and slowly stir the egg-cream sauce into the hot stock. Return the casserole to very low heat and stir constantly until the sauce thickens; this should take no more than a minute. Do not allow the sauce to boil or the egg yolks will curdle and the sauce will separate. It is better to undercook than overcook the sauce. Taste for salt and pepper and correct if necessary.

TO SERVE

With a skimmer lift out the vegetables from the sauce and arrange them over the top of the chicken. Then ladle a liberal amount of sauce over the chicken. Pass a sauceboat with extra sauce. Serve at once.

COOKING AHEAD

The chicken can be cooked in the stock, cooled, and refrigerated. The egg-cream addition should be done when reheating at serving time. The flavor of the dish will improve for having stood for a day.

LOW-CHOLESTEROL VERSION

Use 4 celery ribs instead of 3. Substitute 3 tablespoons of cornstarch for the 4 egg yolks and 1 cup of evaporated skimmed milk or polyunsaturated dairy substitute (or a combination) for the cream. Stir the skimmed milk into the cornstarch to make a smooth paste; add it to the sauce and stir. Add to the sauce 1 tablespoon of polyunsaturated margarine and an additional tablespoon of whiskey. Simmer for 2 minutes and taste for salt and pepper.

Poulet yvonne

Yvonne, an enchanting Frenchwoman, serves chicken in many ways to her Parisian family. But this version, her own creation, is their favorite, hands-down. It has great French flair to it, without the usual complications. The chicken is simmered with vegetables—tomatoes, mushrooms, and artichokes—making it a complete main course. Yvonne browns the chicken in a skillet, but I prefer doing it under the broiler to prevent all the splattering. Also, far less oil is used this way, which means fewer calories. Both frozen and canned artichokes are listed. I prefer the canned bottoms, but they are more expensive.

SERVES 4

WORKING TIME: 18 minutes

COOKING TIME: 45 minutes

INGREDIENTS

3½ **pounds chicken, cut in pieces**
   about 6 tablespoons oil
   salt and pepper
1 **medium onion, chopped**
2 **tomatoes (or a 1-pound can)**
1 **garlic clove, minced**
2 **tablespoons brandy**
¼ **cup dry white wine**
   Optional: 1 tablespoon tomato paste
¼ **pound mushrooms**
1 **9- or 10-ounce package frozen artichoke hearts, or 6 canned artichoke bottoms cut into quarters**
1 **egg yolk**
1 **teaspoon cornstarch**
¼ **cup heavy cream**

PREPARATION

1   Preheat the broiler. Rinse the chicken pieces and dry well on paper towels. Place the chicken on a baking sheet and brush with oil, sprinkle with salt and pepper. Broil until the chicken is golden brown; this should take 3 to 4 minutes. Turn the chicken and brush again with oil; sprinkle with salt and pepper. Broil until the second side is brown.

2   While the chicken is browning, pour ¼ cup of oil in a skillet large enough to hold the chicken. Heat the oil while peeling and chopping the onion. Add the onion to the oil, cover, and simmer gently for 5 minutes. Rinse and quarter tomatoes; peel and chop garlic.

3   Add the chicken to the onions along with the tomatoes, garlic, brandy, and white wine. If the tomatoes are not of best quality add the tomato paste. Cover and simmer gently for 30 minutes. Turn the chicken once or twice, crushing the tomatoes as you do.

4   While the chicken is simmering, rinse the mushrooms and cut in halves or quarters depending on size. After the chicken has simmered for 30 minutes, add the mushrooms and artichoke hearts and sprinkle with salt and pepper. Cover and simmer for 15 minutes.

5   Put the egg yolk in a small bowl. Add the cornstarch and beat together. Add the cream and beat again. Take a ladleful of sauce from the skillet and slowly pour it into the cream while whisking vigorously. Repeat with another ladleful of sauce. Slowly pour the cream sauce over the chicken. Turn the chicken so all sides are covered with the sauce.

TO SERVE

Place the pieces of chicken in the center of a deep serving platter. Arrange the mushrooms and artichoke hearts around the chicken and spoon a little sauce over the chicken and vegetables. Pass remaining sauce separately.

COOKING AHEAD

Proceed with the recipe as above through step 4, but once the mushrooms and artichokes are added, simmer for only 5 minutes. Finish the remaining 10 minutes of cooking and preparation of sauce just before serving.

LOW-CHOLESTEROL VERSION

Eliminate the egg yolk and heavy cream. Stir ⅓ cup evaporated skim milk into 2 teaspoons cornstarch and stir this paste directly into the simmering stock. Add 2 tablespoons of polyunsaturated margarine.

Lemon chicken

Today's supermarket chicken is convenient to buy, but in quality is a far cry from the fresh-killed farm chicken of bygone years. A simple roasting no longer gives the succulent results it once did. Other ways with modern poultry are clearly in order. I know many cooks who sprinkle lemon juice over chicken to "freshen its taste." Lemon does seem to add something. But to do even better, try marinating chicken in lemon juice. That's a way to make the flavor really wake up and sing. Make plenty of Lemon Chicken while you're at it. Though it's mighty good hot, it's equally delicious cold.

SERVES 6

WORKING TIME: *10 minutes*

MARINATING TIME: *at least 6 hours*

COOKING TIME: *25 minutes*

INGREDIENTS

4	**pounds chicken, cut in pieces**
	salt and pepper
1	**cup lemon juice**
½	**cup oil**
½	**cup dry white wine**

PREPARATION

1   Rinse the chicken and dry on paper towels, sprinkle salt and pepper on both sides of the chicken, then transfer to a nonmetal dish that holds the pieces snugly.

2   Squeeze the lemons. Add ¼ cup oil to the juice and beat together with a fork. Pour this marinade over the chicken. Turn pieces so all surfaces are coated with the marinade. Cover tightly and keep in a cool place for at least 6 hours. Overnight in the refrigerator is better yet. Turn pieces once or twice.

3   Preheat the broiler. Lift chicken pieces out of marinade and dry on paper towels. Place them on a baking sheet and brush them with oil and sprinkle with salt and pepper. Broil the chicken to a golden brown. Turn the pieces over and repeat.

4   Put the chicken pieces in a large frying pan or casserole and pour over them the marinade and white wine. Cover and simmer for 20 to 25 minutes, or until the pieces are tender.

TO SERVE

Place the chicken pieces on a serving platter and spoon some cooking sauce over them. Pass the rest of the sauce separately.

TO SERVE LEMON CHICKEN COLD

Chill the chicken in the refrigerator in its cooking liquid which will turn into a jelly. Scrape the lemon jelly into a small bowl and place spoonfuls of it around the chicken pieces. Decorate with a few black olives.

COOKING AHEAD

The entire recipe can be completed, cooled, and refrigerated in the sauce. Reheat slowly in the sauce at serving time. The flavor will improve with the reheating.

LOW-CHOLESTEROL VERSION

Use polyunsaturated oil; no other changes in the recipe are necessary.

Coq au vin

Coq au Vin is one of the most widely known of the classic French dishes. Its popularity is justified. The lusty flavor and rich wine sauce sum up the best of Gallic cuisine. This streamlined version gives you the same results without the usual amount of time-consuming fuss. Three basic variations are used in this recipe: (1) the chicken is marinated before cooking, ensuring a stronger flavor; (2) the chicken pieces are not browned in fat, thus avoiding an oil-splattering operation and all the calories that go with it; (3) the sauce is thickened before the chicken is added, not after. This last step preserves the full flavor and moisture of the chicken. When cooking any meat in a large quantity of thin liquid, the meat tends to flavor the liquid rather than the other way around. Here all the goodness of the thick sauce penetrates the chicken.

Although Coq au Vin can be prepared the day it is to be served, it improves considerably if done at least a day ahead. Cooling, chilling, and reheating do more for it than you can possibly imagine.

SERVES 6

WORKING TIME: *20 minutes*

MARINATING TIME: *8 to 24 hours*

COOKING TIME: *1¾ hours*

INGREDIENTS

3½	pounds chicken, cut in pieces
4½	cups red wine
½	cup white wine
¾	cup brandy
½	teaspoon thyme
½	cup olive oil
1½	teaspoons salt
½	teaspoon pepper
4	carrots, sliced
2	medium onions, quartered
6	whole garlic cloves
4	parsley sprigs
2	bay leaves
1	cup chicken broth
3	tablespoons tomato paste
3	tablespoons butter, room temperature
½	cup flour
1	teaspoon gravy coloring (Kitchen Bouquet)
½	pound mushrooms
	Optional: 1-pound jar white onions, drained

PREPARATION

1 Put the chicken in a large, deep bowl. In another bowl combine 4 cups of red wine, the white wine, ½ cup brandy, thyme, oil, salt, and pepper. Beat this marinade with a fork or whisk and pour it over the chicken, which should be completely covered. Prepare the carrots, onions, and garlic and add them to the wine. Tuck in the parsley and the bay leaves. Cover and marinate the chicken for a full day in the refrigerator or overnight in a cool spot.

2 Lift the chicken pieces out of the marinade and transfer them to another deep bowl. Pour the marinade into a deep, nonaluminum pot or casserole. (Don't wash the marinade bowl yet.) Add the remaining ¼ cup brandy, chicken broth, and tomato paste to the marinade. Put the pot on the fire and bring to a boil. Reduce the heat and simmer for 45 minutes to 1 hour, or until the vegetables are soft.

3 Strain the sauce into the marinade bowl, pressing the vegetables to get as much liquid out as possible. Return the sauce to the pot.

4 In a small bowl, cream the butter with a fork and work the flour into it until it is completely incorporated into the fat. This thickening agent is called *beurre manié* in French cooking. Add about ½ the *beurre manié* and the gravy coloring to the sauce and simmer for 5 minutes. Check the thickness of the sauce. It should be the consistency of a thick syrup since the chicken and mushroom juices will thin it somewhat. Add as much flour-butter as necessary, simmering for 5 minutes after the final addition.

5 Add the chicken pieces and simmer for 45 minutes or until the chicken is tender. If the sauce seems a little thin, stir ½ cup red wine into ¼ cup of flour, to make a thin paste. Stir this paste into the sauce.

6 While the chicken is cooking, rinse the mushrooms and cut into halves or quarters, depending on size. Add the mushrooms and onions for the final 10 minutes of cooking. The *Coq au Vin* can be served at once, or cooled, refrigerated, and reheated.

TO SERVE

If an attractive pot was used for the cooking, serve directly from it; otherwise transfer the *Coq au Vin* to a deep serving bowl. Serve chicken, mushrooms, and onions in each portion, liberally spooning the sauce over them.

COOKING AHEAD

As indicated above, *Coq au Vin* improves by standing for at least a day. If possible, reheat it once, cool and refrigerate again. The mushrooms, however, should be added only in the final reheating before serving. Their texture and flavor should remain distinct. *Coq au Vin* can be frozen; add mushrooms and onions when reheating to serve.

LOW-CHOLESTEROL VERSION

The only substitutions necessary are polyunsaturated oil for olive oil, and polyunsaturated margarine instead of butter.

REMARKS

Now that domestic rabbit is found in so many frozen food counters, enjoy this lean meat often. This same recipe will give you *Lapin au Vin* (Rabbit in Red Wine). If you are lucky enough to have a hunter in the family, this recipe can turn wild rabbit into *Civet de Lièvre.* Traditionally this full-bodied dish utilizes the hare's blood and liver in the sauce. But even the liver alone would enhance the dish.

Prepare the hare according to the *Coq au Vin* recipe. Meanwhile cut the liver in four pieces and sauté it in a small skillet just until it stiffens, about 2 minutes. Remove the liver to a blender. Add ¼ cup brandy to the skillet and boil rapidly while stirring to scrape up all the coagulated juices from the bottom. Reduce the heat and stir in 2 tablespoons butter. Add this liquid to the blender and process until quite smooth. If you have time push the liver paste through a strainer to remove any small filaments. Stir the liver paste into the sauce and simmer very gently for 1 or 2 minutes.

Whether you have cooked chicken, rabbit, or hare according to this recipe, you will produce a delicious sauce. If any sauce is left over it can be frozen and used later to cook more chicken without any preliminary preparations, though you may want to add a little more red wine. Tiny beef or pork meatballs can also be poached in the simmering sauce for an entirely different dish. Serve the meatballs with a generous amount of sauce over cooked noodles or spaghetti.

Milky-way chicken

While we're used to cooking poultry in liquid — chicken stock, red wine, white wine, brown sauce — the idea of using milk may seem unusual. It is, despite the fact that Central Europeans have long appreciated this delicate combination. Few recipes could be easier than this one, and for the few minutes spent in the kitchen you have the whole main course all done .The quantities of sugar, garlic, and gin (yes, gin) specified are timid. They can be increased as you wish, but should not be omitted. One point about cooking with milk — it can scorch easily. To prevent that, coat the bottom of the pot with oil and bring the milk to a simmer slowly, not on high heat.

SERVES 6

WORKING TIME: 4 *minutes*

COOKING TIME: 1 *hour*

INGREDIENTS

3	**tablespoons oil**
1	**quart milk**
3	**pounds chicken, cut in pieces**
	salt and pepper
2	**teaspoons sugar**
1	**teaspoon ground coriander**
1	**tablespoon gin**
3	**cloves garlic, pierced on toothpicks**
	aluminum foil
1	**cup rice**

PREPARATION

1 Smear the oil in the bottom of a large heavy casserole, preferably enameled cast iron. Then pour in 1 cup of the milk. Rinse the chicken pieces and place them in the casserole. Sprinkle with salt and pepper. Pour in the rest of the milk; it should almost cover the chicken. Add the sugar, coriander, gin, and garlic. Use only 2 garlic cloves if you prefer.

2 Put the pot on a low fire and gently bring the milk to a simmer. Fit a piece of aluminum foil directly over the chicken, then place a lid on the pot. Reduce the heat and simmer for 30 minutes.

3 Remove the foil and discard. Add the rice, cover, and simmer for 20 minutes more. Remove the garlic.

TO SERVE

If the cooking casserole is good-looking, serve directly from it. Spoon out the chicken pieces and some cooked rice at the same time.

COOKING AHEAD

The entire recipe can be completed in advance and reheated carefully when needed. A little more milk should be added when reheating. A safer method is to cook just the chicken, cool, and refrigerate. Twenty-five minutes before serving time, bring back to a simmer and add the rice.

LOW-CHOLESTEROL VERSION

Substitute skimmed milk for whole milk and add an extra ½ teaspoon of sugar and coriander, plus 1 tablespoon of polyunsaturated oil. If possible, chill the casserole after cooking the chicken, then remove the fat that has congealed on the surface. Proceed as above.

Baked chicken cacciatore

Everyone has his favorite recipe for that Italian classic, Polla Alla Cacciatore (Hunter's-style Chicken). This is mine for several practical reasons. First of all, the chicken doesn't have to be browned, which automatically eliminates hundreds of calories and possibly a splattering mess in the kitchen. The slow oven baking allows the tomato sauce to penetrate the meat thoroughly. And the good news for those on K.P. is that this excellent main course leaves only one small saucepan and the baking dish to be washed.

SERVES 6

WORKING TIME: *11 minutes*

COOKING TIME: *approximately 2 hours*

INGREDIENTS

Sauce (2 cups)

1	**2-pound 3-ounce can Italian plum tomatoes**
2	**tablespoons pure olive oil**
½	**cup dry white wine**
½	**cup chopped onion**
2	**garlic cloves, mashed**
1	**small piece orange rind, about 1 by 1½ inches**
1	**bay leaf**
½	**teaspoon fennel seeds**
½	**teaspoon basil**
½	**teaspoon coriander**
¼	**teaspoon cinnamon**
	salt and pepper
3½	**pounds chicken cut in pieces**
	Garnish: black olives

PREPARATION

Preheat oven to 350°.

1   Drain the tomatoes (reserve the juice) and crush the tomato pulp with your hands into a small saucepan. Add the remaining sauce ingredients, cover and simmer for 30 minutes.

2   Meanwhile, arrange the chicken pieces in a baking dish, and sprinkle with salt and pepper. Pour the sauce over the chicken, making certain that all pieces are covered. Cover the dish with a lid or aluminum foil and bake for about 1½ hours or until the chicken is tender. (If the sauce seems a little dry during the baking, add some of the reserved tomato juice.)

TO SERVE

Remove the cover and decorate the top of the baked chicken with the black olives. Serve directly from the baking dish.

COOKING AHEAD

Baked Cacciatore can be cooked a day or two before serving and refrigerated. Its flavor will improve. Reheat the dish in a 350° oven for 20 minutes or until heated through. It can also be frozen.

LOW-CHOLESTEROL VERSION

Substitute polyunsaturated oil for the olive oil. No other changes are necessary.

Marinated turkey drumsticks

Once upon a time turkey meant Christmas or Thanksgiving. No more. Serving turkey all year long has become one way to ease the strain of food budgets, since turkey remains good food value for the dollar. Undoubtedly, a big fat browned roasted turkey is a beautiful sight. But for a small family, it means an endless parade of leftovers. Now, however, when the frozen-food industry is cutting up the large birds and offering a choice of pieces, turkey can be enjoyed on a one-meal basis at reasonable cost.

Turkey drumsticks, it turns out, are usually the best buy, offering a lot of meat for the money. For some inexplicable reason, the less meaty turkey wings often cost more. In this recipe the individual one-pound drumsticks are easiest and nicest to serve. If only the larger ones are available, slice them before serving.

This recipe has an unexpected bonus: The slightly spicy marinade gives the flavor of game to the dark meat of plebeian turkey drumsticks.

SERVES 4

WORKING TIME: 9 minutes

MARINATING TIME: at least 3 hours

BAKING TIME: 1 hour

INGREDIENTS

4   1-pound turkey drumsticks, thawed
½   cup dry white wine
½   cup olive oil
1   teaspoon oregano
½   teaspoon thyme
1   teaspoon cayenne pepper
2   garlic cloves, sliced
     salt and pepper
2   bay leaves
¾   cup water
1   tablespoon oil
1   teaspoon brandy
1   teaspoon aromatic bitters

PREPARATION

1   Place the drumsticks in a deep ovenproof dish. In a jar shake the wine, olive oil, oregano, thyme, cayenne, garlic, salt, and pepper. Pour this marinade over the drumsticks, turning them so that all surfaces are coated. Break the bay leaves in half and tuck around the meat. Cover and let stand at room temperature for 3 hours; or refrigerate for at least 6 hours, 24 is better. Turn occasionally.

Preheat oven to 375°.

2   Lift the drumsticks out of the marinade and dry them on paper towels. Strain the marinade into a small pot. Rinse the ovenproof dish with ½ cup water, then add the water to the marinade. Wipe the baking dish with paper towels and grease it with the oil. Return the drumsticks to the dish.

3   Place the drumsticks in the hot oven for 15 minutes. Brush them with the marinade and bake for another 15 minutes. Twice more, turn the drumsticks, brush with the marinade and bake for 15 minutes each time. They will have baked 1 hour in all. To test for doneness, pierce the fleshy part of the leg with a small sharp knife; if the juices run clear or pale rose, the meat is done.

4   To the strained marinade add ¼ cup water, the brandy, and bitters. Place the pot on the fire, bring to a boil and simmer slowly for 2 minutes. Strain the sauce into a sauceboat.

TO SERVE

Place the drumsticks on large dinner plates and spoon a little sauce over each one. Pass the rest of the sauce separately.

COOKING AHEAD

The drumsticks can be marinated and partially baked in advance. At serving time bake for the final 15 minutes in a 400-degree oven.

LOW-CHOLESTEROL VERSION

Substitute polyunsaturated oil for the olive oil.

Terrine de foies de volaille

Twenty minutes might seem like a lot of time to spend on something that seemingly can be bought at the delicatessen counter. Only it can't —not a good one, that is. And those small specialty shops that prepare their own pâtés for sale know what a fine thing they have, and charge accordingly. If you can make a meat loaf, you can make a good, inexpensive pâté. . . it's that easy. But one would never think so from the heady French flavor of the final product.

SERVES 8 AS A MAIN COURSE; 12 AS FIRST COURSE

WORKING TIME: *20 minutes*

MARINATING TIME: *2 hours*

BAKING TIME: *1 ¾ hours*

MATURING TIME: *at least 2 days*

INGREDIENTS

1 **pound fresh pork, ground twice (pork should be rather fatty)**

1 **pound chicken livers**

Marinade

¼ **cup dry white wine**

¼ **cup brandy**

¼ **cup Madeira**

¼ **teaspoon tarragon**

½ **teaspoon thyme**

2 **bay leaves**

½ **teaspoon allspice**

3 **garlic cloves, minced**

1 **onion, minced**

 salt and pepper

3 **tablespoons bread crumbs**

1 **egg**

 oil

PREPARATION

1 Put the ground pork and chicken livers in separate bowls. Mix together all the marinade ingredients and divide it between the two bowls. Let stand at least 2 hours.

2 Remove the bay leaves and reserve. Chop half the livers coarsely and add them to the pork along with the marinade drained from the livers. Add the bread crumbs and beaten egg to the pork and mix well. Fry a spoonful of the pork mixture, let it cool and taste for seasonings; correct if necessary.

Preheat oven to 350°.

3 Select an 8-cup loaf pan or pâté mold. Oil the mold heavily. Pack half the pork mixture into the mold. Then layer in the whole chicken livers, and cover with the remaining pork. If any marinade remains in either of the bowls, pour it over the meat. Smear oil on top, and press the reserved bay leaves in the center of the top of the pâté. Cover the mold tightly and place it in a pan with hot water that reaches a level of ¼ the depth of the dish. Place the pâté in the oven and bake for 1½ to 1¾ hours, or until a metal skewer plunged in the center will be hot to the wrist. Remove from the oven and cool.

4 Place weights on top and refrigerate for at least 2 days; 3 is better. The weights are not essential, but they help produce a closer-textured pâté which is easier to cut. Weights can be removed after 24 hours. The pâté will be good for at least a week.

TO SERVE

Cut directly from the mold and serve with crusty bread and pickles.

COOKING AHEAD

For best flavor, the pâté should be prepared at least 2 days in advance of serving. It will keep in the refrigerator for at least a week.

Mousse de foies de volaille

Perhaps this recipe should be in the section on Cocktail Hors d'Oeuvres, since that is how it is usually served. However, this mousse is just too good to be limited in that way. It can be a first course of great distinction at dinner or take star billing as the main course. In the latter case, the menu could start with a good soup, Crème Portugaise (page 15) for example, then Chicken Liver Mousse with toast and potato chips, followed by a hot vegetable course like Tomato Bake (page 172), Gratin Parisienne (page 157), or Spinach Gratin (page 168). Apricot Sherbet (page 202) or Coffee Granita (page 204) would be a perfect light finale to this dinner. Add up the cost of such a menu and you'll be surprised to find how low-budget it is despite its high style.

SERVES 12 AS COCKTAIL HORS D'OEUVRE;

6 AS FIRST COURSE;

4 AS MAIN COURSE

WORKING TIME: *8 minutes*

MARINATING TIME: *at least 4 hours*

COOKING TIME: *12 minutes*

MATURING TIME: *2 or 3 days*

INGREDIENTS

½   **pound chicken livers**

¼   **teaspoon allspice**

¼   **teaspoon salt**

⅛   **teaspoon pepper**

⅓   **cup Madeira, or Port**

2   **tablespoons plus ½ teaspoon brandy**

8   **tablespoons butter**

½   **cup chopped onions**

PREPARATION

1   Carefully pick over the chicken livers and remove any clinging fat and membranes. Put the livers in a small nonmetal bowl and sprinkle with allspice, salt, and pepper. Pour the Madeira and 2 tablespoons of brandy over the livers. Cover and let stand at least 4 hours at room temperature, or overnight in the refrigerator. (The livers can remain in the marinade in the refrigerator for as long as 2 days.)

2   Melt 4 tablespoons of butter in a heavy skillet, while chopping the onion. Add the onions to the skillet, cover, and simmer them slowly for about 7 minutes. They must not brown.

3   Increase the heat and push the onions to one side of the skillet. Lift the livers out of the marinade and fry quickly in the other side of the skillet for about 3 minutes, turning them almost constantly. Part of the secret of the mousse is not overcooking the livers, which toughens them and gives them an astringent flavor. Sprinkle with salt and pepper. Scrape the onions and livers into a blender. Pour the marinade into the same skillet and reduce it by boiling briskly for about ½ minute. Scrape it into the blender.

4   Return the skillet to medium heat and melt the remaining 4 tablespoons of butter in it. Add the melted butter and ½ teaspoon of brandy to the blender and purée the contents. Taste for salt and pepper and correct if necessary, blending again after any addition. Scrape the mousse into a 2-cup container, cover tightly and refrigerate for at least 2 or 3 days; 4 or 5 is even better.

TO SERVE

Place the chicken liver mousse in its mold on a small dish. At the table scoop out the mousse with a spoon, just the way many French restaurants do when serving fresh *foie gras*. Pass with warm toast.

COOKING AHEAD

This is another dish which must be prepared several days in advance.

Sautéed chicken livers

This recipe is based on the dramatic flavor marinating gives to chicken livers. Instead of puréeing them into a mousse as in the preceding recipe, this time they are sautéed with a generous amount of onions and served hot. Polenta (page 180), Sunny Rice (page 181), or Puréed Chick-peas (page 177) would be excellent accompanying vegetables.

SERVES 4

WORKING TIME: *8 minutes*

MARINATING TIME: *at least 4 hours*

COOKING TIME: *15 to 20 minutes*

INGREDIENTS

1	**pound chicken livers**
½	**teaspoon allspice**
½	**teaspoon salt**
¼	**teaspoon pepper**
⅔	**cup Madeira or Port**
3	**tablespoons brandy**
4	**tablespoons butter**
2	**tablespoons oil**
2	**medium onions, thinly sliced**
¼	**cup beef broth**
2	**tablespoons chopped parsley**

PREPARATION

1 Carefully pick over the chicken livers and remove any clinging fat and membranes. Put the livers in a small nonmetal bowl and sprinkle with allspice, salt, and pepper. Pour the Madeira and brandy over the livers. Cover and let stand at least 4 hours at room temperature, or overnight in the refrigerator.

2 While melting 2 tablespoons of butter and 1 tablespoon of oil in a heavy skillet, peel and slice the onions and add them to the skillet. Cover and simmer very slowly for 10 to 15 minutes or until the onions begin turning a golden color. Scrape the onions out of the skillet and into a small bowl.

3 Using the same skillet, melt the remaining 2 tablespoons of butter and 1 tablespoon of oil until very hot. Lift the livers out of the marinade and add them to the hot fat. Keep the heat high while cooking and turning the livers to sear them all over. Once the outside of the livers have turned a dark golden brown (this should take 2 or 3 minutes), scrape in the cooked onions, stir, cover and simmer for 2 minutes.

4 Spoon the liver and onions into a warm serving dish and keep warm. Pour the marinade and beef broth into the skillet, stir, and boil briskly for about 1 minute. Pour this reduction over the cooked livers and onions. Sprinkle with parsley and serve at once.

COOKING AHEAD

The onions can be cooked a day in advance and kept tightly covered in the refrigerator. The sautéing of the marinated livers must be done at serving time, but since only a few minutes are needed, it is easy to do between courses.

Gavin's rabbit

Gavin is a witty young man who knows absolutely nothing about cooking. His fondness for rabbit and sour cream, though, was the inspiration for this dish. I haven't told him yet, but it works equally well with chicken.

SERVES 4 TO 5

WORKING TIME: *17 minutes*

COOKING TIME: *50 to 60 minutes*

INGREDIENTS

3	tablespoons butter
1	tablespoon oil
1	medium onion, chopped
1	carrot
1	celery rib
3	pounds rabbit, cut in pieces
1½	cups chicken broth
½	cup dry white wine
	pinch of saffron
¼	teaspoon allspice
	salt and pepper
2	egg yolks
1	tablespoon dark prepared mustard
2	tablespoons flour
1	cup sour cream

PREPARATION

1 In a heavy nonaluminum casserole or pot, melt the butter and oil slowly while peeling and chopping the onion. Add the onion to the butter, cover and simmer gently while preparing the vegetables.

2 Peel the carrot and cut in half lengthwise, then cut in half crosswise. Scrub the celery rib and break in half.

3 Pull off and discard any fatty portions of the rabbit. Add the rabbit to the onions. Pour on 1 cup of chicken broth and the wine. The liquid should come to ¾ the level of the meat; if not, add the remaining ½ cup of broth. Tuck in the carrot and celery pieces. Add the saffron, allspice, salt, and pepper. Cover and simmer gently for 45 minutes, or until the meat is tender. Remove the carrots and celery.

4 Put the egg yolks in a small bowl with the mustard and beat together. Add the flour and mix to a smooth paste, then beat in the sour cream. Take a ladleful of stock from the pot and slowly beat it into the sour cream mixture. Repeat with a second ladleful. Pour this cream over the rabbit, turning the pieces of meat so that all surfaces are covered with the sauce. Cover and reheat gently for 5 minutes. Do not allow the sauce to boil.

TO SERVE

Remove rabbit pieces to a deep serving dish and spoon some sauce over the meat. Pass the remaining sauce separately.

COOKING AHEAD

Complete the cooking of the rabbit (through step 3), cool, and refrigerate, for as much as a day. At serving time, remove the carrot and celery pieces and bring the meat and stock back to a gentle simmer. Proceed with step 4 to finish the sauce. If the sauce has been finished, add ¼ cup of milk when reheating very slowly.

LOW-CHOLESTEROL VERSION

Substitute 3 tablespoons polyunsaturated margarine for the butter. To make the sauce: put 3 tablespoons flour in a small bowl, stir in ½ cup yogurt and ¼ cup mustard; slowly stir in ¼ cup evaporated skimmed milk or polyunsaturated cream substitute, plus the juice of ½ lemon. Proceed with recipe as in step 4.

Lapin au diable

Americans tend to think of rabbit as a European food. However, Indians enjoyed wild rabbit long before Columbus arrived on the scene. Rabbit also was a staple in the diet of early settlers and frontiersmen. It eventually found its way from the huntsmen's tables to the elegance of the dining room at Monticello. Thomas Jefferson especially liked rabbit marinated, then simmered in red wine. He called it a fricassee.

Without a hunter in the family it can be difficult to get wild rabbit, fresh or frozen. Domestic rabbits are quite a different breed, but they are now available frozen almost always in supermarkets and poultry shops. It's no accident that poultry shops carry rabbit. The flavors of chicken and rabbit are rather similar, as is the texture of the meat. But rabbit is less fatty and firmer. Your favorite recipes for veal or chicken would work well with rabbit.

SERVES 4

WORKING TIME: 17 minutes

DRYING TIME: 30 minutes

BAKING TIME: 1 hour

INGREDIENTS

2	pounds rabbit, cut in pieces
9	tablespoons butter (1 stick plus 1 tablespoon)
¼	cup prepared mustard
1½	cups bread crumbs
¾	cup cream
½	cup chicken broth

PREPARATION

1 Rinse the rabbit pieces and dry them on paper towels. Cream together 3 tablespoons of butter and the mustard. Pour the bread crumbs in a dish.

2 Using a pastry brush, paint each piece of rabbit liberally on all sides with the mustard-butter. Then roll it in the crumbs, patting the crumbs to make them adhere. Place the rabbit pieces in a baking dish and let them dry at least 30 minutes.

Preheat oven to 375°.

3 Put the baking dish with the rabbit in the oven for 10 minutes. Meanwhile, melt 6 tablespoons of butter. Pour half the butter over the rabbit, reduce the heat to 350° and bake for 15 minutes.

4 Turn the rabbit pieces and pour the rest of the melted butter over them. Return the dish to the oven for another 15 minutes.

5 Pour ¼ cup of cream over the rabbit and bake for 10 minutes more. Turn the pieces again and pour over them the remaining ½ cup of cream and bake for 10 minutes.

6 Remove the rabbit to a warm serving platter and keep it warm. In a small pot, bring the chicken broth to a boil and pour it into the baking dish. Stir the broth with a wire whisk to scrape all the juices from the bottom.

TO SERVE

Pour the sauce from the baking dish over the rabbit and serve at once.

COOKING AHEAD

The rabbit can be coated with the mustard and crumbs and refrigerated early in the day for the evening. Proceed with the recipe at dinnertime. If the rabbit also must be baked in advance, proceed only through step 4. At serving time pour on the cream and continue with step 5.

LOW-CHOLESTEROL VERSION

Substitute polyunsaturated margarine for the butter and ½ cup evaporated skimmed milk mixed with ¼ cup dry white wine for the cream. In making the final sauce, add ¼ cup dry white wine after the chicken broth has been stirred into the pan.

MEAT

Meat, in one form or another, is America's favorite food. So cutting down the preparation time of meat dishes alone will save the cook countless hours over a year. That is what I've tried to do in this chapter.

One timesaving device is to eliminate the browning of beef before simmering it in a broth or sauce. Happily, the finished product is moister than when browned. Delicious French pâtés can be made in well under 30 minutes by discarding a number of time-consuming steps, such as lining the mold with pork fatback. A liberal smearing of oil gives the same moistness, without intruding fatback's flavor. Also I don't brown beef tongue before braising it. Why should it be browned, other than because recipes always say so? There is no blood to be sealed into the meat, which is the usual explanation for the process.

The longest recipe in this section is Boeuf Mode en Gelée (Beef in Aspic) which requires 35 minutes of working time. But for those 35 minutes you serve 10 people a complete main course with vegetables, and you serve them beautifully.

For most of the dishes in this section red wine is the obvious choice. A rosé would be lovely with Baked Lamb Curry, Gratin Campagne or Pâté Panaché en Aspic. For veal, or pork treated like veal, I suggest a Beaujolais, light Bordeaux (particularly a Médoc), or a California Cabernet Sauvignon. The beef dishes go well with a fuller wine like a Beaune, Nuits-Saint-George or Aloxe-Corton from Burgundy; Saint-Emilion from Bordeaux; Pinot Noir or another of the better Burgundy-type wines from California. Robust dishes like Cassoulet or Ragout de Mouton are very good with a big Burgundy, a Châteauneuf-du-Pape, a California Pinot Noir, or a Cahors from central France.

Escalopes à la colonnade

Originally this dish was made with thin veal slices. But when veal prices went out of sight I switched to butterfly pork chops and found that they worked perfectly. Since the chops are quite thin, they need not be cooked very long. A quick simmering in the white wine will keep them moist and tender. Escalopes à la Colonnade are handsomely presented — each golden brown cutlet is crowned with a pale green artichoke brimming with bright red tomato sauce. An attractive and unusual dish with a marvelous blend of flavors.

SERVES 6

WORKING TIME: 12 minutes

COOKING TIME: 8 minutes

INGREDIENTS

8	**tablespoons butter (1 stick)**
2	**tablespoons oil**
	flour
6	**boneless veal slices or butterfly pork cutlets**
1¼	**teaspoons sage**
1¼	**teaspoons rosemary**
	salt and pepper
1½	**cups dry white wine**
6	**artichoke bottoms (the flat kind, not the small round hearts)**
½	**cup Quick Tomato Coulis (page 225), or other tomato sauce**
¼	**teaspoon oregano**

PREPARATION

1   Melt 3 tablespoons of butter and 1 tablespoon of oil in a large skillet. Meanwhile, spread some flour on waxed paper or a dish and dip each cutlet into the flour. Flour both sides, patting the flour into the meat. Shake off the excess.

2   When the butter is hot and foamy, add the meat, keeping the heat moderately hot. Sprinkle the meat lightly with sage and rosemary, rubbing the herbs into it. When the underside of the cutlets are a golden brown, turn the meat and sprinkle with salt and pepper. Add butter as needed. Fry for 1 minute, then pour in the wine to a level of about ¼ inch. Reduce the heat, cover, and simmer for 5 minutes.

3   While the meat is simmering, prepare the sauce and the artichokes. Place the artichokes on paper towels to dry. Put the tomato sauce in a small pot, add the oregano and simmer slowly. Melt 2 tablespoons of butter and 1 tablespoon of oil in another skillet. When the butter is hot and foamy add the artichokes and fry them on both sides until the edges brown lightly. Add butter as needed. Sprinkle the artichokes lightly with salt and pepper.

TO SERVE

Place the cutlets on a warm serving platter or individual dinner plates. Arrange an artichoke bottom in the center of each cutlet and fill it with the hot tomato sauce. Serve at once.

COOKING AHEAD

For best results *Escalopes à la Colonnade* should be cooked and assembled just before serving.

LOW-CHOLESTEROL VERSION

Use polyunsaturated margarine instead of butter and sprinkle the cutlets a little more generously with the sage and rosemary. No other changes in the recipe are necessary.

Vitello tonnato

Even though it's served cold, Italians don't reserve this classic dish just for summertime eating. They enjoy it all year round. You can, too, especially since its complexities have been streamlined down to an easy 23 minutes. Vitello Tonnato is really festive fare, a company dish that always pleases. Yet there is not one bit of last-minute flurry involved, since the whole platter has to be done ahead.

Traditionally in this dish slices of the delicate veal are coated with a zesty tuna-anchovy sauce. That's the way I used to do it. But as American veal has deteriorated in quality, and pork has become finer and leaner, I now substitute lean pork loin. It works beautifully. Try it with veal or pork, but do try Vitello Tonnato.

SERVES 8 TO 10

WORKING TIME: *23 minutes*

ROASTING TIME: 1 ¾ *hours*

COOLING TIME: *about 2 hours*

CHILLING TIME: *at least 3 hours*

INGREDIENTS

1   **3-pound boned veal roast; or lean, rolled pork loin**

2   **tablespoons butter, room temperature**

1   **teaspoon rosemary**

   salt and pepper

1   **medium onion, quartered**

1   **bay leaf, broken in half**

½   **cup dry white wine**

   Sauce
½   **cup liquid from roast, degreased**

   juice 1 lemon

1   **6½-ounce can tuna in oil, drained**

6-8   **anchovy fillets**

2   **tablespoons capers, drained**

2   **cups mayonnaise (p. 226)**

   Optional decoration: rolled anchovy fillets, capers, black olives

PREPARATION

Preheat oven to 350°

1   Lay a large piece of heavy aluminum foil in a roasting pan, put the meat on the foil and smear it with butter; sprinkle with rosemary, salt, and pepper. Scatter the onion and bay leaf pieces around the meat. Lift the edges of the foil, carefully pour in the wine and completely seal the foil over the meat. There should be no open seams through which the juices can escape. Place the pan in the oven for 1¾ hours. (If you are not sure about the degree of doneness, carefully open the foil and insert a meat thermometer; it should read 180°. You can also test by piercing with a fork—the juices should run pale-clear, with just a touch of pink.) Cool the meat in the sealed foil.

2   Lift the meat out of foil, carefully pour off the juices and strain them. Chill the meat and juices separately.

3   Sauce: remove the congealed fat from the juices and discard. Measure out a ½ cup of juice and pour it into a blender. Add all the remaining sauce ingredients, except the mayonnaise, and blend to a smooth purée. Put the mayonnaise in a bowl and beat the purée into it. Chill well.

4   About 3 hours before serving, cut the meat into thin slices. If you are using rolled pork, remove all string and the layer of fat on the outside. One by one, lay the slices of meat on the serving platter, liberally coating one side with the tuna sauce. Stack them together with the uncoated side of the one slice against the sauced surface of the previous slice. Reshape to resemble the original roast and coat the entire surface with the sauce.

TO SERVE

Decorate the *Vitello Tonnato* with any one or a combination of rolled anchovy fillets, capers scattered about, and black olives. Pass the extra sauce in a sauceboat.

COOKING AHEAD

The meat is best roasted the day before, so it can chill thoroughly. The sauce can also be prepared the day before, leaving only the slicing and arranging to do several hours before serving.

LOW-CHOLESTEROL VERSION

Use veal or very lean pork. Substitute polyunsaturated margarine for the butter. No other changes in the recipe are necessary.

Steak au poivre

Most men I know order Steak au Poivre every chance they get. The paralyzing fire of the hot peppercorns is a sensation they relish for some reason, perhaps as an excuse to quaff chilled Beaujolais. The Steak au Poivre fancier around my house declared this fast version sensational, even though it wasn't quite as fiery as usual. The secret comes in a little cardboard box from France . . . Boursin pepper cheese. Boursin au Poivre is spread on the grilled steak, which then is slipped under the broiler for ½ minute. The result is a lot, but a civilized amount, of pepper on the steak.

The first Boursin cheese to come to this country was flavored with garlic and herbs (Boursin à l'ail et fines herbes). When it is substituted for the pepper cheese, it produces an herb-flavored steak with a flavoring that resembles maître d'hôtel butter or béarnaise sauce. Wisconsin now produces an excellent imitation of both Boursin cheeses. Rondolé is one brand that will give you either the pepper or garlic and herb flavors at half the price of the imported.

There is another advantage to preparing steak with these seasoned cheeses — a less expensive cut of meat can be used. Top round is perfect. Pound the meat a little, then moisten it and sprinkle with meat tenderizer. Under the spicy cheese it is hard to tell it from fillet.

SERVES AS MANY AS YOU LIKE

WORKING TIME: *3 minutes*

GRILLING TIME: *5 to 10 minutes*

INGREDIENTS

top round steak, ½ pound per person

meat tenderizer

oil

Boursin pepper cheese, or Boursin garlic and herb cheese

brandy

PREPARATION

Preheat broiler.

1 Tenderize the steak and grill it according to your favorite method. I like to do it on a heavy cast-iron grill or skillet. Once the steak has been turned sprinkle it with salt and pepper and smear Boursin cheese over it. Sprinkle brandy over the cheese.

2 When the steak has been grilled to the desired degree of rareness (the timing will depend on the thickness of the steak) slip the skillet under a hot broiler for ½ minute, just long enough to melt the cheese a little. Serve at once.

LOW-CHOLESTEROL VERSION

The above method cannot be used for low-cholesterol diets since Boursin is a whole-fat cheese. In an earlier cookbook (*Haute Cuisine for Your Heart's Delight*), I adapted the classic procedure to eliminate all animal fat in the sauce. It is prepared this way to serve 6:

1 Trim all fat off 6 individual steaks or 3 pounds of lean beef. Dry the meat on paper towels and rub a little polyunsaturated oil on both sides. Crush slightly 2 tablespoons of black and white peppercorns and press them into the surfaces of the meat. Put the seasoned meat aside for at least 2 hours. (A blender can be used for grinding the peppercorns, but don't crush too fine.)

2 Heat polyunsaturated oil in a heavy skillet until quite hot. Add the meat and sauté it on both sides according to the degree of doneness desired. Salt the steak after it has been turned. Remove the steak to a warm platter and keep warm.

3 Pour out all the oil from the skillet and add 1 cup of white wine and ¾ cup of beef broth. While the liquids simmer, mix 2 teaspoons of cornstarch with ¼ cup beef broth and add it to the sauce, stirring with a wire whisk and scraping up the coagulated juices from the bottom of the pan. When the sauce has thickened, add ¼ cup brandy and 2 tablespoons evaporated skimmed milk or polyunsaturated cream substitute. Simmer the sauce for ½ minute, remove it from the fire, and stir in 3 tablespoons polyunsaturated margarine. Spoon the sauce over the meat and serve at once. Have lots of red wine on hand to put out the fire.

Tranche de boeuf au madère

Well-prepared braised beef is one of the easiest, and best, dishes a busy cook can offer. The cooking time is long because less-expensive cuts of beef are used, but the simmering pot demands no attention. This particular version is more flavorful than most because of its long marinating period and the use of Madeira instead of the usual red wine. A fortified wine from a Portuguese subtropical island, Madeira produces a sauce that is mellow and rich in flavor. The finished dish has a stewlike appearance—a real treat for family and friends. The final garnish of black olives, a Mediterranean touch, is unusual and striking.

SERVES 6

WORKING TIME: *11 minutes*

MARINATING TIME: *at least 4 hours*

COOKING TIME: *3 to 4 hours*

INGREDIENTS

3	**pounds chuck steak, 1½ inches thick**
	salt and pepper
	allspice
2	**onions, sliced**
4	**carrots, sliced**
3	**garlic cloves**
1½	**cups Madeira, or Port**
½	**cup dry white wine**
¼	**cup brandy**
⅛	**teaspoon thyme**
6	**sprigs parsley**
2	**bay leaves**
½	**cup beef broth**
18	**pitted black olives**

PREPARATION

1 Place the meat in a deep nonmetal dish. Sprinkle it with salt, pepper, and allspice and rub these seasonings into the meat. Turn the meat and repeat on the other side.

2 Peel the onions and cut them into thick slices. Peel the carrots and slice them into ½-inch rounds. Peel the garlic cloves. Scatter the vegetables over and under the meat.

3 Pour 1 cup of Madeira, the white wine, and brandy over the meat. Sprinkle thyme on the marinade. Tuck in the parsley sprigs and bay leaves. Cover the dish closely and marinate at room temperature for at least 4 hours, or overnight in the refrigerator. Turn the meat once or twice.

4 Transfer the contents of the dish to a large skillet or casserole and add ¼ cup of Madeira and the beef broth. Place a piece of aluminum foil directly over the meat. Bring the liquid to a boil, cover the skillet with a lid, reduce the heat to a slow simmer and cook for 3 to 4 hours, or until the meat is tender. The amount of cooking will depend on the quality of the meat.

5 For the last 15 minutes of cooking, add the remaining ¼ cup of Madeira. Rinse the olives well under hot water to remove all the brine and add them to the stock for the final 5 minutes of cooking.

TO SERVE

Transfer the meat to a warm serving platter. The meat may break into pieces as you do, but it doesn't matter. Cut the meat into serving portions. Remove the parsley and bay leaves from the stock. (The garlic will have turned sweet during the long cooking.) With a skimmer, lift out the vegetables and olives and scatter them over the top of the meat. Spoon enough of the stock over the meat to wet it thoroughly and let some collect in the platter. Pass a sauceboat of extra stock separately.

COOKING AHEAD

So much the better. Braised Beef in Madeira will improve if allowed to stand for a day. In this case, do not add the final ¼ cup of Madeira and olives until reheating the dish.

LOW-CHOLESTEROL VERSION

No changes in the recipe are necessary. Select the leanest beef possible.

Tomato-noodle casserole

Many people look upon casseroles as the busy cook's solution to entertaining. This may be true, but it's not the only solution. Any dish that can be prepared in advance and reheated falls into the "Entertain with Ease" category. But there are times when a real casserole is just what you want. Then, I think, this may be the one. Its layers of meat sauce and noodles look especially pretty in a glass baking dish. Another reason I'm partial to this recipe is that the noodles are not pre-cooked, which means one less pot to wash. Be precise when selecting a 2½-quart baking dish since the casserole will shrink some as the noodles soften and will not look nice in a large dish.

SERVES 6 TO 8

WORKING TIME: 14 minutes

COOKING TIME: 55 minutes

INGREDIENTS

3   tablespoons oil
1   pound ground beef
2   medium onions, sliced
1   garlic clove, mashed
1   2-pound 3-ounce can tomatoes
½   cup tomato paste
1   cup red wine, or water
½   teaspoon paprika
1   tablespoon salt
1   bay leaf
⅛   teaspoon thyme
1   teaspoon marjoram
1   teaspoon Worcestershire sauce
½   teaspoon Tabasco
8   ounces uncooked broad noodles
¼   cup grated Parmesan cheese

PREPARATION

Preheat oven to 375°

1   Heat the oil in a large heavy skillet until it is hot, then add the meat, keeping the fire rather high. Stir the meat with a wooden spoon or fork, breaking it into small pieces.

2   Peel and slice the onions while the meat is cooking; add the onions and garlic. Cover and simmer for 2 minutes.

3   Add the tomatoes, tomato paste, wine (or water), paprika, salt, bay leaf, thyme, marjoram, Worcestershire sauce, and Tabasco. Stir the meat and seasonings well, cover, and simmer slowly for 5 minutes.

4   Select a 2½-quart baking dish, preferably a deep one. Spoon ½ the sauce into the baking dish, then add the uncooked noodles. Cover the noodles with the remaining sauce.

5   Bake the casserole for 45 minutes. Sprinkle it with cheese and bake 5 minutes more. Serve directly from the casserole dish.

COOKING AHEAD

Tomato-Noodle Casserole can be prepared, covered, and refrigerated until needed. Add 5 to 10 minutes additional oven time, depending on how cold the dish is. It can also be frozen before baking.

LOW-CHOLESTEROL VERSION

Use polyunsaturated oil for the frying, increasing the amount to ¼ cup; use very lean beef; use low-fat cheese or omit it.

Pot-au-feu

The difference between plain boiled beef and Pot-au-Feu is roughly the same as the difference between scrambled eggs and a puffy truffled omelet. This streamlined Pot-au-Feu also borrows a little from the Italian Bolliti Misti (mixed boiled meats), so popular around Bologna. I find that the lightly smoked sausage added to the misti does a lot for the entire dish. Since most sausages available in the United States are quite fatty, I have substituted smoked pork shoulder. If you are lucky enough to have a supplier of fresh smoked farm sausages, use them instead.

This is a very hearty dish, hearty enough to be served to grape pickers at harvest time in France, especially around Bordeaux. It is better not to start the dinner with anything else since the soup of Pot-au-Feu is served with its meats and vegetables. Afterwards serve some cheese or a light dessert and you will give your guests and family a good idea of why the French and Italians eat so well.

Caution: Before starting this recipe, make certain you have a really big kettle, at least 12 quarts in capacity.

WORKING TIME: 25 minutes

COOKING TIME: 4 hours

INGREDIENTS

4	pounds chuck, rump, sirloin tip, or brisket
3	cups beef broth
12	cups water

Soup seasonings

1	onion studded with 2 cloves
3	carrots, peeled and cut in chunks
1	celery rib, broken in half
1	turnip, peeled and cut in quarters
	herb bouquet (6 parsley sprigs tied around 2 bay leaves)
½	teaspoon thyme
4	garlic cloves
½	teaspoon pepper
1	teaspoon salt

1	2-to-2½-pound head cabbage
2½	pounds smoked pork shoulder roll, or 2 pounds sausage
2½	pounds chicken, cut in pieces
6	potatoes, peeled and cut in halves or quarters
8	carrots, peeled and cut in chunks
	Optional condiments: mustard, horseradish, salsa verde (page 228)

PREPARATION

1 Rinse the beef and place it in a 12-to-14-quart soup kettle. Add the beef broth and just enough water to cover the meat. Bring the liquid to a simmer while preparing the vegetables for the seasoning. Skim off any foam that rises to the surface. This will have to be done several times during the cooking.

2 Add all soup seasonings: the onion with cloves, carrots in chunks, celery rib, turnip, herb bouquet, thyme, garlic, pepper, and salt. Do not oversalt at this point since the beef broth is already salted. Cover and simmer for 1½ hours.

3 While the beef is cooking, prepare the cabbage. Rinse it, then quarter and remove the hard center core. Cook the cabbage for 2 minutes in a pressure cooker or in a large quantity of unsalted boiling water until it is almost soft. Drain at once and rinse under cold running water. Cut the quarters into 2 or 3 slices, depending on the size of the cabbage.

4 Add the smoked pork to the kettle. Add more water if necessary to cover the meats. Bring the broth back to a simmer and cook for 1 more hour.

5 Add the chicken pieces and cook for 20 minutes. If a foam residue clings to the sides of the kettle, wipe it off with a wet paper towel.

6 Turn off the heat and let the pot stand for 30 minutes so the fats rise to the surface. Spoon off the fat, or draw pieces of paper towels across the top to absorb the fat. Or, best of all, cool and refrigerate overnight, then remove the layer of congealed fat on top.

7 Add the potatoes and carrots and cook for about 25 minutes or until they are tender. Add the cabbage for the last 10 minutes of cooking. Remove the beef and pork to a carving board and cut in slices.

TO SERVE

Obviously, large, wide soup dishes are called for, not small consommé cups. The soup bowls should be placed on dinner plates. Put some of each of the sliced meats, plus a piece of chicken, in each of the bowls; then add a selection of vegetables. With a ladle pour in broth to reach half the level of the contents. Provide guests with knife, fork, and soup spoon. Pass optional condiments.

COOKING AHEAD

The recipe can be completed to step 7, but the potatoes and carrots should be cooked for only 10 minutes. Finish cooking them and the cabbage when reheating the *Pot-au-Feu*. It can be refrigerated for two days before serving.

LOW-CHOLESTEROL VERSION

Use lean meats and lean smoked pork instead of sausage. It is essential to chill overnight to remove all congealed fat.

REMARKS

Since *Pot-au-Feu* is an unusual party dish, guests often ask how they should eat it. I suggest they put the condiments on the edge of the soup dish, if it has a wide rim, or on the dinner plate underneath. A piece of meat is cut and, with the knife, a dab of the condiment is added before eating. The soup broth is taken intermittently with the meat and vegetables. Before refilling the soup bowls, remove the chicken bones.

Meat loaf à la pâté

One by-product of my learning to make French pâté was greatly improved meat loaf around our house. Actually French pâté is not too different from our familiar meat loaf. But usually there are vast differences in moisture and taste. I think you'll find that just by adopting the technique of covered baking, the meat loaf will achieve a stronger flavor and a beautifully moist texture. For meat loaf any kind of loaf pan will do, as long as it is covered with a lid, heavy aluminum foil, or what have you. Fill the mold completely. During the baking the loaf will shrink as fats and juices cook out. Bread crumbs are included in the recipe since they expand during the cooking and replace the space given up by the melting fat.

SERVES 4 TO 6

WORKING TIME: 12 minutes; add 3 minutes for gravy

BAKING TIME: 1 hour

INGREDIENTS

2	teaspoons oil
1	pound beef, ground twice
2	tablespoons dried onion soup
½	cup condensed tomato soup
¼	cup bread crumbs
1	tablespoon prepared mustard
1	teaspoon Worcestershire sauce
1	tablespoon chopped parsley
1	garlic clove, minced
	salt and pepper
1	beaten egg
2	tablespoons catsup
1	tablespoon grated Parmesan cheese

Gravy

	drippings from meat loaf
1	tablespoon flour
½	cup milk
¼	teaspoon Worcestershire sauce
	salt and pepper
	few drops gravy coloring (Kitchen Bouquet)

PREPARATION

Preheat oven to 350°.

1 Select a 1-quart loaf pan and smear it with the oil. Put in a mixing bowl all the ingredients except the egg, catsup, and cheese. Knead with your hands to thoroughly mix all seasonings into the meat. Add the egg and mix again with your hands to blend it in.

2 Scoop the seasoned meat into the loaf pan and smooth the top with your hands. Spread the catsup evenly over the meat. Cover and bake for 45 minutes.

3 Remove the cover, sprinkle with cheese and bake for another 15 minutes.

4 Lift the meat loaf out of the pan with two spatulas and onto a warmed serving dish. Keep warm while making the gravy.

5 Pour the liquid from the meat loaf pan into a small pot. Spoon out the excess fat that floats to the top. Put the pot on heat and bring to a slow simmer.

6 Meanwhile, put the flour in a small bowl and stir milk into it slowly to keep the mixture smooth. Pour the flour paste into the meat juices while stirring with a wire whisk. Add Worcestershire sauce, salt, pepper, and just a few drops of gravy coloring. This should not be a dark gravy, but nut brown in color. Simmer for 1 minute and pour into a sauceboat.

TO SERVE

Tuck a few sprigs of parsley at both ends of the meat loaf. Slice it either in the kitchen or at the table. Pass gravy separately.

COOKING AHEAD

The meat loaf can be baked for 45 minutes, then removed from the oven, leaving the cover in place. Twenty minutes before serving time, remove the cover, sprinkle with cheese and return to 375° oven.

LOW-CHOLESTEROL VERSION

Buy the leanest meat possible. Top round is perfect if the fat around the meat is removed before grinding. (Grinding at home is the surest and safest way of eliminating almost all fat.) Use all seasonings listed above, except the whole egg, substituting 2 egg whites. Add 2 tablespoons of polyunsaturated oil to the meat mixture to replace the fat that has been trimmed off. The grated cheese topping can be eliminated for strict diets. In making the gravy, substitute evaporated skimmed milk for the whole milk.

Hearty beef stew

Every busy cook needs at least one good stew in his repertoire. This is mine. Though stew is often thought of as a dish for the family, I can't imagine why guests should be deprived of something so good. Since all stews improve with standing, they are an ideal choice for parties. Cooked one or even two days in advance, there is no last-minute fuss, just a gentle reheating.

Instead of using meat cut into chunks, I much prefer cooking a braising roast in one piece and slicing when needed. I think the lean slices make a more handsome presentation. Contrary to tradition, the meat is not browned in hot fat. Nevertheless, it achieves a dark color during the long, slow cooking in red wine.

SERVES 8

WORKING TIME: *22 minutes*

COOKING TIME: *2½ to 3½ hours*

INGREDIENTS

¼ **cup oil**
1 **medium onion, chopped**
1 **rib celery, sliced**
1 **tablespoon currant or plum jam**
2 **tablespoons tomato paste**
3 **tablespoons flour**
2 **cups beef broth, possibly more**
5 **cups red wine**
¼ **teaspoon powdered thyme**
4 **garlic cloves, mashed**
   salt and pepper
4 **pounds beef arm, rump roast, or similar braising cut**
   herb bouquet (6 sprigs parsley tied around 2 bay leaves)
4 **medium potatoes, quartered**
5 **carrots, cut into chunks**
½ **head of cauliflower**

PREPARATION

1 Pour the oil in a large heavy casserole and put the casserole on medium heat while peeling and chopping the onion and slicing the celery. Add the vegetables to the oil, cover and simmer for 3 minutes. Add the jam and tomato paste and stir until they melt. Add the flour, stir, and simmer for 1 minute. Add 1 cup of beef broth and 4 cups of wine. Bring the liquid to a simmer while adding the thyme, mashed garlic, salt, and pepper.

2 Add the meat to the casserole. Tuck in the herb bouquet. The meat should be almost completely covered by the sauce, if not add more wine or broth or both. Cover and simmer gently, turning the meat from time to time. Cooking time will depend on the quality and thickness of the meat; 2 to 3 hours should be about right. When pierced with a small sharp knife, the meat should be tender.

3 While the meat is cooking, peel and quarter the potatoes, peel the carrots and cut into 2-inch chunks. When the meat is tender add the potatoes and carrots and simmer for 20 minutes.

4 Break the cauliflower into flowerets and add them to the stew. Continue cooking until all the vegetables are soft, but not mushy.

TO SERVE

Remove and discard the herb bouquet. Remove the meat from the stew and cut away any strings. Cut the beef into thin slices and return them to the pot to reheat. Serve directly from the casserole or transfer the stew to a large serving platter, arranging the meat and vegetables in an attractive pattern.

COOKING AHEAD

Hearty Beef Stew improves measurably if prepared a day or two in advance. The meat also will slice into neater slices once it is chilled.

LOW-CHOLESTEROL VERSION

Buy very lean beef and trim off any remaining fat. In this case the stew must be made at least a day in advance so that all chilled, congealed fat on the surface can be removed.

Boeuf à la mode en gelée

The various times listed below may seem complicated at first glance, but don't let that dissuade you from trying this exceptionally good and easy variation on a great French classic. Each step is simple and done at a time of your own choosing. Although 35 minutes of work is longer than for most recipes in this book, it should be kept in mind that it includes the preparation —in grand style —of the meat and vegetable courses for ten people. This is a wonderful party dish that is completely ready hours ahead of time, even the day before. There is absolutely nothing to do at the last minute, not even slicing the meat.

Though Boeuf à la Mode en Gelée is generally considered a summertime dish, I serve it all year round. It is a hearty dish that can stand up to any temperature. A favorite menu at our home is: Roquefort Soufflé (page 32), Boeuf à la Mode en Gelée, Baked Ratatouille (page 149) served hot as a separate course, and a cooling dessert like Frozen Maple Mousse (page 206). As mentioned elsewhere in this book, a completely prepared cold main course gives the chef great peace of mind at dinner-party time.

SERVES 8 TO 10

WORKING TIME: 35 minutes
MARINATING TIME: 6 hours or more
COOKING TIME: 3 to 4 hours
SETTING OF ASPIC: 2 hours or more

INGREDIENTS

4	pounds eye of round or rump roast, well larded by your butcher and prepared as for a roast, with a covering of fat
	(a few bones, if possible)
	salt and pepper
5	carrots, sliced
3	large onions, quartered
4	garlic cloves
2	bay leaves
½	teaspoon thyme
4	cups red wine
2	cups beef broth
2	beef bouillon cubes
1-4	tablespoons gelatin
2	tablespoons Madeira

PREPARATION

1 Sprinkle salt and pepper all over the meat and place it in a deep bowl or enameled Dutch oven in which it can be cooked. Peel the carrots and slice in thick, about ½-inch, rounds and place around the meat. Peel the onions, cut them into quarters, and place them around the meat. Peel the garlic and add to the vegetables. Tuck in the bay leaves and sprinkle with thyme. Pour in the wine and broth and turn the meat so all surfaces are moistened. Cover and let stand in a cool place for at least 6 hours, or refrigerate overnight.

2 Put the Dutch oven directly on heat, or transfer the meat and marinade to a heavy nonaluminum pot or casserole. Add the bones and bouillon cubes and sprinkle the meat again with salt and pepper. Bring the marinade to a fast simmer, reduce the heat and simmer gently for 3 to 4 hours or until the meat is tender when pierced with a long fork or a small sharp knife.

3   Remove the meat to a deep dish, cool it slightly and refrigerate. Pour the stock through a sieve. Let the vegetables drip awhile to collect all the stock; discard the bay leaves. Refrigerate the stock and vegetables separately. When the stock is cool, remove the layer of congealed fat from the surface.

4   If bones were used in the cooking, less gelatin will be needed to make the aspic. Without any bones, the stock will require 4 tablespoons of gelatin. Check the consistency of the chilled stock to determine the exact quantity—for a slightly jellied stock use 2 or 3 tablespoons; in any case use a minimum of 1 tablespoon of gelatin. Soften the gelatin in a small bowl with the Madeira; for 4 tablespoons of gelatin add 2 tablespoons of water to the Madeira.

5   Ladle or slowly pour the stock from the bowl into a pot, carefully leaving behind the residue at the bottom of the pot. This is an important precaution since we eliminate clarifying the stock in this recipe. Reheat the stock slowly and when it is hot add the softened gelatin and stir until dissolved. Cool the stock until slightly syrupy.

6   Pour about ½ cup of the aspic into a chilled serving platter. Chill until it is fairly thick, but not completely set. Meanwhile remove the fat and strings from the meat and slice it evenly in thin slices. Since the meat is cold it will slice quite easily and neatly.

7   Place the thick slice from the end of the roast at one end of the platter; this will act as a support for the other slices. Dip each slice into the aspic and place on the platter, so that the slices slightly overlap each other. Make a pattern of carrot slices down the center of the meat slices. Brush on aspic 1 or 2 times, chilling after each addition of aspic.

8   Place the remaining carrots and onions in separate mounds around the meat. Liberally spoon aspic over the vegetables and chill. This can be repeated one more time. Any leftover aspic can be chopped and spooned onto the meat or the platter just before serving.

9   When ready to serve, decorate the platter with a few parsley leaves along the center and a tomato rose or tomato wedges at the top. Serve directly from the platter at the table.

COOKING AHEAD

It's all done; in fact, if the dish is finished the day before, the flavor will be even better.

LOW-CHOLESTEROL VERSION

Eliminate the larding of the meat and the addition of the outside layer of fat. Add ¼ cup polyunsaturated oil to the marinade.

REMARKS

If you have an enormous amount of refrigerator space, *Boeuf à la Mode en Gelée* can also be prepared on individual dinner plates and perhaps garnished with a tomato wedge or two. Many French bistros mold the meat, vegetables, and aspic in a loaf dish and cut slices of it at the table. In this case, the beef is sliced a little thicker and then cut into pieces 2 or 3 inches square. A very sharp knife is necessary to achieve neat slices of jellied meat and vegetables. This is a less formal presentation, but equally flavorful.

Boeuf à l'estouffade des mariniers du rhône

SERVES 8

WORKING TIME: *15 minutes*

MARINATING TIME: *at least 12 hours*

BAKING TIME: *about 5 hours*

Ignoring common wisdom about what ingredients do not go together, a French sailor-cook of long ago married two wildly different flavors: beef and anchovies. To compound the error he threw in pickles and capers. The happy result is now called Estouffade des Mariniers du Rhône (Rhone Sailors' Stew). The Rhône, a main waterway in France, plunges south through the heart of Provence before emptying into the Mediterranean near Marseilles. Sailors who plied the river were accustomed to the pungent, spicy cooking of the Mediterranean coast and were probably seeking a way to give extra snap to ordinary beef stew when their unlikely combination occurred. The estouffade in the title refers to the very long, very slow cooking. Traditionally the pot would be hermetically sealed with a thick flour paste, but a close covering of aluminum foil under the lid works just as well. Best of all for a busy hostess, the dish improves by standing for a day or two.

There is no real recipe for this stew, just a lot of strong opinions about how it should be done. Some Provençal cooks like to simmer it in red wine, others prefer white. Some marinate it, others wouldn't dream of doing so. Whether to preslice or not is another area of controversy. It's even called by several names—Boeuf à la Façon des Marins du Rhône (Rhone Sailors' Beef), Boeuf à la Façon d'Avignon (Avignon-style Beef), or Grillade des Marins du Rhône (Rhone Sailors' Grill). The only point everyone agrees on is that the sauce must contain anchovies, capers, and pickles.

The estouffade usually is served with the capers and pickles chopped very fine, while the anchovy melts away in the hot sauce. The Rhône sailors never had a blender, but I like to use one to purée the sauce ingredients, deepening the taste mystery. You can see the intrigued look on guests' faces: There is a special flavor, but what is it? After trying many versions of this unusual beef stew, this is the one I recommend.

INGREDIENTS

4	**pounds boneless rump roast, round of beef, or similar cuts**
¼	**cup olive oil**
2	**cups wine, red or dry white**
1	**2-ounce can anchovies**
¾	**cup chopped sour pickles**
3	**tablespoons capers, drained**
4	**garlic cloves, sliced**
¼	**teaspoon thyme**
1	**1-pound can tomatoes**
1	**celery rib, broken in half**
2	**bay leaves**
	pepper
	salt if necessary

PREPARATION

1 Place the meat in an enameled cast-iron casserole. Pour the olive oil and ½ cup of wine into a blender; add the anchovies, pickles, capers, garlic, thyme, and tomatoes. (Add ¼ cup more pickle and an extra garlic clove for stronger flavor.) Blend to a purée and pour this over the meat, adding more wine until the sauce almost covers the meat. Wrap the celery around the bay leaves and tie them together into a small bundle. Tuck this into the marinade. Cover and marinate the meat in a cool spot for at least 12 hours. Turn the meat occasionally.

Preheat oven to 250°.

2 Put the casserole on a medium fire and slowly bring the marinade just to the boil. Sprinkle with pepper. When the marinade is warm, taste for salt and correct if necessary. Remember the anchovies and pickles are salty. Place a sheet of aluminum foil over the casserole, then cover the pot with its lid. Place the casserole in the oven and cook slowly for about 5 hours or until the meat is tender. Turn the meat once or twice during the cooking. (The meat can be cooked faster, say for 3 hours in a 350° oven, but the slower cooking is better. Besides, at 250° the simmering stew needs almost no attention.)

Transfer the meat to a carving board and slice. Remove the celery from the sauce. Arrange the meat slices in the center of a warm platter and spoon the hot sauce liberally over the meat.

COOKING AHEAD

The stew will improve if allowed to stand for 1 or 2 days. Cool the stew then refrigerate. Remove any fat that may have congealed on the surface. Cut the meat into slices while it is cold; it will slice more neatly. Return the meat to the casserole and reheat slowly in a 325° oven.

LOW-CHOLESTEROL VERSION

Use polyunsaturated oil instead of olive oil and drain the oil from the anchovy can and discard. No other changes in the recipe are necessary.

Liver strips in red wine

Thanks to the high cost of food these days, nutritious beef liver has at last been rediscovered. Unfortunately, most preparations do little to capitalize on the stronger flavor of beef liver (as compared to calf's). This recipe and Venetian Liver (page 116) both do. In these two versions the liver is cut into strips, which calls for fast cooking and consequently tender liver. Good accompanying dishes would be Polenta (page 180), mashed potatoes, boiled noodles, or rice. An attractive presentation is to make a ring of the starch and heap the liver strips in the center.

SERVES 6

WORKING TIME: *7 minutes*

COOKING TIME: *1 to 2 minutes*

INGREDIENTS

5   **cups red wine, approximately**

2   **bay leaves**

4   **tablespoons butter**

    salt and pepper

2   **pounds beef liver**

PREPARATION

1   Pour the wine into a nonaluminum pot; add the bay leaves, butter, salt, and pepper. Bring the wine to a boil, reduce the heat, cover, and simmer while preparing the liver.

2   Cut the liver into long, thin strips, about ½ inch wide.

3   Turn up the heat under the wine and add the liver. As soon as the wine returns to a boil, remove the pot from the heat.

TO SERVE

Lift the liver strips with a skimmer onto a serving dish. Spoon some wine over the meat.

COOKING AHEAD

The wine sauce can be cooked in advance and the liver cut into strips. Closely cover and refrigerate both the wine and the liver separately. Just before serving, bring the wine back to boiling and proceed as in step 3.

Beef liver venetian style

Calf's liver can be substituted in this recipe. The results will be more delicate, but the cost will be three times as much. Budget-priced beef liver contains as much protein as calf's liver and is far richer in iron. Besides there is less reason to use the more delicate product here, since a lot of onions are mixed with the meat and both are blended together with a fairly sharp sauce. Save calf's liver for serving plain and simple, which is a pretty fast kitchen operation, too.

In Venice, where this is a traditional dish, Polenta (page 180), a cornmeal porridge, would automatically be served. If you prefer, mashed potatoes or boiled noodles can be alternate starches. As with any liver, the cooking must be done quickly, on high heat. This is especially important in this recipe since the meat is cut into strips.

SERVES 4

WORKING TIME: 8 minutes
COOKING TIME: 15 minutes

INGREDIENTS

4	tablespoons butter (½ stick)
2	tablespoons oil
2	medium onions, thinly sliced
¼	teaspoon powdered sage
1	pound beef liver
	salt and pepper
½	cup flour
	juice of 1 lemon
1	cup dry white wine
2	tablespoons chopped parsley

PREPARATION

1 While melting ½ of the oil and butter in a heavy skillet, peel and slice the onions and add them to the skillet. Sprinkle on the sage, stir, cover and simmer very slowly for 10 to 15 minutes or until the onions begin turning a golden color. Scrape the onions out of the skillet into a small bowl.

2 While the onions are simmering, dry the liver slices on paper towels, and cut them into ¼-inch strips about 3 or 4 inches long. Put the strips on a plate, sprinkle with salt, pepper, and flour and toss with both hands until all pieces of meat are coated with flour.

3 In the same skillet heat the remaining butter and oil until very hot. Lift the liver strips out of the flour, shake off excess flour, and add the meat to the hot fat. Keep the heat high while cooking and turning the meat to sear all over. Once the meat is brown (this should take just a minute or two), scrape in the cooked onions, add the lemon juice and wine, cover and simmer for 2 minutes.

4 Taste for salt and pepper and correct if necessary. Add parsley and mix.

TO SERVE

Spoon the liver and onions into the center of a warm platter. Make a border of neat mounds of mashed potatoes, or polenta, or a ring of noodles. Serve at once while still very hot.

COOKING AHEAD

The onions can be cooked anytime, even the day before, then covered and refrigerated. The cutting and flouring of the liver, however, should not be done until needed or the final results will be pasty. Actual preparation of the meat takes only 3 or 4 minutes.

Garniture italienne pour viande

The garnish gets star billing in this recipe because it is the real magic. This extremely simple and attractive sauce will turn ordinary meat into lavish fare. Italians particularly like it with tender calf's liver, which is an inspired combination. You'll find it does as much for chops or chicken breasts. (Meat recipes listed below.)

INGREDIENTS

Garnish

3   **tablespoons butter**

2   **shallots, or 2 tablespoons chopped onion**

2   **garlic cloves, minced**

¼   **pound mushrooms, chopped**

    salt and pepper

1   **ripe tomato**

½   **cup dry white wine**

2   **slices boiled ham**

PREPARATION

1   Melt the butter in a skillet while chopping the shallots or onions, garlic, and mushrooms. Add the vegetables to the butter. Sprinkle with salt and pepper. Cover and simmer.

2   Chop the tomato coarsely and add it and the white wine to the sauce. Cover and simmer for 5 minutes.

3   While the sauce is simmering, cut the ham slices into ¼-inch squares and put aside.

4   At serving time, reheat the sauce and add the diced ham; simmer for 2 minutes. Spoon the garnish liberally over sautéed meat.

Calf's liver   SERVES 6

INGREDIENTS

    flour

1½   **pound calf's liver**

5   **tablespoons butter**

    salt and pepper

PREPARATION

1   Spread flour in a dish. Dip the liver slices in the flour and coat both sides of the meat. Shake off excess flour.

2   Melt 3 tablespoons of butter in a large skillet. When hot and foamy, add the liver slices; do not overcrowd. Brown the meat well over high heat for 2 or 3 minutes, turn and brown the other side. Add butter as necessary, salt, and pepper. Remove to a warm platter.

Pork or veal chops   SERVES 6

INGREDIENTS

6   **pork or veal chops, 1 inch thick (or 6 chicken breasts)**

4   **tablespoons butter**

    salt and pepper

⅓   **cup dry white wine**

PREPARATION

1   Melt the butter in a skillet until hot and foamy; add the chops or chicken. Brown the meat well on each side; add salt and pepper.

2   Pour in the wine, reduce heat, cover and simmer for 25 minutes for chops and 15 minutes for chicken breasts. Turn the meat occasionally. Remove to a serving platter.

COOKING AHEAD

The garnish can be prepared in advance and refrigerated. Add the boiled ham when reheating the sauce. The chops are better if done just before serving. The liver must be done at serving time.

LOW-CHOLESTEROL VERSION

Substitute polyunsaturated margarine for butter and increase shallots or onion by 1 teaspoon. Do not use liver. Trim chops of fat.

Langue de boeuf dossilier

Despite its good value and good taste, tongue is not one of our popular meats. I have very rarely seen it served in a private home in the United States (except my own), or listed on a restaurant menu. French bistros know a good thing and serve tongue quite often. This braised version should be accompanied by a starch to soak up the flavorful sauce, perhaps Polenta (page 180), Chick-pea Purée (page 177), or boiled noodles.

SERVES 6

WORKING TIME: *22 minutes*

COOKING TIME: *1 ½ to 2 hours*

INGREDIENTS

1	**3-pound smoked beef tongue, uncooked**
2	**onions, sliced**
1	**carrot, sliced**
6	**garlic cloves**
⅓	**cup oil**
2	**bay leaves**
1	**cup dry white wine**
2	**tablespoons tomato paste**
1	**tablespoon meat extract (like BV), or 4 beef cubes**
½	**teaspoon allspice**
¼	**teaspoon thyme**
	pepper
6	**cups beef broth, approximately**
½	**cup flour**
3	**tablespoons gravy coloring (like Kitchen Bouquet)**
1	**tablespoon brandy**
½	**cup Madeira, or Port**
½	**cup sour pickles**

PREPARATION

Preheat oven to 325°.

1 Cut off any excess fat from the tongue and rinse the meat well. Place the tongue in a heavy casserole and cover it with cold water. Bring the water to a boil and cook the tongue for 15 minutes. Discard the water, rinse the pot and wipe it dry.

2 While the tongue is cooking, prepare the onions and the carrot and peel the garlic. Heat the oil in the casserole and add the onions and carrots. Cook the vegetables over medium heat until they turn a light golden brown. Add the garlic, bay leaves, wine, tomato paste, meat extract, allspice, thyme, and pepper. Put the tongue in the casserole and add enough beef broth to cover almost half of it. Put a lid on the casserole and place it in the oven. Cook for 1 to 1½ hours, or until the meat is tender when pierced with a long fork.

3 Remove the meat from the casserole and strain the vegetables. Discard the bay leaves. Pass the vegetables through a food mill or purée them with some of the stock in a blender. Return the puréed vegetables and the stock to the pot and bring them to a gentle boil. In a small bowl mix the flour with cold water to make a smooth paste. Add this paste to the sauce, a little at a time, until the sauce has thickened to the consistency of heavy cream.

4 Add the gravy coloring (begin with 2 tablespoons, add more if needed), brandy, and Madeira. Slice the pickles thinly (the amount depends on their size and your preference) and add to the sauce at the last minute. While the sauce is simmering remove the skin from the tongue.

TO SERVE

Slice the tongue and reshape it on a platter. Spoon a liberal amount of sauce over the tongue and pass some sauce separately.

COOKING AHEAD

The tongue can be completely cooked and the sauce completed the day before serving. For a less fatty sauce, cook the tongue through Step 2, leave in the pot, and cool at room temperature. Cover and refrigerate overnight. The congealed fat can be easily lifted from the surface. Add the pickles after the sauce and meat have been reheated. Beef Tongue Dossilier will improve in flavor for having matured a day or two.

Langue de boeuf lucullus

Too many people treat organ meats, including tongue, like the ugly ducklings of the meat counter. I hope this recipe changes a lot of minds about tongue at least. Langue de Boeuf Lucullus is a treat to present at your fanciest dinner parties. Plain old tongue is sliced and stuffed with a mousse of goose liver pâté, then reassembled and given a shimmering coat of aspic. This ugly duckling turns into a swan before your eyes.

SERVES 8 TO 10

WORKING TIME: *22 minutes*

COOKING TIME: *1 to 1½ hours*

COOLING TIME: *about 2 hours*

CHILLING TIME: *at least 2 hours*

INGREDIENTS

1   **3-pound smoked tongue, or 1½-pounds cooked tongue, sliced ¼ inch thick**

2   **garlic cloves**

1   **bay leaf**

1   **medium onion, quartered**

6   **peppercorns**

2   **tablespoons gelatin**

¼   **cup plus 2 tablespoons Madeira or Port**

3   **cups beef broth**

1   **8-ounce can imported smoked goose liver pâté**

4   **tablespoons butter (½ stick), room temperature**

     salt and pepper

PREPARATION

1   Cook the tongue the day before, assembling it and the goose liver filling. Place the tongue in a heavy casserole, cover it with cold water, and add the garlic, bay leaf, onion cut into quarters, and the peppercorns. Bring the water to a boil and simmer slowly for 1 to 1½ hours, or until the tongue is tender. Drain the tongue, cool it, remove the skin, cover tightly with plastic wrap, then refrigerate.

2   Put the gelatin in a small bowl and pour ¼ cup of Madeira over it. Meanwhile, bring the beef broth to the boiling point in a small pot. Add the softened gelatin to the hot broth and stir to dissolve the gelatin. Put aside to cool.

3   Prepare the stuffing by creaming together the liver pâté and the butter. Add 2 tablespoons of Madeira, salt and pepper, and 2 tablespoons of the cool beef broth and mix well.

4   Cut the tongue into ¼-inch-thick slices. Leave a piece about 2 inches thick at the larger end. Select a rectangular serving platter and place this 2-inch piece of tongue at one end of the platter. Put aside ½ cup of the pâté stuffing. Smear a slice of tongue with the stuffing and place it against the piece of tongue on the platter, the side with the stuffing facing up. Take another slice of tongue and again smear the stuffing over one side and place it against the previous slice—plain side down, the side with the stuffing up. Continue with all the slices, arranging them next to each other to reform the tongue in its original shape. Smear the reserved ½ cup of stuffing over the entire surface of the tongue. Chill well.

5   With a pastry brush, paint on a coating of the cool beef broth aspic. Chill the tongue and repeat 1 or 2 times. Then chill the remaining aspic.

TO SERVE

Remove the tongue from the refrigerator at least one hour before serving. Chop the leftover aspic into small pieces and scatter them along the sides of the rearranged tongue and some along the top.

COOKING AHEAD

Like all dishes containing aspic, *Langue de Boeuf Lucullus* must be prepared in advance. It can be finished the day before it is to be served.

Leg-of-lamb steak

Leg of lamb is an admirable cut of meat. Its flavor is emphatic, it is easy to cook, and it is lean. Pound for pound it is cheaper than lamb chops, which generally have a good deal of bone and fat. Usually leg of lamb is roasted. Good as that method is, there is a new dining experience to be enjoyed by boning the meat and treating it like a steak. Ask your butcher to butterfly it.

In this recipe the meat is marinated, as in the Provence region of France, with some garlic, sage, and rosemary. Then the outside is seared crisp while the interior meat is cooked to the degree of rareness desired. The only thing that can be done to spoil this exceptional dish is to overcook it; the meat should be pink. There is another advantage for timid carvers—lamb steak takes no technique at all; it slices like any steak. Grilled lamb steak would also make a wonderful barbeque treat. As with all lamb, this meat is equally delicious cold.

SERVES 6

WORKING TIME: *6 minutes*

MARINATING TIME: *1 to 2 hours*

GRILLING TIME: *15 to 20 minutes*

INGREDIENTS

1	**boned leg of lamb, weighing 4 to 4½ pounds with bone**
1	**garlic clove**
1½	**teaspoons sage**
1½	**teaspoons rosemary**
	salt and pepper
¼	**cup whiskey (straight or blended), or brandy**
2	**tablespoons oil**

PREPARATION

1 Lay the boned meat flat and cut small incisions right under the skin on both sides. Cut the garlic into thin slices and slip them into the incisions. Rub the sage, rosemary, salt, and pepper into the meat on both sides. Put the meat in a nonmetal dish and pour on the whiskey. Turn the meat so that all surfaces are moistened by the whiskey. Cover tightly and let stand for 1 or 2 hours.

2 Rub the oil on the bottom of a heavy cast-iron grill (preferably one with ridges) or a frying pan. Heat the grill until it is very hot. Lift the meat out of the dish and place it, completely flat, on the grill.

3 After 2 minutes the first side of the lamb should be seared. Turn to sear the other side for another 2 minutes. Reduce the heat to medium, sprinkle the meat with salt and pepper and pour the marinade over it. If possible, place a cover over the meat; this is not essential, but it produces moister meat. Cook the lamb for 10 to 15 minutes depending on the desired degree of rareness. Ten minutes will give you quite rare meat, 15 pink. Baste once or twice during the cooking.

TO SERVE

Transfer the meat to a carving board and cut it across in fairly thick slices, ½ to 1 inch. Serve hot.

COOKING AHEAD

The marinade can be rubbed on the lamb several hours in advance, even the day before if refrigerated. The grilling must be done at serving time, except if you plan serving the meat cold.

LOW-CHOLESTEROL VERSION

No changes in the recipe are necessary, but make sure the meat is very lean and remove all surrounding fat. Use polyunsaturated oil.

Baked lamb chops

Lamb chops lend themselves to many, many preparations, all the way from just plain grilling to fancy stuffing and braising. This easy recipe falls between the two extremes. The only thing you might want to add for the main course is a salad. You'll find that the communal baking of the chops and the vegetables results in a wonderful blending of flavors.

SERVES 6

WORKING TIME: *18 minutes*

FRYING TIME: *about 8 minutes*

BAKING TIME: *1 hour*

INGREDIENTS

5   tablespoons butter or margarine

6   shoulder lamb chops

3   medium onions, thinly sliced

1   garlic clove, chopped

1   cup beef broth

    salt and pepper

4   potatoes

PREPARATION

Preheat oven to 400°.

1   Melt 3 tablespoons of butter in a skillet until foamy and hot. Add the chops and brown well on both sides. Add more butter as necessary. Remove the browned chops to a dish.

2   While the chops are browning, peel the onions and slice; peel and chop the garlic.

3   When the browned chops have been removed, add 1 tablespoon of butter to the skillet with the onions and garlic. Stir to loosen the coagulated juices from the bottom of the pan and simmer slowly for 2 minutes. Select a baking dish that will hold the chops snugly. Scrape the softened onions and garlic into the dish and pat into a smooth layer.

4   Place the chops on top of the onions. Pour in ½ cup of broth and sprinkle with salt and pepper. Place in the hot oven, uncovered, and bake for 30 minutes.

5   While the chops are baking, peel the potatoes and slice thin, using either a knife or the slicing side of a grater. Place the potato slices over the chops, covering the meat completely. Pour in the remaining ½ cup of broth and sprinkle with salt and pepper. Return to the oven for about 30 minutes more, or until the potatoes are soft. Baste occasionally during the baking.

TO SERVE

Serve from the baking dish at the table. Use a spatula and spoon to lift the chops out with the onions beneath and the potatoes on top.

COOKING AHEAD

After the potatoes are in place, bake for only 20 minutes. Cool and refrigerate. To reheat, bring the dish to room temperature and bake in 375° oven for 20 minutes.

LOW-CHOLESTEROL VERSION

Substitute polyunsaturated margarine or oil for the butter and select lean lamb chops.

Lamb sauté touteron

This sauté offers an interesting blend of two rather distinctive Provençal flavors —lamb and green peppers. I also like to add water chestnuts. That unusual note provides a bland buffer between two strong tastes, as well as a crackling texture. Though they would never find their way into a cooking pot in Provence, I find that the water chestnuts from Chinese cuisine are another kind of international détente. The lamb tends to exude a good deal of juice, so the dish is best served with rice or broad noodles.

SERVES 6

WORKING TIME: *12 minutes*

COOKING TIME: *15 minutes*

INGREDIENTS

3	tablespoons butter
1	tablespoon oil
1½	pounds lamb shoulder or leg, cut into 1-inch cubes
	salt and pepper
1	medium onion, chopped
1	green pepper, seeded
1	garlic clove, mashed
¼	teaspoon cayenne pepper
½	teaspoon vinegar
1	8-ounce can water chestnuts
2	tablespoons chopped parsley

PREPARATION

1 Heat the butter and oil together in a large skillet. Add the lamb and fry until lightly browned. Sprinkle with salt and pepper.

2 While the lamb is frying, peel and chop the onion and add to the skillet; cover and simmer for 5 minutes.

3 Meanwhile, cut the green pepper in half and remove the seeds and filaments, then cut the pepper into ½-inch pieces. Add it to the meat, along with the garlic, cayenne, and vinegar. Cover and simmer for 5 minutes more.

4 Slice the water chestnuts about ⅛ inch thick and add to the skillet. Re-cover and cook for another 2 minutes.

TO SERVE

Spoon the lamb sauté into a warm deep serving dish and sprinkle with chopped parsley.

COOKING AHEAD

Once finished, Lamb Sauté Touteron can be kept on a very low fire for 10 to 15 minutes. Otherwise, prepare the sauté in advance and refrigerate, but do not add water chestnuts at this point. Add them when reheating. Reheat thoroughly, but do not overcook or the green peppers will be soft and mushy.

LOW-CHOLESTEROL VERSION

Substitute polyunsaturated margarine for the butter and make certain the lamb is trimmed of all fat.

Agneau des alpes

The two main ingredients in this recipe are handy to the Swiss Alps: lamb and white wine. The craggy mountain ranges provide excellent grazing land for sheep. Not too far away are valleys where white wine grapes are cultivated. Villagers often bring these two local products together in a pot, adding a few herbs, for a simple but inspired dinner. At other times veal is used, since as many cattle graze in the mountain foothills as do sheep. To make a more copious dish, strips of green pepper can be added and an extra potato.

SERVES 4 TO 5

WORKING TIME: *11 minutes*

COOKING TIME: *50 minutes*

INGREDIENTS

1½	**pounds boneless lamb shoulder or leg, cut into 1-inch pieces**
1	**medium onion**
1	**clove**
2	**garlic cloves on toothpicks**
2½	**cups dry white wine**
½	**cup water**
1	**small bay leaf**
1	**teaspoon coriander**
	salt and pepper
3	**medium potatoes**
3	**tablespoons flour**
¼	**teaspoon saffron**
¼	**teaspoon turmeric**
1	**teaspoon lemon juice**

PREPARATION

1 Put the lamb in a nonaluminum pot and cover it with cold water. Bring the water to a boil, simmer for 2 minutes, and drain. Rinse the meat under cold running water. Rinse out the pot and return the meat to it.

2 While the meat is blanching, peel the onion and stud it with the clove. Peel the garlic cloves and spear them on toothpicks.

3 Add 2 cups of wine and the water to the pot. Then add the onion, garlic, bay leaf, coriander, salt, and pepper. Put the pot on medium heat and bring the wine to a boil; reduce the heat, cover the pot, and slowly simmer the lamb for 30 minutes.

4 While the lamb is cooking, peel the potatoes and cut them into ½-inch cubes. Put the flour, saffron, and turmeric in a small bowl and stir. Slowly stir ½ cup of wine into the flour and mix it to a smooth paste.

5 Remove the onion, garlic, and bay leaves from the stock. Pour the flour paste into the pot while whisking vigorously to keep the sauce smooth. Add the potatoes and lemon juice. Cover the pot and simmer for 20 minutes or until the potatoes are soft.

TO SERVE

If an enameled cooking pot was used, serve directly from it, or transfer the Alpine Lamb to a deep serving bowl. Spoon lamb and potatoes and a liberal amount of the pale yellow sauce onto each dinner plate. The potatoes can be mashed with a fork to absorb the sauce.

COOKING AHEAD

Alpine Lamb can be completely cooked, cooled, and refrigerated. Reheat at serving time.

LOW-CHOLESTEROL VERSION

Buy leg of lamb, which is leaner than shoulder. No changes in the recipe are necessary.

Baked lamb curry

This is one of the prettiest presentations of curried lamb that I know of. It also is a clever way of using leftover roast lamb, although the directions given here are for freshly ground meat. For a particularly unusual touch, try baking it in a pastry shell. I've never been able to decide if I prefer Baked Lamb Curry hot or cold. Both are delicious. Once the baked lamb is cold it cuts into nice neat wedges and makes perfect picnic fare. If you plan serving the lamb cold, use a bit more curry since its strength is weakened when chilled.

SERVES 8

WORKING TIME: *22 minutes*

BAKING TIME: *30 minutes*

INGREDIENTS

2	tablespoons oil
2	pounds ground lamb shoulder
2	apples, sliced
2	medium onions, sliced
4	tablespoons butter
1½	tablespoons curry (to taste)
¼	cup chopped almonds
¼	cup seedless raisins
	juice ½ lemon
	salt and pepper
1	thick slice white bread
1	cup milk
2	eggs
	chutney

PREPARATION

Preheat oven to 350°.

1 Heat the oil in a large skillet and fry the lamb in it for about 10 minutes, mixing often. If the meat gives off a lot of liquid, drain most of it off before putting the meat into a mixing bowl.

2 While the meat is cooking, quarter and slice the unpeeled apples and peel and slice the onions. After removing the meat, put the butter in the skillet and fry the apples, onions, curry, almonds, raisins, lemon juice, salt, and pepper. Mix these seasonings well, cover, and cook for about 5 minutes. Add the meat, cover, and cook another 5 minutes.

3 While the meat is cooking, soak the bread in the milk, then squeeze the bread dry but reserve the milk. Break 1 egg into the softened bread and beat with a fork until light and frothy. Remove the meat from the fire and beat in the bread-egg combination.

4 Butter a 10-cup baking dish and spoon in the meat mixture. Beat the other egg with the reserved milk, add salt and pepper, and spoon this over the surface of the meat. Bake for 30 minutes or until the custard on top is set.

TO SERVE

At the table cut the Baked Lamb Curry into pie-shaped wedges and serve with chutney.

COOKING AHEAD

Baked Lamb Curry can be baked for 20 minutes, or until the custard topping is just set. Cool and refrigerate. At serving time reheat in a 375° oven for 10 minutes.

LOW-CHOLESTEROL VERSION

Use lean lamb. Substitute polyunsaturated margarine for the butter, ½ cup liquid egg substitute for the whole eggs, and skimmed milk for the whole milk. Increase the lemon juice to juice of 1 lemon and add an extra 2 tablespoons of raisins.

Ragoût de mouton

Mouton *in French means mutton,
which is not all that easy to find now
that everyone is so lamb conscious. If
you can buy mutton, so much the better
for this recipe; if not, don't worry: the
delicate lamb that goes into the oven
loses its innocence during the baking
and emerges with a very forceful
character. This is another recipe I first
tried with the pieces of meat browned
in oil. The next time I eliminated that
step (but added the marinating) and the
meat was just as good and less fatty.
Potatoes can be added to the stew to
make it a complete main course, though
I prefer serving plain* ragoût *with Baked
Gnocchi (page 179) or Polenta (page
180).*

SERVES 8

WORKING TIME: *13 minutes*

MARINATING TIME: *1 or 2 hours*

BAKING TIME: *approximately 2½ hours*

INGREDIENTS

2   medium onions, sliced

4   carrots, sliced

3   garlic cloves, minced

¼   pound cured ham or Canadian bacon

Optional: 3 potatoes

3   pounds lean shoulder or leg of lamb
    without bones, cut into 2-inch pieces

salt and pepper

3   bay leaves

1   1-pound can tomatoes, drained, or 2 or
    3 fresh tomatoes

4   cups red wine

PREPARATION

1   Peel and cut the onion into thick slices;
peel and cut the carrots into ¼-inch pieces;
peel and mince the garlic. Dice the ham into
¼-inch pieces. Peel the optional potatoes
and cut them into 1½-inch chunks.

2   Select a 5- or 6-quart casserole (preferably an enameled cast-iron Dutch oven from
which the stew can be served). Put half the
lamb pieces in a layer in the casserole and
sprinkle with salt and pepper; scatter half
the diced ham over the lamb. Layer in half
the onions, carrots, optional potatoes, and
garlic and tuck in 1 bay leaf. Repeat with the
remaining lamb and other ingredients.

3   Plunge the tomatoes into a small pot of
boiling water, lift them out with a skimmer
and slip off the skins. Crush the tomatoes
with your hands and spread them over the
top of the stew. Pour in the wine which
should cover at least two-thirds of the stew.
Cover the casserole closely and let it stand
for 1 or 2 hours.

Preheat oven to 375°.

4   Place the casserole in the preheated oven
for 15 minutes; reduce the heat to 350° and
bake the stew for 2 hours. Test a piece of
meat for tenderness, if it is not soft return
the casserole for another 15 minutes of baking.

TO SERVE

Take the casserole to the table and serve directly from it.

COOKING AHEAD

Ragoût de Mouton will be even better if
made the day before serving and reheated in
a 350° oven for 15 or 20 minutes.

LOW-CHOLESTEROL VERSION

Buy lean leg of lamb instead of shoulder; no
other changes in the recipe are necessary.

Szekely gulyas

There are several explanations for the name of this particular Hungarian goulash. It is most probably named after a Transylvanian branch of the Magyar race. It is also known in Austria. This version makes it a complete main course.

SERVES 6

WORKING TIME: 11 minutes

COOKING TIME: 55 minutes

INGREDIENTS

3   tablespoons oil

1   large onion, sliced

2   pounds lean pork, cut into 1-inch cubes

2   teaspoons sweet rose paprika

¼   teaspoon caraway seeds

1   1½-pound can sauerkraut

½   pound mushrooms

½   cup dry white wine

1   cup canned or frozen peas

2   tablespoons flour

1   cup sour cream

PREPARATION

1   Heat the oil in a heavy casserole while peeling and slicing the onion. Add the onion, stir, cover, and simmer gently for 5 minutes.

2   Add the pork, paprika, and caraway seeds to the onions. Stir well to mix all the ingredients. Cover and simmer for 30 minutes. (If the meat seems dry, add ¼ cup of the wine.)

3   While the pork is simmering, drain and rinse the sauerkraut and squeeze out excess water. Rinse the mushrooms and cut them in halves or quarters, depending on size.

4   Add the sauerkraut and the wine to the meat and simmer 15 minutes. Add the mushrooms and peas and simmer 5 more minutes.

5   Meanwhile, stir the flour into the sour cream. Remove from heat and slowly stir in sour cream. Return to heat, uncovered, and simmer 5 minutes without boiling. Serve directly from the casserole.

COOKING AHEAD

As much as two days in advance, the entire recipe can be completed except for step 5.

LOW-CHOLESTEROL VERSION

Increase paprika to 1 tablespoon, caraway seeds to ½ teaspoon, and wine to ¾ cup. Also increase the flour to 3 tablespoons and substitute low-fat yogurt for sour cream. Three tablespoons of polyunsaturated margarine can be stirred in to add richness.

Piquant pork chops

Here is a sauce to really wake up pork chops. It is not thick, heavy, or overwhelmed with tomatoes. Instead you have a snappy blending of sharp flavors that recalls Provence or southern Italy. This is also an attractive-looking dish. The browned, thick chops arrive gilded with the red-tinged sauce, ready to delight the eye and the palate.

SERVES 4

WORKING TIME: 8 minutes

COOKING TIME: 30 minutes

INGREDIENTS

3   tablespoons butter

4   extra thick (1 to1½-inch) pork chops
    pepper

1   tablespoon chopped parsley

2   teaspoons minced capers

2   teaspoons anchovy paste, or 1 fillet

½   cup dry white wine

½   cup canned tomatoes, crushed

1   tablespoon tomato paste

½   teaspoon basil

PREPARATION

1   Melt 1 tablespoon of butter in a skillet that will snugly hold the four chops. When the butter is hot, quickly brown the chops on both sides and sprinkle with pepper. Remove the chops from the skillet, pour out the fat, rinse the skillet, and wipe it clean.

2   While the chops are browning, mince the parsley and capers.

3   Add the remaining 2 tablespoons of butter to the skillet and melt. Add the anchovy paste and stir for a minute or so, until the anchovy paste has melted. Add the wine, tomatoes, tomato paste, parsley, capers, and basil. Stir.

4 Return the chops to the skillet, cover, and reduce the heat. Simmer the meat and sauce for 30 minutes, turning the chops 2 or 3 times.

TO SERVE

Place the chops on a serving dish and spoon the sauce liberally over each chop.

COOKING AHEAD

Piquant Pork Chops can be prepared ahead, but they should be cooked for only 15 minutes. The final 15 minutes of cooking should be done just before serving.

LOW-CHOLESTEROL VERSION

Buy very lean pork chops and trim off all fat. Use polyunsaturated margarine.

Pork chops with mustard sauce

Putting mustard on meat is nothing new. But putting it in the sauce instead is sheer kitchen wizardry. It gives pungency to a rich cream sauce, then tarragon is added to soften the overall effect. This is a real man-pleaser.

SERVES 4

WORKING TIME: *10 minutes*

COOKING TIME: *20 minutes*

INGREDIENTS

4 tablespoons butter

4 loin pork chops, ¾ to 1 inch thick

salt and pepper

1 egg yolk

1 tablespoon mustard

¼ cup heavy cream

½ cup white wine

2 tablespoons water

1 garlic clove, mashed

1 teaspoon tarragon

½ teaspoon brandy

Optional: 2 teaspoons chopped fresh tarragon, for garnish

PREPARATION

1 In a heavy skillet, melt 2 tablespoons of butter until foamy and hot, then add the pork chops and brown well on both sides. Sprinkle the chops with salt and pepper. Cover, reduce the heat, and simmer for 15 minutes. (If the butter in the pan has burned, remove chops, pour out the fat, and wipe the skillet; melt 2 tablespoons of fresh butter, return the chops and proceed as above.)

2 While the chops are cooking prepare the sauce flavorings. In a small bowl, beat together the egg yolk and mustard. Stir in the cream and put aside.

3 Remove the chops to a warm serving platter and keep warm. Turn up the heat under the skillet, pour in the wine and water, scraping all the juices from the bottom. Add the garlic, tarragon, and a little salt and pepper; boil for 1 minute.

4 Remove skillet from the heat, add the mustard-cream, and stir for a few seconds. Return to heat, stirring until the sauce thickens. Do not allow it to boil. Add the brandy. Taste for salt and pepper; correct if necessary.

TO SERVE

Spoon the sauce liberally over the cooked pork chops. If fresh tarragon is in season, chop a little and sprinkle over the sauce. Serve at once.

COOKING AHEAD

The chops are best if prepared just before serving, to prevent their drying out. If the dish must be prepared ahead, return the cooked chops to the completed sauce, turn once to cover both sides with the sauce, cover and cool. Refrigerate if there will be more than an hour's delay before serving. Reheat the chops in the sauce on a very low fire until warmed through. A few tablespoons of milk may be added if the sauce seems thick.

LOW-CHOLESTEROL VERSION

Buy lean pork chops and trim off all fat around the meat. Use polyunsaturated margarine to brown the chops. Prepare the sauce flavoring with ¼ cup liquid egg substitute and evaporated skimmed milk. Once the sauce thickens, stir in another ¼ cup white wine.

Jambon à la crème

When it comes to ham, America has a bountiful choice of strong, mild, and in-between flavors. For this particular recipe, based on a French country version, a mild ham is best. The sauce has a piquant but delicate flavor and should not be overpowered by the meat.

SERVES 6

WORKING TIME: 5 minutes

COOKING TIME: 15 to 20 minutes

INGREDIENTS

1	cup heavy cream
¼	cup beef broth
1	tablespoon Madeira
3	tablespoons tomato paste
½	teaspoon meat extract (like BV)
½	teaspoon Worcestershire sauce
	good pinch of cayenne pepper
	black pepper
6	slices mild, ready-cooked ham, ¼ inch thick

PREPARATION

Preheat oven to 375°.

1 In a saucepan combine all the ingredients except the ham. (No salt is included at this point since the meat and the broth already include salt.) Stir to mix well, put the saucepan on medium heat and simmer, uncovered, for 15 to 20 minutes, or until the sauce thickens enough to coat a spoon. Taste for seasoning and correct if necessary.

2 Stack the ham slices and wrap in aluminum foil, making a complete seal. Put the wrapped ham on a baking dish and place in the oven for 10 minutes to heat the slices through.

TO SERVE

Lift ham slices out of the foil package and place on a serving platter or individual plates. Spoon some sauce over each slice. Pass the remaining sauce separately.

COOKING AHEAD

The sauce can be prepared, cooled, and refrigerated in a tightly covered container. Reheat the sauce slowly at serving time. Pour 2 tablespoons of milk into the saucepan before adding the sauce. Heat the ham slices in the oven while the sauce is reheating.

LOW-CHOLESTEROL VERSION

Substitute evaporated skimmed milk or polyunsaturated dairy substitute for the cream; add 1 teaspoon cognac to the sauce. Buy very lean ham and trim off all fat.

Ham steak with sherry sauce

Ham steak is a very handy item to have in the refrigerator. It will keep far longer than fresh meats, in fact as much as a week in the hermetically sealed packages many stores now use. Once you know how to dress it up with this fast sherry sauce, last-minute guests need no longer be feared.

SERVES 6

WORKING TIME: 6 minutes

COOKING TIME: 5 minutes

INGREDIENTS

1	3-pound slice ham steak (or 2 1½-pound slices)
3	tablespoons butter
1½	cups sherry
2½	teaspoons prepared mustard

PREPARATION

1 Trim the ham steak of all fat while heating the butter in a large skillet (or 2 skillets if the ham is in 2 slices). Pat the ham dry with paper towels. When the butter is really hot, add the ham and fry on high heat until brown. Turn and brown the other side. Remove the ham to a warm platter.

2 Pour out the fat from the pan, add the sherry, and return the pan to the heat. (Make the sauce in only 1 pan even if 2 were used for the frying.) Stir with a wooden spoon to scrape up the coagulated juices from the bottom. Add the mustard, stir a few seconds then let the sauce simmer for about 2 minutes to reduce it slightly.

3 While the sauce is simmering, cut the ham steaks into individual portions.

TO SERVE

Spoon the sauce over the ham and serve at once.

COOKING AHEAD

This is a dish to be prepared at the last minute. But since only 6 of those minutes are needed, it easily can be cooked while guests finish cocktails.

LOW-CHOLESTEROL VERSION

Buy very lean ham and remove every trace of fat around it. Substitute polyunsaturated margarine for the butter.

Canadian bacon roast

Most cooks ignore Canadian bacon, except to slice it and fry it to serve with eggs. Its potentials are greater than that. This recipe is one example —treating it like a roast. Canadian bacon also is economical since it is solid meat —usually very lean and always boneless. Don't worry about baking more than you need, it is delicious served cold, especially with the mustard sauce on page 227.

Using Coca-Cola for basting meat may seem like an American idiosyncrasy, but it's a trick I learned from Louisette Bertholle (co-author of Mastering the Art of French Cooking). *She developed this technique for basting her Easter ham to the delight of many friends who visited her home in the Sologne region of France.*

SERVES 4

WORKING TIME: *5 minutes*

BAKING TIME: *40 minutes*

INGREDIENTS

1 **tablespoon prepared mustard**

¼ **cup brown sugar**

   salt and pepper

1½ **pounds Canadian bacon**

½ **cup Coca-Cola**

2 **tablespoons water**

PREPARATION

Preheat oven to 350°.

1 In a small bowl mix the mustard, sugar, salt, and pepper to a paste.

2 Remove the heavy cellophane wrapper around the Canadian bacon and place the meat in a baking dish. Smear the mustard paste over the top of the bacon. Pour the Coca-Cola directly into the dish, not over the meat. Place in the oven.

3 Bake for 20 minutes, then baste; baste once more during the final 20 minutes of baking. Remove the meat to a carving board and pour the liquid into a small pot. Add the water to the sauce in the pot and bring to a boil.

TO SERVE

Slice the Canadian bacon thin and place in the center of a platter. Add just a small spoonful of sauce to each slice and pass the rest of the sauce separately.

COOKING AHEAD

Canadian Bacon Roast can be prepared in its dish several hours in advance and refrigerated. To retain its moistness, however, the baking should be done just before serving. Since it takes almost no attention once in the oven, this is an easy dish to handle for a dinner party.

LOW-CHOLESTEROL VERSION

Buy the leanest possible Canadian bacon. No changes in the recipe are necessary.

Gratin de campagne

This is a very simple, tasty one-dish meal that is open to any kind of variations you may like to make. Diced green peppers, chopped pimentos, or peas can be added. I would suggest, though, trying it first as described below. You may not want to change it at all.

SERVES 6

WORKING TIME: 13 minutes

BAKING TIME: ¾ to 1 hour

INGREDIENTS

4   tablespoons butter
2   onions, sliced
3   Idaho or russet potatoes, sliced
1   pound Canadian bacon
1   cup tomato sauce
    thyme
    salt and pepper
3   tablespoons grated Parmesan cheese

PREPARATION

Preheat oven to 375°.

1   Melt 2 tablespoons of butter in a skillet while peeling and slicing the onions. Add the onions, stir, cover, and simmer slowly.

2   Meanwhile, peel the potatoes and cut in ½-inch slices. Peel the covering off the Canadian bacon and cut in ¼-inch slices.

3   Pour ¼ cup of tomato sauce in the bottom of a large gratin or baking dish. Arrange a layer of Canadian bacon to completely cover the bottom; cut pieces to fit if necessary. Arrange a layer of potato slices over the meat; again cutting pieces to achieve a solid layer. Sprinkle with thyme, pepper, and a little salt (the meat and tomato sauce have salt in them).

4   Dice any leftover pieces of bacon and potatoes and scatter over the potatoes. Pour on the remaining ¾ cup of tomato sauce. Spread the softened onions over the top. Return the skillet to the fire and melt the remaining 2 tablespoons of butter while sprinkling salt and pepper over the gratin. Pour the butter over the surface. Cover the dish.

5   Bake for ¾ to 1 hour, or until the potatoes are tender when pierced with a small sharp knife. Increase the oven heat to 450°. Uncover the dish and sprinkle with the grated cheese. Return the dish to the oven and bake for 15 minutes more.

TO SERVE

Serve directly from the baking dish, using a serving spoon and fork to cut portions of *Gratin Campagne* at the table.

COOKING AHEAD

Complete the preparation and baking until the potatoes are tender. Cool and refrigerate. Remove from the refrigerator 1 hour before baking again. Heat the oven to 450°. Sprinkle cheese on the gratin and bake for 15 to 20 minutes.

LOW-CHOLESTEROL VERSION

Substitute polyunsaturated margarine for butter; use very lean Canadian bacon and low-fat grated cheese. Slice 3 onions instead of 2.

Paté panaché en aspic

It seems hard to believe that a dish as extravagant looking as Pâté Panaché en Aspic is not a strain on the budget. But it enables 1¾ pounds of meat to serve six people nicely. The stretching magic is done with a strong aspic and vegetables. Nothing is wasted, not even the onion used in cooking the meat. Only fat and bone are discarded. Lean pork —but not beef —can be substituted for veal. The color and flavor of beef would be wrong in this recipe. Other vegetables can be used, but the proportion of vegetables to meat should not be exaggerated. Now with insulated picnic hampers in everyone's car trunk, this pâté would be appreciated at your next picnic with people who care about food.

SERVES 6

WORKING TIME: *16 minutes*

COOKING TIME: *1 hour, 5 minutes*

COOLING TIME: *approximately 1 hour*

CHILLING TIME: *3 hours*

INGREDIENTS

2   **carrots, sliced**

1¼   **pounds veal or pork chops (1 thick chop)**

2   **cups chicken broth**

1   **medium onion, quartered**

1   **teaspoon basil**

1   **bay leaf**

    salt and pepper

2   **tablespoons gelatin**

½   **cup dry white wine**

1   **slice of ham, ½-pound**

¾   **cup canned small peas, drained**

    For garnish: lettuce leaves and quartered tomatoes

PREPARATION

1   Peel and slice the carrots in ¼-inch rounds. Put the veal or pork in a small pot; pour in the chicken broth and add the carrots, onion, basil, bay leaf, pepper, and a pinch of salt. Cover the pot, put on the fire, and bring the broth to a boil. Then reduce the heat and simmer gently for 1 hour. Remove from heat and cool the meat in the broth.

2   Strain the broth then return it to the rinsed pot and put on the fire. Bring the broth to the boiling point. While the broth is heating, soften the gelatin in the wine, and add it to the hot broth; stir to dissolve the gelatin completely. Remove the broth from the fire and cool.

3   Meanwhile remove the bay leaf from the meat and vegetables. Select a 6-cup loaf pan and make a pattern of carrot rounds in the bottom. Remove the fat and bone from the chop and shred the meat coarsely with your fingers, placing it directly into a mixing bowl. Add the remaining carrots and onion, squashing the onion somewhat between your fingers as you do. Cut the ham into cubes, approximately ¼ to ½ inch, and add to the bowl. Add the drained peas. Mix the meat and vegetables together gently with your hands and carefully place in the loaf pan so as not to disturb the carrot slices, which will be the decoration for the finished pâté. Smooth the top of the filling.

4   Pour in the cool aspic and refrigerate for at least 3 hours; overnight is better for a stronger flavor. (If the aspic is not ready, refrigerate the loaf pan with the filling.)

TO SERVE

Run a hot knife around the pâté, dip the bottom of the pan in hot water; place a chilled serving dish over the pâté and reverse the two. The pâté should ease out onto the platter. Decorate with lettuce leaves and quartered tomatoes. Slice the pâté at the table, using a sharp knife with a sawing motion.

COOKING AHEAD

Any recipe calling for gelatin as this one does, must be prepared at least several hours in advance. *Pâté Panaché en Aspic* will keep for several days.

LOW-CHOLESTEROL VERSION

Use veal or very lean pork. No other changes necessary.

Pâté de poulet et jambon

I suppose the mystique about the making of pâtés comes from their extraordinary flavor. The thinking goes: anything that good just has to be difficult to do. As I've mentioned in other places in this book, if you can make a plain old American meat loaf you can make a heady French pâté, especially since this recipe eliminates some time-consuming steps.

For example, classic French recipes call for a bard (fresh pork fatback) to envelop the loaf while it is baking. Where fatback is difficult to come by, recipes have been adapted for the use of bacon. I find that neither is necessary. Right in the kitchen cupboard is a substitute that is far easier to use and adds no intruding flavor to the meat —vegetable oil. Yes, the same oil used for salad dressings can also moisten a pâté with all the exterior fat necessary. And believe me, it's far faster to smear oil into the mold and over the pâté than it is to carefully layer in pork or bacon. So much for mystiques, now let's make a delicious pâté . But note, you will need a meat grinder.

SERVES 8 AS MAIN COURSE;
12 AS FIRST COURSE

WORKING TIME: 25 minutes
MARINATING TIME: 3 hours to overnight
BAKING TIME: 1 ½ to 1 ¾ hours
MATURING TIME: 2 days

INGREDIENTS

1	whole skinless, boneless chicken breast
¼	pound thinly sliced, cured ham (prosciutto, Westphalian, or country style)
½	pound ready-cooked, lightly smoked ham (or Canadian bacon)
1	teaspoon allspice
½	teaspoon thyme
¼	teaspoon cayenne pepper
	salt and pepper
1	medium onion, sliced
2	garlic cloves
¼	cup plus 1 tablespoon Madeira, or Port
¼	cup dry white wine
¼	cup brandy
2	bay leaves
1	slice white bread
1	pound fatty pork, ground twice
1	egg
2	tablespoons oil

1 Cut away the tendons and cartilage from the chicken breasts. Slice ¾ of the chicken meat into long strips, ¼ to ½ inch wide, and cut the rest into chunks. Place the chicken in a small deep dish. Cut the cured ham into pieces. Cut ½ the ready-cooked ham into strips about the same size as the chicken strips and cut the remaining ham into chunks. Put the cured and ready-cooked ham together in another deep dish.

2 Divide between the two dishes ½ teaspoon of allspice, the thyme, cayenne, and pepper. Sprinkle salt on the chicken only. Slice the onion and scatter it over the two dishes. Peel the garlic and tuck a clove into each dish. Pour ¼ cup Madeira over the chicken and the white wine over the hams; divide the brandy between the two dishes. Turn the meats with your hands so all surfaces are covered by the liquors. Tuck a bay leaf in each dish, cover the dishes, and let them stand for at least 3 hours; overnight in the refrigerator is better. Mix occasionally.

Preheat oven to 350°.

3 Remove the bay leaves and reserve them. Lift the chunks of ham, chicken, onion, and garlic out of the marinade and put them through a grinder. Only the meat strips are not ground. After grinding the meat and vegetables, grind the slice of bread. Put all the ground ingredients in a large mixing bowl and add the ground pork.

4 While grinding the meat, pour the marinade into a small skillet and reduce it by half over fast heat. Then pour it over the ground meats. Add to the mixture ½ teaspoon allspice, ½ teaspoon pepper, and 1 teaspoon salt. Mix the meats and flavoring very well; it is best to knead it with your hands. Beat the egg in a small cup, pour it over the meat and mix again.

5 Fry a teaspoon of the pâté mixture in the small skillet used for the marinade reduction. Cool, then taste for seasonings. Correct if necessary.

6 Select a 6-cup pâté or loaf dish and oil it heavily with 1 tablespoon of oil. Layer in ⅓ of the ground stuffing and pat it smooth. Place alternating rows of chicken and ham strips over the stuffing so that they run the long way in the dish. Cover the strips with another ⅓ of the stuffing. Repeat again with the strips, and finally pat in the last ⅓ of stuffing. Smooth the top. Lightly press the reserved bay leaves on the center of the pâté top and spoon 1 tablespoon of Madeira over the pâté. Smear the remaining tablespoon of oil over the surface of the meat.

7 Cover the dish tightly with aluminum foil, then place a cover on the foil. Put the baking dish in a pan holding enough water to reach ⅓ the height of the dish. Bake for 1½ to 1¾ hours, depending on the depth of the dish used. Test for doneness by inserting a skewer into the center of the meat, then quickly touch it to the inside of your wrist. If the skewer feels hot, the pâté is finished; if it feels only warm continue the baking. Remove from the oven and cool.

8 Place weights on top of the pâté and refrigerate for at least 2 days; 3 is better. The weights are not essential, but they help produce a closer-textured, finer looking pâté which is easier to cut. The weights can be removed after 24 hours.

TO SERVE

Cut directly from the mold and serve with crusty bread and pickles.

COOKING AHEAD

For best flavor, the pâté should be prepared at least 2 days in advance of serving. The pâté will be good for at least a week.

Cassoulet

There are as many recipes for cassoulet as there are for martinis, and people are as fiercely loyal to their own recipes as are martini drinkers. In France where the dish originated, different regions have strict rules about what goes into this bean and meat casserole. There is agreement about one cardinal ingredient—goose, either fresh or preserved (confit d'oie). An earthenware casserole for the baking is another "must." I don't insist on either because of practical considerations: Except for the holiday season, goose is rarely on the market; and an enameled cast-iron Dutch oven will do as well for baking and serving as an earthenware casserole. Duck is a good substitute for goose, as is turkey. To my way of thinking, lamb, pork, and sausage are the vital ingredients, but the meat content can be varied to one's taste.

First decide when you want to make the cassoulet and plan in advance. During the week before, roast a little more lamb, pork, and poultry than you need and save the leftovers for this great party dish. If you want to splurge, a small can of imported confit d'oie can replace the poultry and add authenticity. A big salad and some fruit complete a perfect menu when cassoulet is starred. By making cassoulet according to this plan, after the cooking and serving, only two pans and one bowl have to be washed.

This is definitely a cold-weather dish — in fact, the colder the better. High in protein, cassoulet has a filling and warming effect. When buying red wine to serve with it, please remember that guests seem to drink a little more with a cassoulet dinner.

SERVES 8

WORKING TIME: 25 minutes

COOKING TIME: approximately 2½ hours

INGREDIENTS

1	**pound dried Great Northern or pea beans**
3	**medium onions, 2 sliced**
2	**cloves**
4	**garlic cloves, minced**
1	**rib celery, with leaves**
2	**teaspoons salt**
2	**bay leaves**
½	**teaspoon basil**
½	**teaspoon thyme**
6	**parsley sprigs**
	Optional: meat bones
½	**pound cooked pork**
½	**pound cooked lamb**
½	**pound cooked fowl (goose, duck, or turkey)**
1	**pound pork sausage**
1	**cup tomato sauce**
1	**tablespoon tomato paste**
½	**cup leftover meat gravy, roast drippings, or 1 teaspoon meat extract (like BV)**
	salt and pepper
1	**cup bread crumbs**
2	**tablespoons oil**

1   Select a heavy, enameled cast-iron casserole in which the *cassoulet* can be baked
and served. Rinse the beans, put them in the
casserole, cover with 2 inches of cold water
and soak overnight. (Or if pressed for time,
bring the water to a boil, remove from the
fire, and soak for 1 hour.) Drain the beans,
return them to the casserole, and cover with
cold water. Bring the water to a boil, reduce
the heat to medium and, with a skimmer,
remove any foam that rises.

2   Meanwhile, peel 1 onion and stud it with
the cloves. Peel and mince 1 garlic clove and
scrub the celery. When the foam subsides in
the casserole, add the salt, onion, garlic, celery, bay leaves, basil, thyme, and parsley. If
you have any leftover meat bones add them
to the casserole. Cover and simmer the beans
for about 35 minutes, or until they are soft
but still firm. Remember they will be cooked
again. Drain the beans and reserve the liquid.

3   While the beans are cooking, prepare the
meats by cutting the pork, lamb, and fowl
into bite-size pieces. Do not remove all the
fat from the meat, since it helps moisten the
beans during the baking. Cut the pork sausage into 1-inch pieces (or roll loose sausage
meat into 1-inch balls) and brown in a
lightly oiled skillet. Do not cook all the fat
out of the sausage. Leave 2 tablespoons of
the fat rendered by the pork sausage in the
skillet.

Preheat oven to 325°.

4   Peel and slice 2 onions and simmer them
in the pork sausage fat, covered, for about 5
minutes. Add the tomato sauce, tomato
paste, 1 cup of liquid from the beans, 3
crushed garlic cloves, the gravy, drippings,
or meat extract, salt, and pepper. Cover and
simmer this sauce for 5 minutes. The sauce
should be well seasoned since it will flavor
the beans and meat.

5   While the sauce is simmering, remove
the celery, parsley, and bay leaves from the
beans. Remove ⅔ of the beans to a bowl.
Layer in ⅓ of the mixed meats over the layer
of beans remaining. Repeat 2 more times,
finishing with meat on top. Pour the tomato
sauce over the meat and beans and add
enough of the reserved bean liquid to reach
¾ of the level of the *cassoulet*.

6   Sprinkle the crumbs over the *cassoulet*
and dribble the oil over the crumbs. Bake,
uncovered, for about 2 hours. If the sauce
seems a little dry during the baking, add
more bean liquid or diluted tomato paste.

TO SERVE

Serve directly from the baking casserole,
spooning beans and meat onto dinner plates.
Pass crusty bread.

COOKING AHEAD

Cassoulet will improve for having stood a
day. Complete the baking, cool, and refrigerate. Reheat the casserole, covered, in a 350°
oven for about 20 minutes or until heated
through. It would be advisable to make some
extra tomato sauce and reserve 1 cup of it to
pour over the *cassoulet* while it is being reheated.

LOW-CHOLESTEROL VERSION

It is difficult to make an authentic-tasting
cassoulet without all the meat fats indicated
above. A very good cousin to it can be
created by removing all the fats, eliminating
the pork sausage, and using polyunsaturated
oil for simmering the onions. Add ½ cup
polyunsaturated oil to the tomato sauce
while it is cooking.

VEGETABLES

The more than fifty recipes in this chapter testify that I think vegetables should figure more prominently in American menus. Busy cooks have long relied upon canned and frozen vegetables to save precious time, even though they often lack the quality and flavor to "make" a meal. But look at how little working time is needed to produce imaginative dishes from fresh vegetables: Baked Mushrooms, 4 minutes; Stir-fried Bean Sprouts, 3 minutes; Cauliflower Gratin, 7 minutes; Waterford Cucumbers, 5 minutes; Candied Tomatoes, 2 minutes; Braised Lettuce, 6 minutes; New Potatoes Sautéed in Butter, 3 minutes; Baked Onions, 6 minutes. Some vegetable preparations take a bit longer, but all the recipes have been streamlined to produce maximum flavor in little time.

In the Menu chapter in the front of this book, I often suggest that vegetables be served as a separate course, though not necessarily on a different plate. Vegetables have to be quite special to stand up to that kind of spotlight. I believe these are.

Apple compote

Apples do very nicely as an accompaniment to roasts and fowl —if sugar is used sparingly. The uncovered cooking method in this recipe will bring to the table apples still possessing a solid shape.

SERVES 4 TO 6

WORKING TIME: 8 minutes

COOKING TIME: about 10 minutes

INGREDIENTS

4	medium apples (York or Stayman are best, McIntosh next)
1	cup apple juice or cider
½	teaspoon orange liqueur
½	teaspoon brandy
¼	teaspoon cinnamon
1	tablespoon sugar
1	1-inch piece of orange rind
1	tablespoon butter

PREPARATION

1   Peel the apples, cut them in quarters, and cut out the cores. Place the apples in a skillet that will hold them in a single layer.

2   Measure the apple juice into a small bowl, add the liqueurs, and pour the mixture over the apples. Sprinkle on the cinnamon and sugar, then tuck in the piece of orange rind. Dot the apples with butter.

3   Put the skillet on heat and cook at a fast simmer for about 5 to 10 minutes, or until the apples are just tender when pierced with a small sharp knife. Baste once or twice during the cooking. Serve hot.

COOKING AHEAD

The apples can be cooked until just barely tender, removed from fire at once and allowed to cool. Cover and refrigerate if they are to be held more than 3 hours. At serving time, remove cover, return to heat and complete cooking.

LOW-CHOLESTEROL VERSION

Substitute polyunsaturated margarine for the butter.

Stir-fried bean sprouts

Almost everyone likes Chinese food, but almost no one likes to do all the chopping and slicing usually required. Here is one recipe that lets you have it both ways. Bean sprouts need no slicing or chopping at all. Although they are usually used to fill out Chinese meat and chicken dishes, they can be a crisp, clean-tasting vegetable treat all by themselves. At one time you would have had to search out the sprouts in oriental food stores, but now they are found in more and more supermarkets.

SERVES 6

WORKING TIME: 3 minutes

FRYING TIME: 2 minutes

INGREDIENTS

2	pounds bean sprouts, soy or mungo
	about ⅓ cup oil
	salt and pepper
	juice of 1 lemon

PREPARATION

1   Rinse the sprouts in a sieve or colander while heating the oil in a large frying pan.

2   When the oil is almost smoking hot, dump in all the sprouts and turn them over and over with two large wooden spoons. Sprinkle with salt, pepper, and lemon juice.

3   Cover and cook for 1 minute or just until the sprouts begin to reduce in bulk but are still crisp.

TO SERVE

Transfer into a deep bowl and serve at once.

LOW-CHOLESTEROL VERSION

Use polyunsaturated oil for the frying.

Chinese asparagus

As with many Chinese preparations, thin slicing is called for in this recipe. But Chinese asparagus is a time saver nevertheless. The thin diagonal cutting eliminates the need to peel the asparagus stalks, and slicing is faster than peeling. This vegetable should come to the table still slightly crisp and bright green. The quick cooking guarantees the vivid color. The dull color one usually associates with asparagus stalks comes from slower cooking methods. These delicious morsels can be served as a first course or as a vegetable. I like to serve them as a separate vegetable course, so the delicate and pure flavor can be fully appreciated.

SERVES 6

WORKING TIME: 9 minutes

COOKING TIME: 2 minutes

INGREDIENTS

1½ pounds fresh asparagus
    salt and pepper
3   tablespoons butter
2   teaspoons soy sauce
1   teaspoon lemon juice

PREPARATION

1   Snap off and discard the tough bottom sections of the asparagus. Rinse the stalks under cold water. With a sharp knife cut the stalks and points into long, thin diagonal slices. The longer the better.

2   Put the asparagus slices in a large flat skillet. A single layer is best; overlapping should be kept to a minimum. Sprinkle lightly with salt and pour in enough water to reach a depth of ¼ inch. Cover the skillet.

3   Put it on high heat. Once the water boils, cook for about 2 minutes, or until the asparagus slices are just tender but still crisp.

4   While the asparagus is cooking, put the butter, soy sauce, lemon juice, salt, and pepper in a small pot and bring to a boil. Remove from heat.

5   Drain the asparagus well; scoop it into a serving dish and pour on the sauce. Toss well to coat all pieces with the sauce. Serve at once.

COOKING AHEAD

The asparagus can be cut in advance and kept refrigerated in a plastic bag. The cooking must be done at the last minute. The sauce can be prepared ahead and reheated.

LOW-CHOLESTEROL VERSION

Substitute polyunsaturated margarine for the butter and increase the amount of lemon juice to 2 teaspoons.

Curried carrots

Most of us have got in a rut and cook carrots in only a few routine ways. Here is an unusual treatment combining them with curry and onions.

SERVES 4 TO 6

WORKING TIME: 15 minutes

BAKING TIME: 1 hour

INGREDIENTS

1   pound carrots, 6 or 7
1   medium onion, minced
½   teaspoon celery salt
½   teaspoon curry powder
    salt and pepper
3   tablespoons butter
    juice of ½ lemon
½   cup water

PREPARATION

Preheat oven to 375°.

1   Peel the carrots and grate them with a rotary grater directly into a mixing bowl. Chop the onion fine and add it to the bowl. Sprinkle in the celery salt, curry, salt, and pepper. Toss all together with your hands to mix well.

2 Butter a 9-inch pie dish liberally. Scoop the carrot mixture into the dish and pat it down a little to smooth the top.

3 Mix the lemon juice and water together and pour over the carrots. Cover the dish tightly and bake for about 1 hour.

TO SERVE

Remove the cover and place the baking dish on a platter. Serve from the baking dish at the table, using two large spoons.

COOKING AHEAD

This dish can be done in advance, as much as a day ahead, and reheated at serving time in a 350° oven for 15 minutes.

LOW-CHOLESTEROL VERSION

Substitute polyunsaturated margarine for butter; no other changes in the recipe are necessary.

Cauliflower gratin

In cooking we generally try to preserve the attractive shape of cauliflower. Contrarily, in this gratin recipe it's mashed flat. What we sacrifice in form, though, we more than make up in a new flavor combination. Another bonus—since gratin is a different way to present cauliflower, you can put that dependable vegetable on the menu more often.

SERVES 6

WORKING TIME: *7 minutes*

BOILING TIME: *10 minutes*

BAKING TIME: *30 to 40 minutes*

INGREDIENTS

1   **teaspoon salt**

1   **medium head cauliflower**

½   **cup bread crumbs**

2   **teaspoons paprika**

½   **teaspoon curry**

1¾   **cups buttermilk**

    salt and pepper

PREPARATION

Preheat oven to 375°.

1 Bring a large quantity of water to a boil and add the salt. While the water is heating, prepare the cauliflower by breaking off and discarding all green leaves. Break the cauliflower into flowerets. Discard the core. Add the flowerets to the boiling water and cook for 10 to 12 minutes, or until they are just tender. Drain the cauliflower pieces, dip them into cold water, and drain well again.

2 While the cauliflower is cooking, prepare the topping. Mix together in a small bowl the bread crumbs, 1 teaspoon of paprika and ¼ teaspoon of curry. Stir in 1 cup of buttermilk and let the mixture stand for 10 minutes.

3 Put the cauliflower in a 9-inch pie dish and crush with the heel of your hand. Smooth the surface. Stir ¼ teaspoon curry, salt, and pepper into the remaining ¾ cup of buttermilk and pour this over the cauliflower.

4 Spread the crumb sauce over the cauliflower, sprinkle with 1 teaspoon of paprika, and bake for 30 to 40 minutes or until the top is nicely browned.

TO SERVE

Present in the pie dish and serve with two large spoons.

COOKING AHEAD

Cauliflower Gratin can be prepared and baked in advance, even the day before. Reduce baking time by 10 minutes, or until it just begins to brown on top. Reheat when needed in a 350° oven for 15 minutes. Refrigerate if held for more than 3 hours. Alternatively, crush the cooked cauliflower in the pie dish, prepare the breadcrumb topping, and refrigerate separately. Spread the topping and bake at serving time.

LOW-CHOLESTEROL VERSION

No changes in the recipe are necessary.

Baked celery with herb sauce

The clean flavor of celery combines very well with wine and herbs. This whole dish can be prepared ahead, leaving only the sprinkling of bread crumbs and butter to be done just before baking. Baked Celery is a perfect and economical vegetable to serve with roast meat or fowl.

SERVES 6

WORKING TIME: *13 minutes*
BOILING TIME: *15 minutes*
BAKING TIME: *30 minutes*

INGREDIENTS

- 2   teaspoons salt
- 2   bunches celery
- 1½   cups dry white wine
- 2   tablespoons chopped parsley
- 2   tablespoons chopped basil
- ¾   cup chicken bouillon
-     salt and pepper
- 5   tablespoons butter
- ½   cup bread crumbs

PREPARATION

Preheat oven to 400°.

1   Bring a large quantity of water to a boil and add the salt. Meanwhile cut off and discard the root ends from the celery bunches. Cut off the leafy tops from the celery and reserve for soups or salads. Rinse the celery under cold water. Cut the celery branches into 2- or 3-inch lengths and add them to boiling water. Cook until the celery pieces are almost tender, about 15 minutes. Drain at once.

2   While the celery is cooking, put the wine, parsley, and basil in a small pot and simmer, uncovered, for about 20 minutes. Add the bouillon and salt and pepper to taste. Simmer this herb sauce another 3 minutes.

3   Grease a baking dish with 1 tablespoon of butter and place the celery pieces in the dish. Pour the sauce over the celery. Cover the top completely with the bread crumbs and dot with remaining butter. Bake in the oven for about 30 minutes or until the top is nicely browned.

TO SERVE

Place the baking dish on a platter or trivet and, using two large spoons, serve directly from the dish at the table.

COOKING AHEAD

Prepare the dish and bake for 20 minutes, then cool and refrigerate. It can be done a day ahead. At serving time, cover and reheat the dish in a 375° oven for 15 minutes; remove the cover and bake 5 minutes more.

LOW-CHOLESTEROL VERSION

Substitute polyunsaturated margarine for the butter and add an extra teaspoon of basil.

Gratin de céleri niçois

The crisp flavor of celery can be an unexpected delight when it comes to the table as a cooked vegetable rather than as a salad fixture. Here is a dish to be enjoyed often, since the celery season seems to last the year round. The Niçois name, after the southern French city of Nice, comes from the herbed tomato sauce that is used a lot there and in this recipe is spooned over the celery before broiling. I recommend making that sauce instead of using a canned one. While the work involved is minimal, the flavor will be much better.

SERVES 6

WORKING TIME: *11 minutes*

BOILING TIME: *30 to 40 minutes*

BROILING TIME: *4 to 5 minutes*

INGREDIENTS

3	**bunches of celery**
1	**tablespoon salt**
1	**1-pound can plum tomatoes**
2	**tablespoons oil**
½	**teaspoon oregano**
½	**teaspoon basil**
1	**bay leaf**
	salt and pepper
¼	**cup grated Parmesan cheese**

PREPARATION

1   Bring a large quantity of water to a boil while preparing the celery. Cut off the leafy portions of the celery leaving a piece about 5 inches long, then trim off the root ends. Scrub the celery with a brush under cold running water, separating the ribs a little so the water can rinse the center of the stalks. Add salt to the boiling water, then the stalks. Cover and cook about 30 to 40 minutes, or until the celery is tender when pierced with a small sharp knife. Drain and refill the pot with cold water to cool the celery for a few minutes. Drain again.

2   While the celery is cooking prepare the sauce. Pour the tomato juice from the canned tomatoes into a small pot. Crush the tomato pulp with your hands and add it to the juice. Add the oil, oregano, basil, bay leaf, salt, pepper, and the leafy top from 1 rib of celery. Cover and simmer slowly for 15 to 20 minutes.

3   Gently squeeze each cooked celery stalk to remove the excess water. Cut the stalks in half lengthwise and lay them in a baking dish, cut side down.

4   Preheat the broiler. Remove the bay leaf and celery rib from the sauce and pour it over the celery. Sprinkle with the cheese. Broil for 4 or 5 minutes, or until the cheese melts and turns a golden brown.

TO SERVE

Serve directly from the baking dish, spooning some liquid over each portion.

COOKING AHEAD

Cook the celery and sauce and refrigerate them separately, even the day before. At serving time, drain the celery carefully, cut in half, and place in a baking dish. Reheat the sauce just to the boiling point and pour it over the celery. Bake in a 350° oven for 15 minutes, then sprinkle with the cheese and broil.

LOW-CHOLESTEROL VERSION

Use polyunsaturated oil in the sauce and substitute a low-fat grated cheese for the topping. No other changes are necessary.

Baked corn on the cob

There are at least two advantages to baking instead of boiling fresh corn: (1) no big pot to wash up afterwards; (2) if the corn isn't really farm fresh, as is often the case, this method will improve its flavor a good deal. Moreover, the yellow ears will have a faint taste of having been roasted on a picnic grill. All this for such little effort.

SERVES 6

WORKING TIME: *10 minutes*

BAKING TIME: *30 to 40 minutes*

INGREDIENTS

6	**ears fresh corn**
6	**sheets aluminum foil, approximately 10 x 6 inches**
4	**tablespoons softened butter**
	salt and pepper

PREPARATION

Preheat oven to 400°.

1   Remove the husks and cornsilk from the corn. Lay each ear on a sheet of foil.

2   Smear each ear of corn with 2 teaspoons of butter; sprinkle with salt and pepper. Roll up the ear in the foil, crimping the edges tightly. Place on baking sheet. Repeat with the other ears.

3   Place the corn in the hot oven and bake for 30 minutes. Check at this point: the ears should be fragrant and tender. If they aren't very fresh, they may require another 5 to 10 minutes.

4   Remove to a plate and serve at once, still foil-wrapped. Pass extra butter if desired, but it shouldn't be necessary.

COOKING AHEAD

The ears of corn are best if baked just before serving. If they must be cooked in advance, do not remove the foil wrap after the baking. Reheat the corn still in the foil, in a 350° oven for 10 to 15 minutes.

LOW-CHOLESTEROL VERSION

Substitute polyunsaturated margarine for the butter. Increase slightly the quantity of salt and pepper.

Corn pudding

Canned corn can be rather dull. It also can be turned into something special in just a few minutes. This is a very American dish with universal appeal.

SERVES 4 TO 6

WORKING TIME: *8 minutes*

BAKING TIME: *1 hour*

INGREDIENTS

2	**tablespoons melted butter**
3	**eggs**
2	**tablespoons cornstarch**
2	**teaspoons sugar**
	large pinch nutmeg
¼	**teaspoon allspice**
1	**cup milk**
1	**1-pound can cream-style corn**
2	**teaspoons butter**

Preheat oven to 350°.

1 Put the butter in a small pot to melt slowly. Break the eggs into a mixing bowl. Sprinkle on the cornstarch, sugar, nutmeg, and allspice and beat the mixture with a wire whisk until it is quite smooth. Stir in the milk and finally the corn and melted butter.

2 Grease a 1-quart soufflé dish with butter and pour in the pudding mixture. Put the soufflé dish in a pan containing hot water that reaches ⅓ of the height of the dish.

3 Bake until the pudding is set—about 1 hour or until a knife plunged into the center comes out clean. Serve directly from the soufflé dish.

COOKING AHEAD

The pudding mixture can be prepared and poured into the soufflé dish in advance, and refrigerated for 3 or 4 hours, but the baking must be done when needed.

LOW-CHOLESTEROL VERSION

Make the following substitutions: ½ cup liquid egg substitute for the 3 eggs; 1 cup skimmed milk for the whole milk; polyunsaturated margarine for the butter; polyunsaturated margarine or oil for greasing the soufflé dish.

Baked cranberries

Cranberries should be on the dinner table much more often. Except for Thanksgiving and Christmas dinners, we tend to think of them mostly as a decoration. Here is a recipe to encourage more frequent use of cranberries. It's simple to make, less sweet than most, and has a nice texture that is more interesting than the limp overcooked versions.

WORKING TIME: *4 minutes*

BAKING TIME: *30 minutes*

INGREDIENTS

Cranberries — measure any desired quantity

Sugar — ½ the quantity of cranberries (i.e., for 4 cups of berries, 2 cups of sugar)

PREPARATION

Preheat oven to 350°.

1 Spread the cranberries in a single layer (important) in a baking dish. Pour the sugar all over them. Cover the dish and bake in the preheated oven for 15 minutes.

2 Stir, re-cover, and return to the oven for another 15 minutes.

COOKING AHEAD

As with any cranberry sauce, these baked berries can be made several days before needed.

LOW-CHOLESTEROL VERSION

No changes in the recipe are necessary.

REMARKS

For an extra elegant touch and a sharpened flavor, add finely chopped candied ginger to the cranberries when baking them.

Waterford cucumbers

The cucumber, as a cooked vegetable, is a perfect accompaniment to many dishes. Its flavor is not so strong as to dominate, but at the same time it has a fresh, tangy taste that is pleasantly distinctive. The preparation couldn't be easier, the cooking faster nor the finished results better.

SERVES 4

WORKING TIME: 5 minutes

COOKING TIME: approximately 11 minutes

INGREDIENTS

2	**cucumbers**
2	**teaspoons salt**
3	**tablespoons butter**
¼	**cup bread crumbs**
1	**scant teaspoon tarragon**
	juice of ½ lemon
	¼ cup water
	salt and pepper

PREPARATION

1 While bringing about 2 quarts of water to a boil, peel the cucumbers and cut in quarters lengthwise. With a flexible knife, cut out the seeded centers, then cut each strip across into halves. There will now be 16 pieces.

2 Add salt to the boiling water, then the cucumbers. Bring the water back to a boil, then cook for about 6 minutes or until the cucumbers are just tender and the color a pale translucent green. Pour the contents of the pot into a strainer. Immediately place the strainer under cold running water. Let the cucumbers remain in the strainer so that all excess water drips off.

3 In a skillet melt the butter and add the crumbs. Stir the crumbs over moderate heat until they brown slightly. Lift the cucumbers out of the strainer and into the skillet. (Do not dump the cucumbers directly into the skillet from the strainer to avoid including excess moisture and loose seeds. Add the tarragon, lemon juice, water, salt, and pepper.

4 Stir to coat the cucumber pieces with the crumbs. Cook, uncovered, for 4 to 5 minutes, stirring once or twice. Transfer the cooked and crumbed vegetable to a serving bowl.

COOKING AHEAD

The recipe can be completed well ahead of time, including the browning of the crumbs. The final cooking of the cucumbers with the crumbs should be done when needed. If cooked cucumbers are stored in the refrigerator for any length of time, be careful to lift them out of the liquid that will have collected in the bottom of the dish. Squeeze the pieces slightly to remove the excess liquid.

LOW-CHOLESTEROL VERSION

The only changes necessary are to substitute polyunsaturated margarine for the butter and to add an extra tablespoon of lemon juice.

Mousse aux concombres

There is a constant need in any recipe file for a pretty, tasty, molded garnish for cold meat and fish platters. This pale-green mousse surely fills the bill. Another reason I am partial to it is for its unadulterated flavor. All too often vege-table mold recipes call for an assortment of fruits, vegetables, and even slivered nuts. The end result is a garish-looking mold and confusing tastes. Here is a ver-sion that is purity itself—in appearance and flavor.

SERVES 6

WORKING TIME: 6 minutes

COOKING TIME: 5 to 6 minutes

CHILLING TIME: 2 hours

INGREDIENTS

3   cucumbers

2   teaspoons lemon juice

1   tablespoon gelatin

2   tablespoons hot water

¾   teaspoon salt

½   teaspoon pepper

½   teaspoon Worcestershire sauce

½   teaspoon dillweed

     dash Tabasco sauce

     Optional: few drops green coloring

¼   cup mayonnaise (p. 226)

½   cup heavy cream

2   teaspoons oil

½   cup French dressing

PREPARATION

1   Bring about a quart of water to a boil while peeling 2 cucumbers. Cut them in quarters lengthwise, remove the seeds, and cut the slices in half crosswise. Add the cucumbers to the water with 1 teaspoon of lemon juice and boil for 5 or 6 minutes, or until they just turn transparent. Drain at once and cool under cold running water. Drain well again.

2   Soften the gelatin in the 2 tablespoons of hot water. Put the cucumbers in the blender and purée. Add the gelatin to the hot purée. Add the seasonings: the remaining teaspoon of lemon juice, salt, pepper, Worcestershire sauce, dillweed, Tabasco, and optional color-ing. (The color will be softened with the further additions.) Blend again and scrape into a mixing bowl and cool.

3   Fold in the mayonnaise. Whip the cream until very stiff and gently fold into the purée. Lightly oil a 3-cup ring mold (or other form) and spoon in the mousse. Tap the mold a few times on the counter to settle the mousse well into the container. Chill for at least 2 hours.

4   While the mold is chilling, score the un-peeled remaining cucumber and slice as thinly as possible. Marinate the slices in the French dressing.

TO SERVE

Run a hot knife around the edge of the mousse, dip the bottom of the mold into hot water. Place a chilled serving dish over the top of the mold and reverse the two together. The mousse will ease onto the platter. Drain the marinating cucumber slices and pile into the center.

COOKING AHEAD

The mousse needs at least 2 hours to set, but can also be made the day before.

LOW-CHOLESTEROL VERSION

Substitute evaporated skimmed milk for the cream. Pour the milk into a mixing bowl and place in the freezer until it is almost frozen. Chill beaters as well. Whip the milk until stiff and fold it into the cool mousse carefully and quickly.

Baked cucumbers

Once you stop thinking of the cucumber only as a candidate for the salad bowl and begin viewing it as a cooked vegetable, a whole new range of tasty possibilities opens up. This crisp vegetable can be boiled, sautéed, or baked and lightly sauced as in this recipe. Cooked cucumbers please the eye as well as the palate, since cooking turns them a pretty, translucent pale green. Another plus for dieters: there are only 25 calories in a medium-size cucumber.

SERVES 6

WORKING TIME: *10 minutes*

BAKING TIME: *25 to 30 minutes*

INGREDIENTS

3	**cucumbers**
½	**teaspoon tarragon**
	salt and pepper
¾	**cup chicken broth**
1	**teaspoon cornstarch**
¼	**cup white wine**
½	**teaspoon soy sauce**

PREPARATION

Preheat oven to 375°.

1   Cut ends off the cucumbers and discard. Peel and cut the cucumbers in half lengthwise, then crosswise. Place cucumber pieces, cut-side down, in a baking dish that will hold them snugly. Sprinkle with tarragon, salt, and pepper. Pour in the chicken broth and cover.

2   Bake for about 25 minutes or until the cucumbers are soft when pierced with a small sharp knife and the flesh turns translucent.

3   Remove the baked cucumbers to a serving dish and keep warm. If using a porcelain baking dish, place it on a heat deflecting pad or pour the cooking liquid into a small pot and place it on the heat. Put the cornstarch in a small bowl, then stir in the wine. Pour the cornstarch into the bubbling liquid and stir with a wire whisk. Add soy sauce, salt, and pepper. Taste for seasonings, and correct if necessary. Simmer the sauce until it thickens slightly. The sauce should be fairly clear and not very thick. Drain into the sauce any liquid that has accumulated in the cucumber dish.

TO SERVE

Pour the sauce over cucumbers and serve while hot.

COOKING AHEAD

Bake the cucumbers until barely tender, let cool, then refrigerate, overnight if you like. When needed, reheat the cucumbers in the cooking liquid and proceed as in the recipe above. If the recipe must be completed ahead, mix the baked cucumbers with the sauce, cool, and refrigerate. Reheat the cucumbers in the sauce, adding an extra ¼ cup white wine if more liquid is necessary.

LOW-CHOLESTEROL VERSION

No changes in the recipe are necessary.

Baked ratatouille

Traditional French ratatouille *involves a number of separate steps, most of which are eliminated here. Instead, a long, slow baking in the oven achieves more easily the same mellow results. This vegetable bake can be cooked faster in an oven hotter than I recommend, but since it takes no attention at all, why not let it simmer lazily in its own juice? The results will only be better. This is a substantial vegetable to serve with grilled or roast meats and fowl. Ratatouille is equally good served cold.*

SERVES 6

WORKING TIME: *12 minutes*

BAKING TIME: *4 to 5 hours*

INGREDIENTS

1   **eggplant, 1 to 1½ pounds, unpeeled**

1   **large green pepper, seeds removed**

1   **large onion, peeled and thinly sliced**

   Optional: 1 zucchini, unpeeled and sliced

1   **1½-pound can plum tomatoes, or 4 ripe tomatoes plus 1 cup tomato juice**

   garlic salt (or mashed garlic)

¼   **cup olive oil**

PREPARATION

Preheat oven to 300°.

1   Cut the eggplant crosswise, and the green pepper, into slices ¼ inch thick. Peel the onion and slice thin. In a heavy casserole or large baking dish, make a solid layer of the eggplant slices and sprinkle them very generously with garlic salt. Add separate layers of onion, green pepper, optional zucchini, and tomatoes. Press down with the palms of your hands to make a more compact *ratatouille*.

2   Pour the juice from the canned tomatoes over the vegetables. Crush the tomatoes with your hands and make a layer of the pulp. Dribble the olive oil over the surface and place the casserole in the preheated oven. Immediately reduce the heat to 275°.

3   Bake the *ratatouille*, uncovered, for 4 or 5 hours. It isn't essential, but an occasional basting during the long cooking process blends the flavors more completely.

TO SERVE

Using two large spoons, serve directly from the casserole.

COOKING AHEAD

Baked Ratatouille can be made a day or two before serving. Its flavor will improve. Reheat it in a 300° oven for 20 minutes, or until warmed through. It also freezes well.

LOW-CHOLESTEROL VERSION

Substitute polyunsaturated oil for the olive oil; no other changes in the recipe are necessary.

Grapefruit fritters

Never was grapefruit so spectacularly used as when James Cagney squashed it into the pretty face of Mae Clark in Public Enemy. That's probably carrying the unusual use of the citrus a bit far; one can stop at grapefruit fritters and still get a lot of attention. This may not be the quickest vegetable dish one can put together, but its unexpected and deliciously tart flavor is worth the few extra minutes. And what a treat to face grapefruit other than at the breakfast table. The fritters are excellent with roast meats, game, fried fish, and roasted game birds or duck.

SERVES 6

WORKING TIME: *15 minutes*

STANDING TIME: *2 hours*

FRYING TIME: *10 minutes*

INGREDIENTS

2 **grapefruit**
2 **cups flour**
½ **teaspoon salt**
½ **cup light beer, room temperature**
½ **cup warm water**
1 **teaspoon ground coriander**
1 **tablespoon oil**
1 **egg**
   oil for frying

PREPARATION

1 Cut away all the rind and white part from the grapefruit. Cut the grapefruit across in 4 or 5 slices about ¼ inch thick, then cut each slice in half. Place the slices between paper towels and let them stand for at least 2 hours, changing the paper towels once.

2 Make a batter by mixing together 1 cup of the flour with the salt, beer, warm water, coriander, oil, and egg. Beat the batter until smooth, cover, and set aside in a warm spot for at least 2 hours.

3 When ready to prepare the fritters, transfer the grapefruit slices to a dry dish towel and pat dry. Heat the oil (at least 1 inch deep in the pan) to hot, about 345°. Spread the remaining cup of flour on a dish and dip each grapefruit slice into the flour to coat both sides.

4 Dip the floured slices in the batter, then put them in the hot oil. Turn once to brown both sides. Keep the fire high under the oil. Remove the fritters to paper towels and sprinkle with salt. Serve hot.

COOKING AHEAD

Although the fritters can be fried ahead and reheated in a 375° oven for 5 minutes, the batter coating will not be as crisp.

LOW-CHOLESTEROL VERSION

Use 2 egg whites instead of 1 whole egg in the batter. Use polyunsaturated oil in the batter and for the frying.

Braised lettuce

Lettuce may seem quite ordinary in the salad bowl, but once it is braised and served bubbling hot, it becomes a notable vegetable. Although Boston lettuce is nice to use, iceberg can easily be substituted. Since iceberg lettuce is a solid head, it will provide more servings. This is a lovely dish to serve all by itself, following a cold main course, such as the Mixed Pâté in Aspic (page 131) or other cold pâtés (pages 95 and 132).

SERVES 6 TO 8

WORKING TIME: *6 minutes*

BAKING TIME: *30 minutes*

INGREDIENTS

3	**heads Boston or 2 heads iceberg lettuce**
2	**teaspoons salt**
3	**tablespoons flour**
1½	**cups beef broth**
⅓	**cup Madeira or Port**

PREPARATION

Preheat oven to 375°.

1   Bring a large quantity of water to a boil and add the salt. Meanwhile pick off and discard any bruised outer leaves of the lettuce. Rinse the heads of lettuce and plunge them into boiling water and cover. As soon as the water comes back to a boil, drain the lettuce and plunge the heads into cold water. For iceberg lettuce cook 5 minutes after the water returns to the boil. Drain well again.

2   Put the flour in a small pot and slowly stir in the broth, keeping it very smooth. Put the pot on a medium fire and bring to a simmer. Once the sauce is thick, remove from the heat and add the wine.

3   Gently squeeze each head of lettuce to remove excess water. Cut off the stem ends, then cut each head in half, from top to bottom. Large heads of iceberg can be cut in quarters. Lay the halves in a shallow baking dish, cut-side down. Pour the sauce over the lettuce and cover with a lid or aluminum foil.

4   Place the baking dish in the oven for 30 minutes or until lettuce is tender when tested with a sharp knife.

TO SERVE

Lift the hot baked lettuce out of the baking dish and transfer to a vegetable dish, or place around a carved roast or fowl.

COOKING AHEAD

The lettuce can be blanched, cut, placed in the baking dish, and refrigerated, even the day before. Cook the sauce and chill. Do not pour the sauce over the lettuce until ready to bake. Some water from the lettuce may collect in the dish; it should be drained off before adding the sauce. If all ingredients are cold when placed in the oven, increase baking time by 10 minutes.

LOW-CHOLESTEROL VERSION

No changes in the recipe are necessary.

Creamed lettuce

Iceberg lettuce, which has almost no flavor, is disdained as a salad green by many food-conscious people. For cooking with cream, though, it just happens to be the perfect thing. It cuts nicely into shreds, wilts obligingly under heat, and marries beautifully with a light cream sauce. All in all, this is a rather glamorous presentation for the ugly duckling of the vegetable counter.

SERVES 5 OR 6

WORKING TIME: *7 minutes*

COOKING TIME: *4 to 5 minutes*

INGREDIENTS

4	**tablespoons butter (½ stick)**
1	**large head iceberg lettuce**
1½	**tablespoons potato flour or cornstarch**
1	**cup heavy cream**
⅛	**teaspoon nutmeg**
	salt and pepper

PREPARATION

1   Heat the butter in a large flat skillet while preparing the lettuce. Cut the head of lettuce into halves, top to bottom. Then cut each half in two again, also lengthwise. Lay each section on its side and cut across in ¼-inch slices. It should now look shredded.

2   Add the lettuce to the hot butter, or as much as will fit in the skillet at this point. With two large wooden spoons, turn the lettuce over and over to coat all the pieces with the melted butter. Keep adding more lettuce as its bulk diminishes. Cover and simmer for 1 minute.

3   Meanwhile, put the potato flour in a small bowl and slowly stir in the cream. Use a small whisk to keep the cream smooth.

4   Uncover the skillet and pour in the cream. Sprinkle with the nutmeg, salt, and pepper. Turn the lettuce over and over with the spoons to coat it thoroughly with the cream. Cover the skillet and simmer for 1 minute more.

TO SERVE

Spoon the lettuce into a deep vegetable dish and serve at once while it is still hot.

COOKING AHEAD

Remove the skillet from the fire before adding the cream. Stir in the cream and allow the lettuce to cool, uncovered, then refrigerate, overnight if you like. At serving time, add ⅓ cup cream and reheat in a covered skillet and simmer for 1 minute.

LOW-CHOLESTEROL VERSION

Substitute polyunsaturated margarine for the butter and evaporated skimmed milk for the cream. Increase the quantity of nutmeg to ¼ teaspoon, and stir in 1 tablespoon of polyunsaturated margarine just before spooning the creamed lettuce into a serving dish.

Lima beans with mushrooms

Except for a brief moment in the late summer when fresh lima beans are available, the cook is obliged to rely upon the canned or frozen varieties. Since this vegetable freezes quite well, we can still enjoy its mellow flavor. Furthermore, frozen lima beans are much improved when combined with compatible herbs and vegetables. Basil and fresh mushrooms do the trick here.

SERVES 4 TO 5

WORKING TIME: 6 *minutes*

COOKING TIME: 7 *minutes*

INGREDIENTS

1 **10-ounce package frozen baby lima beans**

4 **tablespoons butter (½ stick)**

¼ **pound fresh mushrooms**

1 **garlic clove**

1 **tablespoon lemon juice**

 salt and pepper

½ **teaspoon basil**

1 **tablespoon chopped parsley**

PREPARATION

1 Cook the lima beans according to the directions on the package, but do not overcook, they should still be fairly firm since they will be cooked again. Drain well and return the beans to the pot.

2 While the beans are cooking, melt 2 tablespoons of butter in a small skillet. Rinse the mushrooms and slice them thin. Add the mushrooms to the skillet along with a peeled garlic clove stuck on a toothpick. Sprinkle with lemon juice, salt, and pepper. Cover and simmer the mushrooms gently for 3 minutes.

3 Remove the garlic from the skillet and scrape the mushrooms into the lima beans. Grind the basil between your fingers until powdery while adding it to the pot. Add the 2 remaining tablespoons of butter to the beans and mix gently. Cover and reheat for 1 minute. Add the parsley, mix, re-cover, and simmer for 1 minute more. Serve hot.

COOKING AHEAD

Cook the lima beans only half as long as the directions call for. Simmer the mushrooms for only 1 minute. Combine the 2 vegetables and the garlic clove in a covered dish. Refrigerate. At serving time, remove the garlic, cover and reheat the beans on a medium fire until warmed through, about 4 to 5 minutes.

LOW-CHOLESTEROL VERSION

Substitute polyunsaturated margarine for the butter and increase the lemon juice to 2 tablespoons.

Lima bean purée

I serve puréed vegetables as often as possible. Somehow, they seem to turn an ordinary vegetable into something quite glamorous. Fortunately, the electric blender makes fast work of reducing, in this case, lima beans to a smooth and novel side dish. And the flavor? See how much horseradish does for it!

SERVES 6

WORKING TIME: *8 minutes*

COOKING TIME: *15 minutes*

INGREDIENTS

2 **cups water**

½ **teaspoon salt**

1 **small to medium onion, thinly sliced**

2 **10-ounce packages frozen lima beans**

¾ **cup heavy cream**

2 **tablespoons butter**

2 **tablespoons grated horseradish, or to taste**

1 **teaspoon Worcestershire sauce**

    salt and pepper

PREPARATION

1 Bring the water and salt to a boil while peeling and slicing the onion. Add the onion and simmer for 5 minutes.

2 Add the lima beans and cook them for 10 minutes once the water returns to a boil. Drain the beans and onion.

3 Pour the cream into a blender, add the drained beans and onions, and purée. Do not overblend—the beans should not be completely smooth. Return the purée to the pot.

4 Add the butter, horseradish (according to taste), Worcestershire sauce, salt, and pepper. Reheat gently. If you feel the purée is too thick, thin it with a little more cream. Makes about 3 cups of purée.

TO SERVE

Heap the purée into a deep dish and serve while still very hot. Lima Bean Purée can also be cooled then chilled in the refrigerator and served as a garnish to cold meat platters. In the latter case, remove the purée from the refrigerator 1 hour before serving.

COOKING AHEAD

The purée can be completely prepared a day or two in advance and refrigerated until needed.

LOW-CHOLESTEROL VERSION

Use a medium-sized onion instead of a smaller one. Substitute evaporated skimmed milk for the cream and 3 tablespoons of polyunsaturated margarine for the 2 tablespoons of butter. Add an extra ½ teaspoon of Worcestershire sauce. Don't be timid with the horseradish.

Baked mushrooms

This is the purest essence of mushrooms. They literally stew in their own juice, which is considerable. The one essential point is to seal carefully the foil in which the mushrooms are wrapped. Although the recipe is listed here as a vegetable, these mushrooms heaped on a slice of toast could do nicely as a main dish at lunch or a first course at dinner. A slice of boiled ham slipped between the bread and the mushrooms makes the dish even more substantial.

SERVES 6

WORKING TIME: *4 minutes*

BAKING TIME: *15 to 20 minutes*

INGREDIENTS

1 **pound fresh mushrooms**

    salt

    juice of ½ lemon

    Optional: ¼ cup water

Preheat oven to 350°.

1 Rinse the mushrooms under cold running water. Leave the stems intact.

2 Line a baking dish with aluminum foil, allowing some foil to hang over the edges. Put the mushrooms on the foil. If the mushrooms seem a little dry, add the water. Sprinkle them with salt and lemon juice.

3 Cover the mushrooms with a second sheet of foil and carefully crimp together the edges of both sheets. The seal must be complete. Place in the oven for 15 to 20 minutes, depending on size of mushrooms.

TO SERVE

Serve directly from the baking dish, opening the foil cover at the table.

COOKING AHEAD

The complete mushroom package can be prepared a half-day in advance and refrigerated. Do not bake until needed or the mushrooms will be limp and somewhat shriveled in appearance.

LOW-CHOLESTEROL VERSION

No changes in the recipe are necessary.

Mushrooms victor

One wonderful thing about mushrooms is their great versatility. They are delicious raw, cooked—plain, fancy, delicate, or spicy. Each version has its very own flavor, especially this recipe for Mushrooms Victor. Its combination of hot spices softened by cream produces a tingling palate sensation. Mushrooms Victor can be served cold as a light first course or as an accompaniment to cold meats, or hot with roasts, chicken, or grilled sandwiches.

SERVES 6

WORKING TIME: *8 minutes*

COOKING TIME: *5 minutes*

INGREDIENTS

½   **cup tomato sauce**

¼   **cup oil**

¼   **cup water**

2   **teaspoons prepared mustard**

⅛   **teaspoon cayenne pepper**

2   **teaspoons sugar**

    salt and pepper

1   **pound fresh mushrooms**

¼   **cup cream**

1   **tablespoon brandy**

PREPARATION

1 In a flat skillet, put the tomato sauce, oil, water, mustard, cayenne, sugar, salt, and pepper. Stir, cover, and simmer slowly.

2 Meanwhile, rinse the mushrooms and cut them in halves or quarters, depending on size.

3 Add the cream and brandy to the sauce and stir well. Add the mushrooms and mix to coat them with the sauce. Cover, bring to a boil, and simmer for 2 minutes.

TO SERVE

Serve hot or cold depending on menu.

COOKING AHEAD

If Mushrooms Victor are to be served hot, cook them for only 1 minute and finish the other minute at serving time.

LOW-CHOLESTEROL VERSION

Use polyunsaturated oil and substitute evaporated skimmed milk for the cream in the sauce.

Dijon-style mushrooms

Dijon *in the name of a recipe almost invariably means mustard will be used. Dijon, the capital of the Burgundy region of France, is also the country's mustard capital. Especially popular is an herb-flavored, pungent variety that enhances everything from sausages to vegetable dressings. Although it is a nice refinement to use Dijon mustard in cooking, it is not absolutely necessary for most recipes. Although this mustard-mushroom combination may seem a bit unusual at first, one taste proves how well matched the pair are, served hot or cold.*

SERVES 4

WORKING TIME: *10 minutes*

COOKING TIME: *9 minutes*

INGREDIENTS

2	**tablespoons butter**
1	**shallot, or 2 scallions, minced**
1	**pound small fresh mushrooms**
	juice of 1 lemon
	salt and pepper
2	**tablespoons flour**
¼	**cup heavy cream**
½	**cup white wine**
1	**tablespoon dark mustard**
	good pinch nutmeg

PREPARATION

1 Melt the butter in a large skillet while mincing the shallot. Add the shallot, cover the skillet, and simmer slowly for 2 minutes; meanwhile rinse the mushrooms under cold running water. If the mushrooms are large cut them into halves or quarters.

2 Add the mushrooms to the skillet, squeeze in the lemon juice, and sprinkle with salt and pepper. Cover and simmer for 2 minutes more.

3 Put the flour in a small bowl; stir in the cream and wine to make a thin paste. Then stir in the mustard and beat to smooth the sauce.

4 Pour the mustard-cream sauce over the mushrooms. Add the nutmeg, cover, and simmer slowly for 5 minutes.

TO SERVE HOT

Spoon the mushrooms and sauce into a deep serving dish.

TO SERVE COLD

Cool the mushrooms, then chill. This is an excellent dish with cold meats.

COOKING AHEAD

When preparing the recipe to serve the mushrooms hot, proceed through step 4, but cook only 2 minutes instead of 5. Finish the cooking at serving time.

LOW-CHOLESTEROL VERSION

Substitute polyunsaturated margarine for the butter and polyunsaturated cream substitute for the cream. Add an extra ½ teaspoon of mustard and 1 tablespoon of polyunsaturated oil to the sauce.

Gratin parisien

Here is still another way to cook the accommodating mushroom. The mushrooms get a quick turn in the pan, then are sprinkled with cheese and slipped under the broiler just long enough to achieve a crisp and speckled brown topping. Although included in the vegetable chapter of this book, Gratin Parisien could be a new way to begin a meal. But in that case it would be better to use just the caps for a prettier presentation. A word about the name of the recipe. In France, where one can buy a variety of mushrooms, the plain white mushroom, much like ours, is called Champignon de Paris or the Mushroom of Paris.

SERVES 6

WORKING TIME: *10 minutes*
COOKING TIME: *6 minutes*
GRILLING TIME: *2 to 3 minutes*

INGREDIENTS

1   **pound mushrooms**
3   **tablespoons butter**
     nutmeg
     salt and pepper
1   **tablespoon lemon juice**
1   **tablespoon flour**
¾   **cup cream or sour cream**
½   **teaspoon meat extract (like BV)**
3   **tablespoons grated Parmesan cheese**

PREPARATION

1   Rinse the mushrooms while melting the butter in a large skillet. When the butter is hot and foamy add the mushrooms and sprinkle them with the nutmeg, salt, pepper, and lemon juice. Stir to mix all the seasonings with the mushrooms, cover, and simmer on a medium fire for 2 minutes.

2   Remove the cover and sprinkle the flour over the mushrooms and cook for 1 minute. Slowly pour in the cream and stir in the meat extract. Stir well to distribute the meat extract evenly. Cover the skillet and simmer the mushrooms on low heat for 3 minutes.

3   Spoon the mushrooms and their sauce into an ovenproof gratin dish and sprinkle all over with the cheese.

TO SERVE

Just before serving, place the gratin dish under a preheated broiler for 2 to 3 minutes or until the cheese turns brown here and there. Place the gratin dish on a platter and serve directly from it, using 2 large spoons so that lots of sauce can be spooned over the mushrooms.

COOKING AHEAD

Gratin Parisien can be prepared in advance through step 3, but without sprinkling with cheese. Refrigerate until needed. Put the gratin dish under the broiler (not preheated) and broil until the sauce begins to bubble; then sprinkle with cheese and complete the recipe.

LOW-CHOLESTEROL VERSION

Substitute polyunsaturated margarine for the butter and evaporated skimmed milk for the cream. Add 1 extra tablespoon of lemon juice to the sauce and an extra ½ teaspoon of meat extract.

Rabat onions

The addition of raisins and a few seasonings to ordinary white onions turns them into a rather exotic treat. Although these onions can be served as a warm vegetable, I find the flavor best when they are served cold. They make an unusual addition to an antipasto tray and bring an element of surprise when served with any cold meats, pâtés or fowl.

SERVES 6

WORKING TIME: *7 minutes*

COOKING TIME: *30 minutes*

CHILLING TIME: *2 hours*

INGREDIENTS

12	small white onions
2	cups white wine, approximately
1	cup water, approximately
1	teaspoon salt
½	cup seedless raisins
1½	cups boiling water
1	tablespoon sugar
1	bay leaf
	Optional: white wine vinegar

PREPARATION

1 Peel the onions and place them in a deep frying pan. Cover them with wine and water to a level of 1 inch above the onions. Add salt, cover, and simmer for 10 minutes.

2 While the onions are simmering, soak the raisins in about 1½ cups of boiling water. Drain the raisins, add them to the onions with the sugar and bay leaf. Cover and simmer the onions for approximately 20 minutes, or until they are soft when pierced with a small sharp knife. Remove the pan from the fire.

3 Cool the onions, then taste the broth. If you would like a slightly sharper flavor, add a bit of vinegar, a teaspoon at a time to suit your taste.

TO SERVE

Chill the onions and broth. Spoon the vegetables and some liquid into a deep serving dish.

COOKING AHEAD

Rabat Onions must be prepared at least 2 hours in advance, but could be cooked as long as 2 days before serving.

LOW-CHOLESTEROL VERSION

No changes in the recipe are necessary.

Baked onions

When onions are served as a vegetable, generally the small white ones are chosen. Good as they are, peeling them is a time-consuming, pesky chore. Regular yellow onions can be turned into a new vegetable presentation with a small amount of effort and tears. Thorough baking destroys their usual pungency and produces a delicious noncliché accompaniment for meats and poultry. An interesting variation on this recipe would be to lift the cooked onions from their broth, place them in another baking dish, sprinkle them with grated Swiss cheese, and slip under the broiler for a minute or so, just until the tops are a pretty golden color.

SERVES 6

WORKING TIME: *6 minutes*

BAKING TIME: *approximately 45 minutes*

INGREDIENTS

6	onions
1	cup beef broth, approximately
	salt

Preheat oven to 400°.

1 Peel the onions and cut in half crosswise. Lay the onions flat side down in a baking dish just large enough to hold them.

2 Pour in enough beef broth to reach ½ the depth of the onions. Sprinkle lightly with salt. Cover the dish and bake for about 45 minutes or until the onions are soft. Baste once or twice during the baking.

TO SERVE

Lift the onions from the broth and place on a platter around the carved meat or fowl.

COOKING AHEAD

It is best to underbake the onions a little, leaving them in the oven for only 35 minutes. Finish baking at serving time.

LOW-CHOLESTEROL VERSION

No changes in the recipe are necessary.

Peas with mint

Even in its dried state, mint has a fresh flavor that can impart new life to frozen peas. Here the mint is a hint, not a strong statement. It doesn't mask the peas or the boiled ham. Peas with mint is a favorite Italian way with the vegetable.

SERVES 4 TO 5

WORKING TIME: 5 minutes

COOKING TIME: approximately 10 minutes

INGREDIENTS

2	**tablespoons butter**
½	**cup sliced onion**
1	**1-ounce slice boiled ham**
1	**10-ounce package frozen peas**
¼	**cup water**
1	**teaspoon mint**
	salt and pepper

PREPARATION

1 In a small heavy saucepan melt the butter, while peeling and slicing the onion. Add the onion to the butter, cover, and simmer slowly. Meanwhile, dice or chop the ham slice into small pieces and add to the onions. Cover and simmer for 5 minutes.

2 Add the frozen peas to the saucepan, pour on the water, and turn up the heat. When the frozen block of peas can be broken up, sprinkle in the mint, salt, and pepper. Reduce the heat and simmer for 2 or 3 minutes, or until the peas are soft. Serve hot.

COOKING AHEAD

Complete the recipe, but cook the peas for only 1 minute and remove from the fire immediately. Reheat the peas at serving time and finish cooking them. A few tablespoons of water may be needed when reheating.

LOW-CHOLESTEROL VERSION

Use polyunsaturated oil and select very lean ham; no other changes in the recipe are necessary.

New potatoes sautéed in butter

Peeling potatoes is a chore most people dislike. In this recipe tiny new potatoes are used, and their delicate skins stay on. Furthermore, during the cooking the skins are thoroughly softened and impregnated with butter, becoming quite delectable. Here is a quick and easy way to prepare potatoes.

SERVES 6

WORKING TIME: *3 minutes*

COOKING TIME: *approximately 45 minutes*

INGREDIENTS

8   **tablespoons butter (1 stick)**

18   **small new potatoes, or 12 medium**

    salt and pepper

3   **tablespoons chopped parsley**

PREPARATION

1   Put the butter in a large heavy skillet or casserole that will hold the potatoes in a single layer. While the butter is melting, briskly scrub the potatoes and dry them on a towel. (If a dish towel is used the potatoes will dry better and can be more easily transferred to the pot.)

2   When the butter is hot and foamy, pick up the ends of the towel and dump the potatoes into the pot. Lift the pot by both handles and roll the potatoes around to cover all surfaces with the fat. (If you find this difficult, use a large wooden spoon for turning the potatoes.) Sprinkle with salt and pepper, cover, reduce the heat, and allow the potatoes to "steam" in the butter until they are soft when pierced with a small sharp knife. This will take about 45 minutes. Roll or turn the potatoes from time to time.

TO SERVE

Lift the potatoes to a deep serving dish and sprinkle with the parsley.

COOKING AHEAD

Cook the potatoes only until they just begin to soften. If possible, refrigerate them in the casserole; or put the potatoes in a deep bowl and scrape all the melted butter over them. Reheat in the original casserole, cooking until they are tender.

LOW-CHOLESTEROL VERSION

Substitute polyunsaturated margarine for the butter and add 1 tablespoon of lemon juice to the melted fat.

Potato pudding

Time was when making potato pudding was a long, knuckle-scraping chore. Happily, the electric blender has changed all that. If the blender is used carefully, the results won't give away your timesaving secret. The potatoes must not be allowed to purée too long, or the batter will lack good texture. Instead, process the potatoes in two batches and they will be turned into fluffy batter in mere seconds. Of the many, many ways to prepare potatoes, you'll find this one a special favorite.

SERVES 6 TO 7

WORKING TIME: *13 minutes*

BAKING TIME: *40 to 45 minutes*

INGREDIENTS

1½	**pounds medium potatoes (5 or 6) cut into chunks**
½	**cup, plus 1 tablespoon oil**
1	**small to medium onion, cut into chunks**
1	**small garlic clove, sliced**
2	**eggs**
1 to 1½	**teaspoons salt**
	pinch pepper
½	**cup flour**

PREPARATION

Preheat oven to 375°.

1 Peel the potatoes and cut them into chunks about 1½ inches thick. Pour ¼ cup of oil into the blender and add a few pieces of potato. Start grating while adding more potato pieces. Stop when half the potatoes have been grated. Do not overblend. Pour the grated potatoes into a mixing bowl and repeat the process with the other ¼ cup of oil and the remaining potatoes.

2 Peel the onion and cut it into chunks. Peel the garlic and slice it. Put the eggs in the blender container. Add the garlic and half the onion pieces. Begin puréeing and continue adding the rest of the onion pieces, a few at a time. This mixture should be processed until quite smooth. Add to the grated potatoes. Stir in the salt, pepper, and flour. Mix well.

3 Smear 1 tablespoon of oil in a deep 9-inch pie dish or other baking dish. Pour in the batter and smooth the top. Bake for 40 to 45 minutes or until the top is a golden brown.

TO SERVE

Cut wedges from the pie dish at the table.

COOKING AHEAD

Potato Pudding can be prepared and baked in advance. Reheat at serving time in a 350° oven for 15 minutes, covering the dish with aluminum foil.

LOW-CHOLESTEROL VERSION

For the 2 eggs, substitute ¼ cup liquid egg substitute or 3 egg whites. Use poly-unsaturated oil.

Baked caraway potatoes

This is a quick and easy way to give bland potatoes a lot of flavor. As a bonus, the lively flavor comes from calorie-free caraway seeds, not from gobs of cream and butter. The amount of fat you smear on the baking dish is a personal matter. A light coating of butter will produce a crisper potato. More butter will give you a richer, moister version. Both are delicious.

SERVES 6

WORKING TIME: 7 minutes

BAKING TIME: 45 minutes to 1 hour

INGREDIENTS

3   Idaho baking potatoes
3   tablespoons butter, or less
    salt and pepper
1½ teaspoons caraway seeds
    Optional: 3 tablespoons oil

PREPARATION

Preheat oven to 350°.

1   Scrub the potatoes and pat them dry. Cut them in half lengthwise and smear each cut side with ½ teaspoon of butter. Sprinkle the cut sides with salt, pepper, and ¼ teaspoon of caraway seeds. Pat the seeds lightly into the butter.

2   Smear butter in a baking dish that will hold the potatoes snugly. Use as much as you like. Place the potatoes in the dish, cut side down. If some seeds fall off, use the potatoes to sweep the seeds underneath them. If desired, brush oil over the skins.

3   Bake in the oven for 45 minutes to 1 hour, or until the potatoes are soft when pinched.

COOKING AHEAD

The potatoes can be completely baked in advance and reheated in a 350° oven at serving time. Add water to the baking dish used for reheating, but just enough to moisten the dish. Alternatively, each baked potato half can be tightly wrapped in aluminum foil (with a teaspoon of water) and reheated in a 350° oven for 15 to 20 minutes.

LOW-CHOLESTEROL VERSION

Use polyunsaturated margarine instead of butter and polyunsaturated oil for brushing on the skins.

Garni à la boulangère

For some strange reason, in French cooking boulangère (baker-style) means that a combination of potatoes and onions is included in the dish. Indeed, the two vegetables are very good together, even when not added to something else. Our popular home-fried potatoes are proof of that. The following is a different, fast, and tasty way to put the classic pair of root vegetables together. Once in the oven this dish needs virtually no attention. Since no fat is called for in the recipe, the calorie count is very low —only about 75 per serving.

SERVES 6

WORKING TIME: 8 minutes

BAKING TIME: approximately 1 hour

INGREDIENTS

1   pound potatoes (3 or 4)
1   medium onion, sliced
    thyme
    salt and pepper
2   cups beef broth

PREPARATION

Preheat oven to 350°.

1   Peel the potatoes and slice them into ¼-inch rounds. Peel the onion and slice it thin.

2   Select a deep, 8- or 9-inch pie plate or similar ovenproof dish. Layer in ½ the onions, then ½ the potatoes. Sprinkle

slightly with thyme, salt, and pepper. Layer in the remaining onions and potatoes and repeat the seasoning.

3 Pour the beef broth into the dish, just enough to almost cover the potatoes. Pour it along the sides so it doesn't disturb the seasoning on the potatoes. Cover the dish and place it in the preheated oven. Bake for 45 minutes.

4 Remove the cover and bake for another 15 minutes, or until the potato slices are soft when pierced with a sharp knife.

5 Serve from the baking dish, spooning a little of the broth over each portion.

COOKING AHEAD

The entire recipe can be done in advance and reheated in a 350° oven when needed. The generous amount of broth prevents it from drying out.

LOW-CHOLESTEROL VERSION

No changes in the recipe are necessary.

Mashed potatoes with red wine

Mashed potatoes undeservedly have gotten a "blue-plate special" kind of reputation—cheap, filling, and not very good. Properly made, mashed potatoes can be very good, even if not very unusual. In this version they are both. Instead of a bland, neutral flavor, the potatoes take on a rich and assertive character. The dish is an excellent accompaniment to Marinated Turkey Drumsticks (page 94), game of all kinds, roast duck, or pork. The potato color, obviously, changes completely. The mashed potatoes become a muted beige-rose that closely resembles puréed chestnuts. Mashed Potatoes with Red Wine only look like puréed chestnuts; they don't cost like them.

SERVES 4

WORKING TIME: *8 minutes*

COOKING TIME: *approximately 25 minutes*

INGREDIENTS

1   **pound potatoes (3 or 4), cut into chunks**

2   **teaspoons salt**

½   **cup red wine**

3   **tablespoons butter**

¼   **teaspoon nutmeg**

    salt and pepper

PREPARATION

1 Bring a large quantity of water to a boil while peeling the potatoes and cutting them into chunks. Add 2 teaspoons of salt and the potatoes to the water. Partially cover the pot and boil until the potatoes are soft, about 20 minutes. Drain well.

2 Mash the potatoes or put them through a food mill. (I prefer the food-mill method.) Pour the wine into the pot, bring to a boil, and simmer for a half-minute. Return the potatoes to the pot and add the butter and nutmeg, stirring to blend all flavors. Taste for seasoning, adding salt, pepper, and nutmeg as needed. The nutmeg flavor should be subtle, but almost identifiable.

TO SERVE

Spoon the mashed potatoes into a deep vegetable dish.

COOKING AHEAD

Cook and mash the potatoes and add the flavorings, but stir in only 6 tablespoons of wine. Cover tightly and refrigerate. At serving time, stir in the remaining 2 tablespoons of wine and reheat thoroughly.

LOW-CHOLESTEROL VERSION

Substitute 4 tablespoons of polyunsaturated margarine for the 3 tablespoons of butter. Add a bit more nutmeg.

Patatas bravas

Spanish peasants like their potatoes very brave. That means lots of hot peppery seasoning. For them the proportions in this recipe are just about right —in other words, much wine is needed to put out the fire. It might be prudent to add the cayenne and Tabasco more timidly than I call for until you are familiar with the recipe and your courage rises. As the potatoes cook in the spicy tomato sauce, the outside turns bright red while the inside remains white, offering an attractive color contrast.

SERVES 6 TO 8

WORKING TIME: *10 minutes*

COOKING TIME: *approximately 20 minutes*

INGREDIENTS

2	**cups tomato sauce**
1	**cup tomato juice or water**
1	**tablespoon oil**
1	**teaspoon cayenne**
½	**teaspoon Tabasco**
1½	**pounds potatoes (5 or 6)**
¼	**cup chopped parsley**

PREPARATION

1   In a covered flat skillet simmer together all the ingredients except the potatoes and parsley.

2   Meanwhile, peel the potatoes and cut them into chunks. Add the potatoes to the sauce, cover, and simmer until the potatoes are soft, about 20 minutes. Turn the potatoes occasionally.

TO SERVE

Transfer the potatoes to a deep serving dish and spoon the sauce over them. The sauce will have thickened considerably during the cooking. Sprinkle with parsley.

COOKING AHEAD

Patatas Bravas can be cooked in advance and refrigerated. Reheat at serving time. They will be even braver.

LOW-CHOLESTEROL VERSION

Use polyunsaturated oil; no other changes in the recipe are necessary.

Roquefort gratin

Although Roquefort Gratin is a member of the scalloped-potato family, there is little family resemblance. The pungent, blue-veined Roquefort cheese brings a strong character to this dish, instead of the usual bland richness. Here is a stylish accompaniment to roasts, grilled meats, chicken, vegetable plates, even stews. By adding diced ham to the potatoes, Roquefort Gratin can become a hearty main course. There are two versions below, one plain and one without a golden topping. You'll like it either way.

SERVES 4 TO 5

WORKING TIME: 11 minutes

BAKING TIME: 1 hour

INGREDIENTS

2 teaspoons butter
3 ounces Roquefort cheese
1½ cups milk
¼ teaspoon freshly grated nutmeg
few drops Tabasco
salt and pepper
1 pound medium potatoes (3 or 4)

PREPARATION

Preheat oven to 400°.

1   Smear the butter in a 9-inch pan or other baking dish. Mash the cheese in a mixing bowl, while heating the milk in a small pot. When the milk comes to a boil, pour about ½ cup of it onto the cheese and beat vigorously with a wooden spoon to smooth a little. Pour in the rest of the milk and beat again. Some lumps will remain. Add the nutmeg, Tabasco, pepper, and a little salt. Do not oversalt; the cheese contains salt.

2   Peel the potatoes, slice them thin, and place in the buttered dish. Pour the Roquefort sauce over the potatoes. The sauce should cover the potatoes; if not, add more milk.

3   Place the dish in the oven and bake for about 1 hour, or until the potatoes are soft and the liquid is almost completely absorbed. Serve directly from the baking dish.

Gilding

The addition of this golden coating will also increase the number of servings to six. The rich smoothness of this creamy addition can also enhance many other vegetable dishes. Use it, Italian style, on asparagus: cook the asparagus and drain well. Stir ¼ cup grated Parmesan cheese into the cream sauce, spread over the asparagus, and bake for 15 minutes in a 375° oven. The same sauce (with or without the cheese) can be used on broccoli or Brussels sprouts.

WORKING TIME: 2 minutes

1   egg yolk
½   cup sour cream
nutmeg

Beat the above ingredients together in a bowl. After the gratin has baked for 45 minutes, reduce the heat to 350°, spread the cream over the top in a smooth layer and bake another 30 minutes.

COOKING AHEAD

Roquefort Gratin can be almost completely done in advance, by baking for about 45 minutes and leaving the potatoes still slightly crisp. To finish, pour on about ½ cup milk and complete the baking. In the gilded version, stop the cooking process before adding the topping and finish when needed.

Radis au beurre

Any time a vegetable doesn't have to be peeled, you're ahead in the timesaving game. You'll find that bright red radishes turn a pale pink when boiled, adding a different color touch to the vegetable platter. The flavor is a surprise —much like young sweet turnips. Also try white radishes. They are equally delicious.

SERVES 6

WORKING TIME: *7 minutes*

BOILING TIME: *about 20 minutes*

SAUTÉING TIME: *2 minutes*

INGREDIENTS

1   **teaspoon salt**

2   **bunches (about 4 cups) radishes**

4   **tablespoons butter (½ stick)**

   salt and pepper

   juice of ½ lemon

PREPARATION

1   While bringing a large quantity of salted water to a boil, snip off the top and stem ends of the radishes. Rinse the radishes and dump them into the boiling water and cook for about 20 minutes, or until they are tender. Do not overcook. Drain well.

2   Melt the butter in a large frying pan. When it is hot, add the radishes and sprinkle with salt, pepper, and lemon juice. Simmer for about 1 minute, stirring from time to time. Serve hot.

COOKING AHEAD

The boiled radishes can keep for several days in the refrigerator in a covered container. Drain off any water they may have exuded before adding them to the hot butter. If they must be fried ahead, reheat in a covered skillet or put in a baking dish and slip under the broiler for a minute or so.

LOW-CHOLESTEROL VERSION

Substitute polyunsaturated margarine for the butter. Add ¼ teaspoon basil while sautéing the radishes.

Improved sauerkraut

Sauerkraut out of the can is not a culinary masterpiece. But a lot can be done to improve it. This recipe borrows hints from cooks in Central Europe who add many refining touches even to freshly made sauerkraut. Though there is a special affinity between roast pork and sauerkraut, it goes equally well with sausages, grilled pork and lamb, and is something different to try with turkey. Central European cooks also insist that sauerkraut is good for the complexion. Serve it often.

SERVES 6

WORKING TIME: *10 minutes*

COOKING TIME: *1 hour*

INGREDIENTS

1   **1-pound 11-ounce can sauerkraut**

2   **tablespoons butter**

2   **onions, sliced**

2   **cups dry white wine**

¼   **teaspoon caraway seeds**

1   **bay leaf, broken in half**

1   **garlic clove, minced**

   salt and pepper

   Optional, but recommended: 12 juniper berries

PREPARATION

1   Dump the sauerkraut into a sieve and rinse it under cold running water. Let the sauerkraut drain.

2 Melt the butter in a large skillet while peeling and slicing the onions. Add the onions to the skillet, cover, and simmer slowly for 5 minutes.

3 Add the sauerkraut to the onions and stir. Add the wine, caraway seeds, bay leaf pieces, garlic, salt, pepper, and optional juniper berries. Cover and simmer slowly for 1 hour.

TO SERVE

Remove the bay leaf pieces. It is not necessary to remove the juniper berries; the diners will push them aside. Spoon Improved Sauerkraut into a deep serving dish and serve hot.

COOKING AHEAD

Complete the recipe and refrigerate the sauerkraut. Reheat at serving time, adding more white wine if necessary. It can be done several days in advance.

LOW-CHOLESTEROL VERSION

Substitute polyunsaturated margarine for the butter; no other changes in the recipe are necessary.

Fried spinach

Fried spinach? Why not? We're used to fried parsley on fish platters, and this variation is larger and crisper. A few seconds in the hot oil and the limp leaves turn crisp and stiff. Nibbling them can become addictive.

WORKING TIME: *3 minutes*

FRYING TIME: *5 seconds*

INGREDIENTS

small fresh spinach leaves

oil for frying

salt

PREPARATION

1 Rinse the leaves and dry them between towels. All moisture must be removed before the leaves are added to the oil. If not, expect a lot of messy splattering. If you want to be extra safe, dry the leaves for a minute in a barely warm oven.

2 Heat at least 1 inch of frying oil in a deep pan until it's almost smoking. If using a French fryer, put the spinach leaves in the basket and lower it into the hot oil. In skillet frying, add the leaves quickly, one after the other. Leave in no more than 5 seconds.

3 Lift the basket out of the oil, or remove the fried leaves with a skimmer. Drain on paper towels. Sprinkle with salt and serve immediately.

COOKING AHEAD

The spinach leaves can be washed and dried several hours in advance. The frying must be done at the last minute.

LOW-CHOLESTEROL VERSION

No changes in the recipe are necessary, but polyunsaturated oil should be used for the frying.

Spinach gratin

Let's face it, when it comes to spinach most people use the frozen variety. Equally undeniable is the fact that its flavor is a far cry from that of fresh spinach. But when one must save time, cleaning fresh spinach leaves is a nuisance. Save the pleasure of unadulterated fresh spinach for days when you have the extra time. However, I don't recommend serving plain frozen spinach. No amount of butter can make up for its lack of flavor. Here is a way to make it really enjoyable.

SERVES 4 TO 5

WORKING TIME: *12 minutes*

COOKING TIME: *35 minutes*

INGREDIENTS

4½	**tablespoons butter (about ½ stick)**
1	**tablespoon minced onion**
½	**cup rice**
1¼	**cups hot water**
	salt and pepper
2	**tablespoons bread crumbs**
½	**cup milk**
1	**12-ounce package frozen leaf spinach, thawed**
4	**tablespoons grated Parmesan cheese**
½	**teaspoon freshly grated nutmeg**
	juice ½ lemon
1	**beaten egg**

PREPARATION

Preheat oven to 375°.

1   Melt 2 tablespoons of butter in a pan while chopping the onion. Add the onion to the pan, stir, cover and let simmer for 1 minute. Add the rice, turn up the heat and stir for about 1 minute or until the rice grains turn opaque white. Add the water and salt and pepper; cover, reduce the heat, and cook for 20 minutes.

2   Meanwhile, in a small bowl, stir the milk into the bread crumbs and put aside.

3   Take a handful of the thawed spinach at a time and squeeze out the excess water. Chop the spinach coarsely, then pull the pieces apart while putting them in a mixing bowl. Add 2 tablespoons of cheese, the nutmeg, lemon juice, salt, and pepper.

4   Scrape the cooked rice from the pan into the mixing bowl. Put 2 tablespoons of butter in the pan and melt. Add the softened bread crumbs to the spinach and rice along with the egg and the melted butter. Mix thoroughly.

5   Butter a 9-inch pie dish with the remaining ½ tablespoon of butter and scoop the spinach-rice mixture into it. Smooth the top and sprinkle with the remaining 2 tablespoons of cheese. Place the dish in the oven for 15 minutes. Serve hot directly from the pie pan.

COOKING AHEAD

The entire preparation can be done in advance and refrigerated. The final baking, however, should be done just before serving. If the dish is taken directly from the refrigerator to the oven, add 5 minutes baking time.

LOW-CHOLESTEROL VERSION

For the butter, substitute polyunsaturated margarine; for the milk, skim milk; for the whole egg, 2 egg whites (or ¼ cup liquid egg substitute), and low-fat cheese for the Parmesan. Add an extra tablespoon of minced onion.

Spinach loaf

Spinach, even frozen spinach, adapts well to special treatment. Here is proof. I call it a loaf because in French the name would be pain (bread), but bread has nothing to do with it. This dish is more like a dense soufflé. It puffs in the oven a little, but not dramatically. I like to bake it in a soufflé dish, but a regular loaf dish would do just as well. Serve Spinach Loaf as a special vegetable or a soufflé-type first course.

SERVES 6

WORKING TIME: *12 minutes*

COOKING TIME: *40 to 50 minutes*

INGREDIENTS

4	**tablespoons butter (½ stick)**
¼	**cup flour**
1¼	**cups milk**
	freshly grated nutmeg
	salt and pepper
2	**12-ounce packages frozen leaf spinach, thawed**
3	**tablespoons sour cream**
2	**eggs, beaten**
½	**cup light cream**
	Optional: 2 tablespoons grated Parmesan cheese

PREPARATION

Preheat oven to 400°.

1   Heat 3 tablespoons of butter in a heavy saucepan until it is foamy. Stir in the flour and cook for ½ minute. Slowly add the milk, stirring with a wire whisk. Add the nutmeg, salt, and pepper. Simmer this white sauce for 2 minutes.

2   While the sauce is simmering, squeeze the water out of the spinach, a handful at a time. Chop the spinach coarsely and put it in a mixing bowl.

3   Add 1 cup of the white sauce to the spinach and mix together. Add the sour cream and beaten eggs and mix well again.

4   Butter a 4-cup soufflé dish or loaf pan with 1 tablespoon of butter. Scrape the spinach mixture into the dish. Place the baking dish in a pan containing about 1 inch of water. Bake for 35 to 45 minutes or until the spinach loaf browns a little on the top and begins pulling away from the sides of the dish.

5   While the loaf is baking, thin the remaining sauce with the cream and season with nutmeg, salt, and pepper. (Add the grated cheese if the loaf will be served as a first course.)

TO SERVE

Reverse the loaf on a serving platter and spoon sauce over the entire top. Pass the rest of the sauce separately.

COOKING AHEAD

Since Spinach Loaf is not cranky, it can be baked for about 25 minutes, cooled, and refrigerated, still in its baking dish. At serving time reheat it in a 400° oven, again putting the dish in a pan of water. Reheat the sauce.

LOW-CHOLESTEROL VERSION

Substitute polyunsaturated margarine for the butter and add 1 additional tablespoon of flour to the sauce base. Substitute evaporated skimmed milk for whole milk and low fat yogurt for the sour cream. To the spinach batter add the juice of ½ lemon and increase the pepper and nutmeg flavorings. Use 3 egg whites, lightly beaten, instead of the whole eggs. Thin the final sauce with evaporated skimmed milk instead of cream, plus 2 tablespoons of low-fat yogurt.

Baked yellow squash

Nature has given yellow summer squash a very pretty shape. Here is one way of showing off its curves while dressing it up with a few subtle flavors. Baked Yellow Squash is excellent with meat dishes. For a change, serve it with egg dishes, or with other vegetables as a vegetarian medley.

SERVES 6

WORKING TIME: *5 minutes*

BAKING TIME: *30 minutes*

INGREDIENTS

2   **tablespoons butter**
1   **pound medium squash (4 or 5)**
    juice of ½ lemon
¼   **teaspoon thyme**
    salt and pepper

PREPARATION

Preheat oven to 375°.

1   Melt the butter directly in a 9-inch pan or baking dish placed in the oven a minute or so. (The butter can also be melted in a small pot and poured into the pan.)

2   While the butter is melting, rinse the squash, cut off the stem ends, then cut each squash in half lengthwise.

3   To the melted butter in the pan add the lemon juice, thyme, salt, and pepper. Stir with a fork to mix. Place the squash in pan, cut-side down.

4   Cover and bake for 30 minutes, or until tender. The timing will depend on the size and quality of the squash.

TO SERVE

If the baking dish is an attractive one, serve directly from it at the table, lifting the baked squash with spatula and spoon. The squash can also be placed around the carved meat on a platter.

COOKING AHEAD

The dish can be prepared a few hours ahead and kept refrigerated before baking. If the cooking must also be done ahead, remove the squash from the oven just before it is completely tender, then reheat in a 375° oven for 5 minutes right before serving.

LOW-CHOLESTEROL VERSION

Proceed exactly as above, but substitute polyunsaturated margarine for butter, and use the juice of 1 whole lemon instead of ½.

Yellow squash, pure and simple

We've become so used to dressing up vegetables with all kinds of sauces that we often overlook the natural way to do them. Yellow squash is a case in point. It has one of the mildest, freshest flavors that the garden produces. It also is very low in calories, a benefit that is capitalized on in this simple preparation. Gobs of butter over the cooked slices would detract from the purity of the dish. In the winter when yellow squash might not be quite so full of flavor as when locally harvested, a bit of chicken bouillon cube added during the cooking will bring the squash back to par.

SERVES 6

WORKING TIME: *6 minutes*

COOKING TIME: *3 to 4 minutes*

INGREDIENTS

1½   **pounds medium yellow squash (6 or 7)**
     salt and pepper
     Optional: ½ chicken bouillon cube
     water

1   Rinse the squash and trim off and discard both ends. Cut the squash into thin—about ⅛-inch—slices.

2   Put the squash slices in a pot that will hold them snugly. Sprinkle with salt and pepper. If using the optional bouillon cube, crumble it and sprinkle on. Pour in enough water to reach half the level of the squash.

3   Cover the pot and put it on high heat. Bring to a boil and simmer for 3 or 4 minutes or until the squash is just tender. The timing will depend on the quality of the vegetables and how thin they were cut.

4   Drain or use a skimmer to lift the squash out of the liquid. Put in deep serving dish and serve immediately.

COOKING AHEAD

Cook the squash for just 2 minutes, cool and refrigerate. At serving time, reheat and cook 1 or 2 minutes more.

LOW-CHOLESTEROL VERSION

No changes in the recipe are necessary.

Provençal string beans

When string beans are really fresh I prefer tasting only their own pure flavor. Given the quality of today's supermarket beans, that is a passing pleasure. So when faced with beans long since off the vine, thick in girth, and full of strings, I toss them up with some of the zippy flavors of Provence. The results make me forget about fresh, fresh beans —almost.

WORKING TIME: *12 minutes*
COOKING TIME: *approximately 20 minutes*

INGREDIENTS

2   **teaspoons salt**
1   **pound string beans**
3   **tablespoons butter (or olive oil)**
3   **tablespoons capers, drained**
1   **tablespoon anchovy paste**
1   **tablespoon lemon juice**

PREPARATION

1   Put the salt in a large quantity of water and bring to a boil while preparing the beans. Snap off the ends and pull off the heavy strings. Boil the beans until tender, this takes 15 to 20 minutes depending on quality. Drain at once.

2   While the beans are cooking, prepare the sauce in a pot large enough to hold the beans, too. Melt the butter, add the capers, anchovy paste, and lemon juice. Cover and simmer for 5 minutes.

3   Add the drained beans and mix together thoroughly, cover, and simmer for 1 minute more. Heap the beans in a deep vegetable dish.

COOKING AHEAD

Plunge the drained cooked beans in cold water and allow to drain thoroughly. Cover tightly and refrigerate. Prepare the sauce and store in a small covered jar. At serving time, scrape the sauce into a large pot; add a little hot water to the jar and shake vigorously to get every bit of the sauce, and add to the pot. Once the sauce is hot, add the beans, mix, cover, and simmer slowly for 5 minutes to heat thoroughly.

LOW-CHOLESTEROL VERSION

Substitute polyunsaturated margarine for the butter; no other changes in the recipe are necessary.

Tomato bake

Just about every kitchen cupboard I know is always stocked with the 9 ingredients listed below. There they sit, waiting to be tossed together into this pie with a summery air. If the canned tomatoes have very little pulp and a lot of liquid, increase the bread by 2 slices or use 2 eggs instead of one.

SERVES 6

WORKING TIME: 8 *minutes*

BAKING TIME: 45 *minutes*

INGREDIENTS

4   slices white bread
1   1-pound, 12-ounce can plum tomatoes, preferably imported
½   cup chopped onion
½   teaspoon sugar
1   teaspoon basil
1   teaspoon sage
     salt and pepper
1   egg
2   tablespoons oil

PREPARATION

Preheat oven to 375°.

1   Break the bread into pieces in a small mixing bowl. Pour the juice from the can of tomatoes directly over the bread and mix to distribute the liquid.

2   Dump the tomatoes into another, larger, mixing bowl and squash with your hands. Add the onion, sugar, basil, sage, salt, and pepper. Mix until all the ingredients are thoroughly blended.

3   With a wooden spoon beat the bread until it becomes quite soft. Beat the egg lightly and add it to the bread. Add the oil. Beat the mixture together vigorously until it is light and fluffy. Mix the beaten bread into the tomatoes.

4   Spoon the tomato batter into a 9-inch pie dish and bake for 45 minutes, or until the top darkens slightly and the batter pulls away from the sides of the dish.

TO SERVE

Tomato Bake should be served while hot. Cut it into wedges at the table.

COOKING AHEAD

Tomato Bake can be prepared in advance, baked for 30 minutes, cooled, and refrigerated. Complete the last 15 minutes of baking time just before serving.

LOW-CHOLESTEROL VERSION

For the whole egg substitute 2 egg whites or ¼ cup liquid egg substitute. Use polyunsaturated oil. No other changes in the recipe are necessary.

Golden grilled tomatoes

A grilled tomato is a grilled tomato is a grilled tomato. But it doesn't have to be. That standard garniture on every conceivable kind of dish really can be turned into something better. In this recipe the tomato also takes on added flavor, which can be a boon eleven months of the year. The light coating on the tomato halves turns a pretty golden brown under the broiler, making the red vegetable somewhat less naked than usual.

SERVES 6

WORKING TIME: 6 *minutes*

GRILLING TIME: *about 3 minutes*

INGREDIENTS

6   ripe tomatoes
     salt and pepper
¾   cup mayonnaise (p. 226)
½   teaspoon curry powder

1 Cut the tomatoes in half, crosswise, and sprinkle with salt and pepper.

2 Spoon the mayonnaise into a small bowl and stir in the curry powder, salt, and pepper.

3 Spread a generous amount of the seasoned mayonnaise over each tomato half. Grill under a hot broiler for about 3 minutes or until the mayonnaise has turned a light golden color. Serve at once.

COOKING AHEAD

The seasoned mayonnaise can be prepared in advance; it will keep for a week in the refrigerator. The tomatoes should not be spread with the topping more than 1 hour before grilling. Grill just before serving.

LOW-CHOLESTEROL VERSION

No changes in the recipe are necessary. For very strict low-cholesterol diets, use one of the polyunsaturated mayonnaises now on the market and add a few drops of Worcestershire sauce to the mixture, or prepare your own mayonnaise using polyunsaturated oil.

Candied tomatoes

The search for good, imaginative garnishes for platters is never ending. A few sprigs of parsley and some tomato wedges seem to be the universal solution. Here is a garnish that is less of a cliché. Small tomatoes are candied very slowly in a spicy syrup and are a delightful surprise whether served hot or cold. Even supermarket tomatoes take on some character with this treatment. Candied Tomatoes are particularly good with roast meats, chicken, and cold platters.

SERVES 6

WORKING TIME: *2 minutes*

COOKING TIME: *2 hours*

INGREDIENTS

6 small tomatoes

2 cups sugar

1 cup water

½ teaspoon cinnamon

½ teaspoon paprika

4 whole cloves

PREPARATION

1 Select a deep heavy casserole or skillet that will hold the tomatoes snugly in a single layer. First put the sugar, water, cinnamon, paprika, and cloves in the pot and bring to a boil.

2 Add the tomatoes and spoon some of the syrup over the top of each one. Cover, reduce the heat to very low, or place the dish on a heat deflecting pad. The syrup should barely bubble. Cover and cook very slowly for 2 hours. Baste occasionally.

TO SERVE

Whether being served hot or cold, drain the tomatoes well before placing on a serving platter.

COOKING AHEAD

Proceed as above. For hot tomatoes, cool and refrigerate; then reheat in the syrup at serving time.

LOW-CHOLESTEROL VERSION

No changes in the recipe are necessary.

Zucchini sauté

For many reasons I consider the zucchini an admirable vegetable. It is not expensive; it keeps well in the refrigerator; it has a fresh, clean flavor; it needs no peeling; and it cooks in just a few minutes. Here is another way to prepare zucchini and take advantage of all its fine qualities.

SERVES 4 TO 5

WORKING TIME: 5 minutes

COOKING TIME: 12 minutes

INGREDIENTS

¼ cup oil

2 medium onions, sliced

1 pound zucchini (3 to 5 medium)

½ cup water

2 teaspoons soy sauce

salt and pepper

PREPARATION

1 Heat the oil in a flat skillet over medium-low heat while peeling and slicing the onions. Add the onions to the skillet, stir, cover, and fry slowly for about 10 minutes. The onions should not be allowed to brown.

2 While the onions are simmering, cut off and discard the ends of the zucchini and slice the rest into thin rounds.

3 Add the sliced zucchini to the onions and mix them together. Pour in the water, cover, and simmer for 1 minute. Add the soy sauce, salt, and pepper and simmer for 1 minute more. The zucchini should remain slightly crisp.

COOKING AHEAD

Cook the onions as described above, add the zucchini, water, soy sauce, salt, and pepper and cook for only 1 minute. Simmer the vegetables for 1 more minute at serving time.

LOW-CHOLESTEROL VERSION

Use polyunsaturated oil; no other changes in the recipe are necessary.

Quick-fry zucchini

Chinese-style stir frying is used for this quick zucchini preparation. It parts company with the Oriental kitchen by grating the vegetable instead of slicing it slowly and uniformly. What you have here is an unusual vegetable dish that also is visually attractive with highlights of red pimento studding the zucchini.

SERVES 6

WORKING TIME: 9 minutes

FRYING TIME: 3 minutes

INGREDIENTS

1½ pounds zucchini (about 6 medium)

2 tablespoons oil

1 4-ounce jar chopped pimentos

salt and pepper

1 lemon

¼ teaspoon oregano

PREPARATION

1 Rinse the zucchini and cut off and discard both ends. Do not peel. Grate the zucchini coarsely (using either an upright or rotary grater). Heap into a bowl.

2 Heat the oil in a large frying pan. Dump zucchini and pimentos with their juice into the frying pan. Salt and pepper lightly, then squeeze in the juice of the lemon, and sprinkle with oregano. Mix thoroughly using a large spoon or spatula. Toss while frying for about 1 minute.

3 Cover the pan, turn off the heat, and let stand for 2 minutes. Spoon zucchini into a deep vegetable dish and serve.

COOKING AHEAD

This preparation is best done when needed. If absolutely necessary, the zucchini can be grated and refrigerated for an hour or two. The frying cannot be done in advance.

LOW-CHOLESTEROL VERSION

Use polyunsaturated oil for the frying; no other changes are necessary.

Lentil salad

Lentils are perhaps the most versatile of the dried legumes. Their musky flavor can add interest at any point in a meal — in soup, as a hot vegetable, puréed, or even as a salad. Given the ease of preparation, modest cost, and rich protein content, it's surprising that lentils don't appear on the table more often. Here is an especially appealing way to enjoy them —as a salad served with cold meats, fowl, or sausages. It will keep beautifully in the refrigerator for days. With the addition of some lettuce, sliced tomatoes, and cucumbers, Lentil Salad is easily turned into a summertime main course dish.

SERVES 8

WORKING TIME: *10 minutes*

COOKING TIME: *approximately 40 minutes*

MARINATING TIME: *2 hours or more*

INGREDIENTS

2	**cups dried lentils, about ¾ pound**
1	**medium onion, halved**
2	**whole cloves**
1	**celery rib**
1	**bay leaf**
1	**teaspoon dry mustard**
3	**tablespoons wine vinegar**
¼	**cup red wine**
¾	**cup oil**
1	**teaspoon tarragon**
3	**tablespoons chopped parsley**
	salt and pepper
2	**tablespoons chopped chives or scallions**

PREPARATION

1   Put the lentils in a sieve and rinse them under cold running water. Dump the lentils into a deep pot and add cold water to a level 2 inches above the beans. Remove any floating husks.

2   Peel the onion, cut it in half, and push a clove into each half. Add the onions to the pot, along with the celery rib, bay leaf, salt, and pepper. Cover and simmer until the lentils are just tender. Do not overcook. The cooking time will vary depending on the quality of the lentils; count on approximately 40 minutes.

3   While the lentils are cooking prepare the dressing. Put the mustard in a small mixing bowl, and stir in the wine vinegar to dissolve the mustard. Add the wine, oil, tarragon, parsley, salt, and pepper. Beat the dressing with a whisk. Stir in the chives or scallions.

4   Drain the lentils and discard the onions, bay leaf, and celery. Transfer the lentils to a mixing bowl, and immediately pour the salad dressing over them. Mix well, cover, and put aside for at least 2 hours. Stir occasionally.

TO SERVE

If served with cold meat, spoon the Lentil Salad at one end of the platter, or pass in a separate lettuce-lined bowl.

COOKING AHEAD

Since it must marinate, the Lentil Salad should be made at least 2 hours in advance. Once the lentils have marinated they can be refrigerated for several days. Remove them from the refrigerator at least 1 hour before serving.

LOW-CHOLESTEROL VERSION

Use polyunsaturated oil; no other changes in the recipe are necessary.

Kidney-bean purée

Plain old kidney beans don't have to remain so plain. They can become quite classy when served this way. Not only are they puréed to a rich smoothness, but red wine is added to intensify the color and flavor. This is a rich and unusual accompaniment for game and roasts of any kind. Leftover purée can be formed into patties, coated with flour and fried in butter for a different treat. Dried beans are specified in this recipe since their texture and flavor are better than the canned variety.

SERVES 6

WORKING TIME: 10 minutes

SOAKING TIME: at least 6 hours

COOKING TIME: about 1 ½ hours

INGREDIENTS

1½	**cups dried red kidney beans, about ½ pound**
1	**teaspoon salt**
1	**bay leaf**
1	**carrot, cut in half lengthwise**
1	**small onion**
1	**clove**
1½	**cups red wine**
¼	**teaspoon nutmeg**
	salt and pepper
	Optional: 3 tablespoons butter

PREPARATION

1 Rinse the beans, put them in a pot, and cover with cold water. Put a lid on the pot and let it stand for at least 6 hours, or overnight. If pressed for time, bring water to boil, remove from fire and soak for 1 hour.

2 Drain the beans and return them to the pot. Pour in enough water to cover the beans by 1 inch. Add the salt, bay leaf, carrot, and the onion studded with the clove. Cover and cook until the beans are tender, about 1½ hours. Drain.

3 Discard the bay leaf and the clove from the onion. Pour half the wine into the blender and purée half the beans with the onion and carrot. Repeat with the remaining wine and beans.

4 Return the purée to the pot, add the nutmeg, salt, pepper, and optional butter, and reheat. Simmer for 5 minutes.

TO SERVE

Either spoon the purée onto the platter around the carved meat, or pass in a separate vegetable bowl.

COOKING AHEAD

The beans can be completely cooked and puréed in advance and kept refrigerated. Reheat at serving time with a little red wine added to prevent scorching.

LOW-CHOLESTEROL VERSION

No changes in the recipe are necessary. Eliminate the optional butter or use polyunsaturated margarine.

Chick-pea purée

Cooks in the Middle East use chick-peas often to capitalize on the nutlike flavor of the legume. This is a habit we can easily adopt now that chick-peas are available in cans. Of course dried chick-peas also can be used, but if they are to be puréed I don't think one gains much for the extra work involved. As a starch, chick-peas are a nice change from the more usual potatoes, pastas, and rice.

SERVES 4

WORKING TIME: 4 minutes

COOKING TIME: 5 minutes

INGREDIENTS

1   1-pound-4-ounce can chick-peas

½   cup milk

    juice ½ lemon

3   tablespoons butter

⅛   teaspoon cayenne pepper

⅛   teaspoon garlic salt

⅛   teaspoon ground cumin

PREPARATION

1   Drain the chick-peas. Put the milk and lemon juice in a blender, then add the peas and purée. Scrape the purée into a pot.

2   To the purée add the butter, cayenne, garlic salt, and cumin. (The seasonings can be used with a stronger hand if you like.) Heat the purée through for 5 minutes.

TO SERVE

Spoon the purée into a bowl and serve hot.

COOKING AHEAD

Chick-pea Purée can be made a day or two before serving and reheated.

LOW-CHOLESTEROL VERSION

Use polyunsaturated margarine instead of butter and a whole lemon. Substitute skimmed milk for whole milk.

Fried chick-peas

Canned chick-peas can be turned into a fast and fine starch to complete your main courses. Here they are fried to make a vegetable that is different, tasty, and astonishingly easy.

SERVES 4
WORKING TIME: *2 minutes*
COOKING TIME: *2 to 3 minutes*

INGREDIENTS

1   1-pound-4-ounce can chick-peas

2   tablespoons oil

    salt and pepper

    paprika

    garlic powder

2   tablespoons chopped parsley

PREPARATION

1   Dump the chick-peas into a sieve and rinse them under hot running water. Put them aside to drain well.

2   Heat the oil in a large skillet. Add the chick-peas and fry them over moderately high heat. Sprinkle with salt, pepper, and paprika. Keep turning the peas with a spatula.

3   In about 2 or 3 minutes the chick-peas will have turned a dark golden brown. Remove the skillet from the heat and sprinkle garlic powder liberally over the peas.

TO SERVE

Transfer the chick-peas to a deep serving dish and sprinkle with the parsley.

COOKING AHEAD

Reheating fried chick-peas takes almost as much time as frying and serving them immediately. Any leftover peas can be reheated by frying in a little oil.

LOW-CHOLESTEROL VERSION

Use polyunsaturated oil; no other changes in the recipe are necessary.

Risotto à la milanaise

Though this risotto is suggested as an accompaniment for meat and poultry dishes, it very easily could become a main course with the addition of another cooked vegetable (peas, lima beans, or carrots) and some sliced meat (cooked lamb, sausage, or ham). The variations are almost endless to this well-prepared rice dish. Quantities of any of the ingredients can be changed —except the rice and water. It is imperative to measure exactly twice as much liquid as rice.

SERVES 6 AS VEGETABLE; 4 AS MAIN COURSE

WORKING TIME: 9 minutes

COOKING TIME: 30 minutes

INGREDIENTS

3	tablespoons oil
1	medium onion, chopped
¼	pound mushrooms, sliced
1	cup raw rice
2	cups water
	pinch of thyme
	pinch of saffron
2	tablespoons tomato paste
1½	teaspoons salt
½	teaspoon pepper
1	bay leaf
2	tablespoons butter
¼	cup grated Parmesan or Swiss cheese
1	tablespoon heavy cream

PREPARATION

Preheat oven to 350°

1 Slowly heat the oil in a 6-cup heavy pot while peeling and chopping the onion. Add the onion to the pot, cover, and simmer slowly while preparing the mushrooms. Rinse and thinly slice the mushrooms.

2 Turn up the heat under the pot and add the rice. Mix the rice with the onions and stir until the grains turn opaque white.

3 Add the water, mushrooms, thyme, saffron, tomato paste, salt, and pepper. Break the bay leaf in half and tuck both pieces into the rice. Cover the pot closely and bake for 20 minutes. Remove the pot from the oven and put it aside, still covered, for 5 minutes.

4 Remove the bay leaf pieces, fluff the rice with a fork, stir in the butter, cheese, and cream. Transfer the risotto to a warm serving bowl.

COOKING AHEAD

Risotto à la Milanaise can be baked in advance and refrigerated. Do not add the cheese, butter, and cream until later. At serving time, fluff again with a fork, add ¼ cup water, cover, and reheat slowly. When the rice is hot stir in the butter, cheese, and cream.

LOW-CHOLESTEROL VERSION

Use polyunsaturated oil for the frying. Increase the quantity of tomato paste to 3 tablespoons. After the risotto has been baked, stir in polyunsaturated margarine instead of butter, low-fat cheese, and polyunsaturated cream substitute or evaporated skimmed milk.

Baked country-style gnocchi

This recipe differs in two respects from those for traditional gnocchi. First, since semolina is hard to find today, cooked Cream of Wheat is used instead. Second, the gnocchi is baked in a layer rather than formed into small individual pieces. The flavor is the same, and a lot of time is saved. There is an extra advantage—any leftover gnocchi can be cut into squares and sautéed lightly in butter or margarine for a brand-new breakfast dish.

SERVES 8

WORKING TIME: *6 minutes*

COOKING TIME: *5 minutes*

BAKING TIME: *40 minutes*

INGREDIENTS

2 **cups milk**

2¾ **cups water**

1 **teaspoon salt**

1¼ **cups 5-minute Cream of Wheat**

¼ **teaspoon nutmeg**

¼ **teaspoon coriander**

3 **tablespoons butter**

½ **cup grated Parmesan cheese**

PREPARATION

Preheat oven to 375°.

1 In a 3-quart pot bring the milk, water, and salt to a boil. Add the Cream of Wheat slowly while stirring with a wooden spoon. Once the liquid is boiling again, reduce the heat and cook for 5 minutes or until the mixture is thick. Remove the pot from the heat. Beat in the nutmeg and coriander.

2 Melt 2 tablespoons of butter in a small pot while smearing the remaining 1 tablespoon of butter in a 9 x 13-inch baking dish. Spread in the cooked cereal and smooth into an even layer.

3 Pour on the melted butter and sprinkle generously with the grated cheese. Bake about 40 minutes or until top is lightly browned.

TO SERVE

Cut into squares at the table.

COOKING AHEAD

The *gnocchi* can be cooked and spread in the baking dish many hours in advance, even a day before if closely covered and refrigerated. Pour on the melted butter and sprinkle with cheese just before baking.

LOW-CHOLESTEROL VERSION

Use 2¾ cups of skimmed milk and 2 cups of water for cooking the cereal. Substitute polyunsaturated margarine for butter and increase the coriander to ½ teaspoon. Use a low-fat grated cheese for the topping.

Polenta

Polenta, *Italy's other starch, is over-shadowed by the pastas. But it is almost a staple in the northern part of the country, especially around Venice. It is automatically served with sautéed Venetian Liver (page 116), Squid in its Ink (Calamari con Inchiostro), or any stew from which it can absorb the sauce. At other times a tomato sauce comes with polenta, or just butter and a sprinkling of freshly grated cheese. The nutmeg is my own touch; I rather like just a hint of it, although I'm sure purists wouldn't.*

SERVES 8

WORKING TIME: *5 minutes*

COOKING TIME: *30 to 40 minutes*

INGREDIENTS

1½   **quarts (6 cups) water**

1   **tablespoon salt**

1½   **cups yellow cornmeal**

⅛   **teaspoon freshly grated nutmeg**

Optional: ¼ cup butter, ¼ cup grated Parmesan cheese

PREPARATION

1   Bring the water to a boil in a heavy 4-quart pot and add the salt. Keep the heat high while *very slowly* pouring the cornmeal into the bubbling water. Use a long wooden spoon to stir the water while pouring the cornmeal. If the stirring is stopped at this point you risk having lumps in the *polenta*. The water and cornmeal will expand at first over the high heat, which is the reason for the large pot.

2   Reduce the heat and cook the porridge uncovered for 30 to 40 minutes, or until the porridge begins pulling away from the sides of the pot and steam rises from around the cooked mass. At this point a heaping spoonful of it will remain firm on the spoon and not slide off. Stir often during the cooking, mashing against the side of the pot any lumps that may have formed. Sprinkle in the nutmeg for the last 10 minutes of cooking.

TO SERVE

If the *polenta* will be served with a dish that has a sauce or gravy, add nothing to it; simply spoon it into a deep vegetable dish. If the *polenta* will accompany roasts or chops, stir in the butter and cheese while it is hot.

COOKING AHEAD

Cook the *polenta* for only 25 minutes, cool, and refrigerate. At serving time, spoon the *polenta* into a pot, stir in ¼ cup of water and continue the cooking until very thick.

LOW-CHOLESTEROL VERSION

No changes in the recipe are necessary. If serving *polenta* with grilled meats, add polyunsaturated margarine, low-fat cheese, or an extra sprinkling of nutmeg.

Fried or baked polenta

Here are two entirely different ways to present polenta at the table. Both are quite good and in no way resemble their porridge origin.

SERVES 8

WORKING TIME FOR BAKING: *2 minutes*

WORKING TIME FOR FRYING: *5 minutes*

BAKING TIME: *20 to 30 minutes*

INGREDIENTS

1   *polenta* **recipe**

for frying: butter and oil

for baking: 2 tablespoons butter

½ cup grated Parmesan cheese

1 While the *polenta* is cooking, oil a 9 x 13 x 1½-inch baking dish. As soon as it is cooked, spoon the hot *polenta* into the dish and spread it into a smooth layer with a spatula.

2 To Fry: Cool, chill, then cut the chilled *polenta* into squares and fry in a combination of butter and oil in a frying pan. Brown on both sides. Grated cheese may be passed with it.

3 To Bake: Melt the butter and pour it over the *polenta*, which does not have to be chilled. Sprinkle generously with the grated cheese and bake in a 375° oven for 20 to 30 minutes or until the cheese on top is brown. Serve at the table from the baking dish.

COOKING AHEAD

For both these recipes the basic cooking is done when the *polenta* is cooked. If the frying must be done in advance, reheat the pieces in a 350° oven for 10 minutes.

LOW-CHOLESTEROL VERSION

Substitute polyunsaturated margarine and oil for the butter and oil and low-fat grated cheese for the Parmesan cheese.

Sunny rice

Yellow kernels of corn peeking among the grains of rice give this dish a bright, sunny look. Flecks of pimento enliven it still more. This is an excellent accompaniment for grilled or roasted meats and fowl, or with fish prepared in just about any manner. Leftover Sunny Rice can be fried in a little hot oil for a crisp, pancakelike treat. Another way to treat leftover rice is to toss it with mayonnaise diluted with a sharp salad dressing. Now you have a salad that can proudly be placed on any cold buffet table. With the addition of cooked or raw vegetables, Sunny Rice becomes an appealing main course.

SERVES 6

WORKING TIME: *5 minutes*
COOKING TIME: *30 minutes*

INGREDIENTS

¼ **cup oil**

1 **cup raw rice**

2¼ **cups chicken broth**

1 **10-ounce package frozen corn, or 1½ cups canned vacuum-packed corn**

⅓ **cup chopped pimento**

1 **teaspoon basil**

  salt and pepper

PREPARATION

1 Heat the oil in a heavy pot. When quite hot add the rice and stir until the grains turn white and opaque. Do not allow the rice to brown.

2 Add the chicken broth, corn, pimento, basil, salt, and pepper. When the liquid comes to a boil, cover the pot closely, reduce the heat and simmer slowly for 20 minutes. Remove the pot from the heat and put aside, still covered, for 5 minutes more. Fluff the rice with a fork before serving.

COOKING AHEAD

Complete the cooking and fluff with a fork. Cool and refrigerate. At serving time, add 2 tablespoons of butter, and reheat slowly in a covered pot.

LOW-CHOLESTEROL VERSION

Use polyunsaturated oil; no other changes in the recipe are necessary.

Flemish noodles

When a recipe has Flemish in the title it usually calls for leeks. What the leeks do in this case is transform plain old noodles into a choice accompaniment for roasts and grilled meats. Since the leeks are separated into long thin strips, they closely resemble the noodles they are mixed with, adding a bit of mystery to what makes the dish taste so good. Though leeks, unfortunately, are expensive in this country, this recipe won't strain the budget. Only 4 or 5 are needed, just enough to deliver their special flavor. In a pinch, scallions can be substituted, cutting away most of the dark green tops, leaving a piece about 5 or 6 inches long. Flemish Noodles can also be served as a main course.

SERVES 6 AS VEGETABLE DISH;

4 AS MAIN COURSE

WORKING TIME: 15 minutes

COOKING TIME: 25 minutes

INGREDIENTS

1	**pound leeks (4 or 5), or 15 scallions**
1½	**teaspoons salt**
3	**tablespoons butter**
3	**tablespoons flour**
2	**cups milk**
½	**cup heavy cream**
	large pinch nutmeg
	salt and pepper
½	**cup grated Parmesan cheese**
8	**ounces broad noodles**

PREPARATION

1 Bring a pot of water to the boil while preparing the leeks. Trim off the roots and cut away all the green leaves. Rinse the leeks well since they can stubbornly hold onto a lot of sand between the layers. Add 1 teaspoon of salt and the leeks to the water; cook for 15 to 20 minutes or until the leeks are soft. (Scallions will cook in about 10 minutes.) Drain at once and rinse the leeks under cold water. Drain again very well. Refill pot with water and put back on fire and bring to a boil.

2 While the leeks are cooking, prepare the white sauce. Heat 2 tablespoons of butter in a saucepan until it is hot and foamy; stir in the flour and cook for 1 minute while stirring. Slowly add the milk while stirring with a wire whisk, then add the cream. Season with nutmeg, salt, and pepper. Add the cheese and stir until it melts.

3 When the water comes to a boil, add ½ teaspoon salt and the noodles and cook for just 3 minutes, or until al dente. Do not overcook. Drain very well. Transfer the noodles to a deep bowl and add 1 tablespoon of butter; toss to melt the butter, which will help prevent the noodles from sticking together.

4 Use the same pot again. Put in the cooked noodles, separate the leeks into their natural layers and add them to the noodles. Pour in the sauce and mix together well so all noodles and leeks are coated with the sauce. Reheat slowly for a few minutes.

TO SERVE

Transfer to a deep serving bowl and use a large spoon and fork for serving.

COOKING AHEAD

All the elements of Flemish Noodles can be prepared in advance but kept separate. At serving time combine together in a pot the noodles, leeks, and sauce and reheat slowly. Since the sauce will have thickened considerably as it cooled, add about ¼ cup of milk to the pot when reheating the noodles.

LOW-CHOLESTEROL VERSION

Use polyunsaturated margarine instead of butter; evaporated skimmed milk instead of milk and cream; add ½ teaspoon Worcestershire sauce to the white sauce and increase nutmeg to ¼ teaspoon.

DESSERTS

Desserts are meant to finish a meal with a flourish, not a stunning blow. Rich and heavy concoctions have a numbing effect at the end of an otherwise well-planned meal. For this reason, elaborate cakes and pies have little place in this book. After a satisfying meal, I think the diner is more inclined to appreciate something like Pear Compote, Tropical Sherbet, Cobbled Peach Bake, or Baked Bananas.

The working time in this chapter is as little as 1 minute for Dulce de Leche, 2 minutes for Coffee Granita, 8 minutes for the Coffee Cream Custard, 9 for Baked Strawberries, and 17 minutes (the longest time) for a delicious Frozen Maple Mousse that will serve 8 to 10 amply.

There are many choices of wine to accompany a dessert. The wine served during dinner can continue through this last course. Champagne is a luxurious choice, especially with Champagne Snow or Champagne Fruit Cup. A full-bodied sweet Port can team up with Six-minute Chocolate Cake, Honey Cake, or cookies like Orange-Mincemeat Squares and Jamaican Squares. Then there is the one wine especially made to accompany the dessert course – sweet Sauterne. Many domestic white wines are sold as "Sauterne" even though they are not sweet nor made from the Sémillon and Sauvignon Blanc grapes. True Sauterne is always sweet, never dry, and is produced in France south of Bordeaux. The most famous of all is Château d'Yquem and it commands a price tag in keeping with its stature. Less expensive but fine Sauternes are Châteaux de La Tour Blanche, de Suduiraut, Guiraud, Doisy-Védrines, Filhot, etc.

Champagne fruit cup

There is no set formula to this recipe because it is meant to take advantage of whatever fruit is in season. Using frozen or canned fruits with champagne would be like spreading Beluga caviar on Ry-Krisp. The amount of sugar used depends on preference and the sweetness of the fruit. Be austere with it.

SERVES 6

WORKING TIME: 6 to 10 minutes depending on the selection of fruits

CHILLING TIME: 3 hours

INGREDIENTS

½   cup each: pineapple, bananas, strawberries, oranges, seedless grapes, and peaches, diced

⅓   cup sugar, approximately

2 to 3   tablespoons kirsch

½   pint lemon sherbet (page 203)

Optional garnishes: mint sprigs, pomegranate seeds, whole strawberries

1   bottle well-chilled champagne

PREPARATION

1   Quantities and fruits are a matter of preference. Basically, use equal amounts of the above list of fruits when in season, or substitute others. Sprinkle with a little sugar and kirsch. Chill at least 3 hours.

2   Spoon the fruit into tall glasses, filling halfway. Add a scoop of lemon sherbet and decorate with any of the optional garnishes. At the table, open the bottle of champagne, pour a little over each fruit cup.

3   All of the above is an excuse for pouring the rest of the champagne into drinking glasses.

COOKING AHEAD

After chilling and marinating the prepared fruits for two hours, they can be spooned into individual glasses and kept refrigerated. The lemon sherbet must be added just before serving.

Frozen banana morsels

Suddenly you have an overabundance of bananas and feel like baking only so many loaves of banana bread. What to do? Slice and freeze the bananas. Now your freezer holds an ever-ready nutritious snack for the children, one that will intrigue them far more than just another banana. In this form bananas also are an easy way to dress up desserts, especially the banana-flavored Tropical Sherbet (page 204). Another way to serve these refreshing tidbits is with after-dinner coffee instead of mints. I got the idea for this use when once served bite-sized ice cream bonbons that were made by a large manufacturer. They were pretty, but, alas, icy and flavorless.

WORKING TIME: 4 minutes per banana

FREEZING TIME: 3 hours

INGREDIENTS

For each banana:

3   tablespoons wheat germ

8 to 10   toothpicks

PREPARATION

1   Peel the bananas and cut them into ½-inch rounds. There will be 8 to 10 pieces depending on the size of the banana.

2   Pour some wheat germ into a saucer and roll each banana chunk in it, patting a bit to make the coating stick. Keep adding wheat germ to the saucer as needed.

3   Stick a toothpick through the side (which is firmer) of each piece and place on a dish. Freeze for at least 3 hours.

TO SERVE

Thaw for about 5 minutes before eating. For garnishing desserts either remove the toothpicks and arrange the morsels in a pattern, or leave the toothpicks intact and spear them into the dessert.

COOKING AHEAD

Frozen Banana Morsels will keep for months in the freezer.

LOW-CHOLESTEROL VERSION

No changes in the recipe are necessary.

Hot banana soufflé

This impressive soufflé need present no timing problem to the chef. It can be prepared and placed in its mold several hours before baking. Depending on the number of courses being served, slip it into the oven in time to be ready for the sweet course. I prefer the soufflé slightly soft in the center, but it can be baked until completely firm, providing larger portions.

SERVES 6

WORKING TIME: 6 minutes

BAKING TIME: 45 to 50 minutes

INGREDIENTS

1	**tablespoon soft butter**
6	**eggs**
½	**cup heavy cream**
	juice ½ lemon
1	**tablespoon kirsch**
¼	**cup sugar**
2	**large bananas**
11	**ounces cream cheese**

Optional: whipped cream flavored with Grand Marnier

PREPARATION

Preheat oven to 375°.

1   Select a 6-cup soufflé dish or other mold and grease it liberally with the butter. Put the eggs, cream, lemon juice, kirsch, and sugar in the blender and blend until the batter is smooth.

2   While the blender is running, peel the bananas and pull off any fibers. Break the bananas into chunks and add them, one at a time, to the blender with the motor still running. Next add the cream cheese in pieces. When all the ingredients are thoroughly mixed, run the blender at high speed for a few seconds.

3   Pour the batter into the prepared dish and place it in the hot oven. Bake until the top is lightly browned and puffy. Shake the dish a little, if the center is still soft it will jiggle. It can be served now or baked longer until the center is firm. Serve at once. Pass the optional whipped cream.

COOKING AHEAD

As noted above, this soufflé can be prepared several hours in advance, placed in its mold, and kept in a cool spot. If the kitchen is very hot put it in the refrigerator, but allow an extra 5 minutes for the baking.

Bananes rôties

If flaming bananas worry you, don't bother with them. Serve baked bananas instead. You'll find the flavor is almost identical and only the fireworks are missing.

SERVES 6

WORKING TIME: 10 minutes

BAKING TIME: 15 minutes

INGREDIENTS

4	**tablespoons butter (½ stick)**
6	**bananas**
	juice ½ lemon
4	**tablespoons dark rum**
2	**tablespoons dark brown sugar**

PREPARATION

Preheat oven to 375°.

1   Melt the butter while peeling the bananas. Place the bananas in a baking dish and sprinkle with the lemon juice.

2   Pour on half the melted butter and half the rum. Sprinkle with the brown sugar and place in the oven for 10 minutes.

3   Pour on the remaining butter and rum and bake for 5 minutes more.

TO SERVE

Serve at once, spooning some sauce over each banana.

The bananas with all their flavorings can be prepared in the dish and kept closely covered in the refrigerator for no more than 2 hours. The baking must be done just before serving.

Substitute polyunsaturated margarine for the butter and sprinkle the bananas with freshly grated nutmeg in addition to the other flavorings.

Pêches caramélisées

This intriguing dessert combines different textures and temperatures. The peaches are soft but still firm and quite cold underneath; the cream is buttery smooth; and the sugar topping is hot and crunchy. This unusual recipe also can be used with nectarines, apricots, or seedless green grapes.

A word about peeling peaches. When doing a large quantity, the most efficient method is to plunge them into boiling water for half a minute, then slip off the skins. This leaves a pretty, smooth fruit. However, if just a few peaches are to be peeled, I find it much easier to use a sharp, swivel-bladed potato peeler. In this recipe, only 6 or 7 peaches are required, which will take less than 5 minutes to peel by hand. Since they are sliced anyway, a perfectly smooth peach is not necessary. Also, a potato peeler is easier to wash than a large pot.

SERVES 6
WORKING TIME: *12 minutes*
DRIPPING AND FREEZING TIME: *4 hours*
GRILLING TIME: *2 or 3 minutes*

2	**pounds ripe peaches (6 to 7)**
1½	**cups heavy cream**
1	**tablespoon vanilla**
1½	**cups firmly packed dark brown sugar, approximately**

1 Peel the peaches and cut into thick slices. Put the peach slices in a colander to allow the excess juices to drip away. Let stand for about 2 hours, mixing the slices a little from time to time. The peach slices will darken a little, but it doesn't matter since they will be completely covered.

2 Place the fruit in an 8-cup freezer-to-oven soufflé dish or a deep pie dish, leaving at least 1 inch of space above the level of peaches. Smooth the top, pressing the slices slightly. Whip the cream until thick; add vanilla and continue beating until the cream is very firm. Spread the whipped cream in an even layer over the peaches. Place the dish in the refrigerator.

3 Put the fruit dish in the freezer 2 hours before serving. Preheat the broiler. Sprinkle brown sugar over the cream to a depth of almost ½ inch. (The amount will depend on size of the dish.) The cream must be completely covered. Place under the broiler no more than 4 or 5 inches away from the heat, and grill for just 2 or 3 minutes, or until the top is hot and crunchy. Serve at once.

The peaches and cream can be put in the dish well in advance and kept in the refrigerator all day. Do not increase time in freezer or the peaches will become icy.

Peach butter

This easy-to-make spread has a suave flavor and is a nice change on breakfast toast, waffles, or pancakes. At dessert time it can be reheated, ever so gently, and poured over vanilla ice cream. Or heap it on a slice of pound cake or in a meringue shell and cover with whipped cream. There ought to be room in the freezer for a few small containers of so versatile a spread.

MAKES 4 TO 5 CUPS OF JAM

WORKING TIME: *12 minutes*

COOKING TIME: *approximately 2 hours*

COOLING TIME: *approximately 1 hour*

INGREDIENTS

3   **pounds ripe peaches (8 to 10)**

½   **cup water**

2½   **cups sugar, approximately**

¼   **teaspoon nutmeg**

½   **teaspoon cinnamon**

½   **teaspoon almond extract**

PREPARATION

1   Rinse peaches and remove any stem ends. Put the peaches in a heavy pot and pour in the water. Cover and bring to a boil, reduce the heat, and simmer for 20 minutes. Put aside to cool.

2   Lift the peaches out of the liquid, but do not discard the liquid. Slip off the peach skins and remove the pits while putting chunks of the fruit into the blender. Purée the pulp and measure it: there should be about 5 cups.

3   Return the purée to the pot with the liquid and add ½ cup of sugar for every cup of purée. (I suggest reducing the total of sugar added by ½ cup and tasting later for sweetness; different quality peaches require varying amounts of sugar.) Add nutmeg, cinnamon, 3 or 4 peach stones, and almond extract, and return to the heat, uncovered. Cook slowly until very thick, about 1½ to 2 hours. Stir occasionally. To test thickness, spoon some peach butter into a cold saucer; no ring of

liquid should separate from the edge. Taste for sweetness and add more sugar if needed, then simmer the peach butter for another 10 minutes.

4   Cool, remove the peach stones, then spoon into individual plastic containers and freeze.

COOKING AHEAD

If using frozen Peach Butter, count on a 2-cup container thawing in 2 hours. To serve for breakfast, place in the refrigerator overnight.

Pear gratin

Since the fresh pear season is a relatively long one, there is ample opportunity to try pears in many guises. This is a particularly easy and savory way to prepare them. Graham crackers are added to the liquid in the final baking, producing a thickened sauce that embellishes the baked pears.

SERVES 6

WORKING TIME: *13 minutes*

BAKING TIME: *35 to 45 minutes*

INGREDIENTS

6   **pears**

⅓   **cup quince or apricot jelly (not jam)**

⅓   **cup dry white wine**

1   **tablespoon fruit liqueur, preferably kirsch or orange-flavored**

½   **cup graham cracker crumbs**

2   **tablespoons butter**

PREPARATION

Preheat oven to 350°.

1   Peel the pears and cut them in half lengthwise; with a grapefruit knife scoop out the center seeds. Place them cut side down in a baking or pie dish that will hold them snugly.

2   In a small bowl beat the jelly with a fork or wire whisk until it is fairly smooth. Beat in the wine and liqueur and pour the mixture over the pears. Cover the dish and bake for 20 to 30 minutes, depending on ripeness of the fruit.

3 Remove the cover, sprinkle about 2 teaspoons of graham cracker crumbs over each pear and the remaining crumbs into the cooking liquid. Dot each pear with ½ teaspoon of butter. Return the uncovered dish to oven for 15 minutes.

TO SERVE

Serve hot directly from the baking dish.

COOKING AHEAD

It is best to do only the covered baking in advance and finish the final 15 minutes of baking just before serving. If the entire recipe must be done in advance, cover and reheat the finished dessert in a 350° oven for 10 minutes, adding an extra ¼ cup of white wine.

LOW-CHOLESTEROL VERSION

Substitute polyunsaturated margarine for the butter; no other changes in the recipe are necessary.

Poires en chemise

Here is a recipe to keep handy when you need a fast dessert that has a bit of show. It doesn't even matter how ripe the pears are; the baking will achieve the right degree of softness. Since the pears are baked in tightly sealed packages, all the good flavors you add stay right there and penetrate the fruit.

SERVES 6

WORKING TIME: *12 minutes*

BAKING TIME: *approximately 1 hour*

INGREDIENTS

aluminum foil

6 **pears**

2 **tablespoons sugar**

½ **lemon**

½ **teaspoon vanilla**

1½ **teaspoons orange liqueur (or kirsch, brandy, or vermouth)**

2 **tablespoons butter**

PREPARATION

Preheat oven to 375°.

1 Prepare six 10-inch-square sheets of aluminum foil. Peel the pears, leaving the stems intact and cutting a slice off the bottom so the pears will stand upright. Place a pear in the center of each foil square.

2 In a small bowl mix together the sugar, lemon juice, vanilla, and liqueur. Stir these ingredients well to dissolve the sugar a little. Pour this sweet dressing over the pears and dot each one with 1 teaspoon of butter.

3 Draw up the sides of the foil and close them around the pears to make a tight seal. Place the pears on a baking dish and bake for about 1 hour or until soft, depending on ripeness.

TO SERVE

Place the pears, still in the foil packages, on a platter. At the table the host or hostess should unwrap each package and transfer each pear to an individual dish, spooning some of the sauce over it. (Although I do not think it particularly appetizing to eat directly from the foil, the escaping perfumed steam from each pear looks and smells nice as the package is opened.) These pears are equally delicious served at room temperature.

COOKING AHEAD

The pears can be baked until they just begin to turn soft, then removed, cooled, and refrigerated, still in the foil packages. Finish the baking at serving time. If they must be completely baked in advance, simply reheat them in the oven in the foil; the taste will be the same but the pears will not be quite so solid looking.

LOW-CHOLESTEROL VERSION

Substitute polyunsaturated margarine for the butter and increase the lemon juice to that of a whole lemon.

Pears with ginger

There is an especially nice affinity between the natural sweetness of fresh pears and the tartness of preserved ginger. I really feel that if the Chinese had the tradition for desserts, they might very well offer this one. It meets all their criteria: pretty to look at, not rich and filling, and an interesting combination of flavors.

SERVES 6

WORKING TIME: *12 minutes*

COOKING TIME: *22 to 32 minutes*

CHILLING TIME: *3 hours*

INGREDIENTS

1½	cups sugar
3	cups, plus 3 tablespoons cold water
2	teaspoons powdered ginger
1	strip of orange rind, about 1 by 1½ inches
½	teaspoon vanilla
6	pears, peeled, stems intact
2	tablespoons chopped candied ginger
	juice of ½ lemon
2	teaspoons potato flour, or cornstarch
2	teaspoons rum

PREPARATION

1   Make a light syrup by boiling together in a large straight-sided skillet the sugar, 3 cups of water, powdered ginger, orange rind, and vanilla. Cover and simmer while preparing the pears.

2   Peel the pears, leaving them whole and with the stems intact. Cut a slice off the bottom so the pears will stand upright when served. Add the pears to the syrup, cover, and simmer for 20 to 30 minutes, or until the pears are soft, but not mushy. Turn the pears once or twice during the cooking. The ripeness of the fruit will determine how long they are to cook. Cool the pears in the syrup, still covered.

3   Remove the pears to a serving dish, cover closely with plastic wrap and refrigerate.

4   Remove the orange rind from the cooking syrup and return the skillet to the heat. Add the chopped ginger and lemon juice. Make a thin paste by stirring 3 tablespoons of cold water into the potato flour. Add the paste to the boiling sauce a little at a time until the sauce thickens. The sauce should have a good syrupy consistency, but not be really thick. Thin honey would be a good comparison. Remove the sauce from the fire, add the rum, cool and chill.

TO SERVE

Whether presenting a large serving dish at the table, or pears on individual plates, spoon about 2 tablespoons of the sauce over each pear and pass more sauce separately.

COOKING AHEAD

Pears with Ginger must be prepared in advance, even the day before. Keep the pears and the sauce refrigerated separately.

LOW-CHOLESTEROL VERSION

No changes in the recipe are necessary.

Alsatian pears

The Alsace region of France is famous not only for its fruity white wines, but also for the heavily perfumed fruit liqueurs called eaux de vie (literally, waters of life). Both raspberries and pears abound in the area and both are distilled into crystal-clear after-dinner liqueurs. Before reaching that part of the evening, though, the same two fruits can also be combined into an attractive and refreshing dessert.

SERVES 6

WORKING TIME: 10 minutes

COOKING TIME: 20 to 30 minutes

CHILLING TIME: 3 hours

INGREDIENTS

2 cups dry white wine

1½ cups sugar

juice of 2 lemons

1 cup water

6 pears, peeled, stems intact

2 10-ounce packages frozen raspberries, thawed

2 tablespoons orange liqueur

Optional: whipped cream flavored with sugar, vanilla, and orange liqueur

PREPARATION

1 In a straight-sided pan put the wine, 1 cup of sugar, juice of 1 lemon, and the water, and bring to a boil. Cover and simmer while peeling the pears.

2 Remove a slice from the bottom of each pear so it will be able to stand on a plate. Drop the peeled pears into the syrup, cover and simmer until the fruit is soft, turning carefully with wooden spoons a few times. Do not bruise the fruit. It will take 20 to 30 minutes of cooking time, depending on the size and ripeness of the pears. They are done when a sharp knife pierces the flesh easily. Remove the pan from the fire, and, if time permits, cool the pears in the syrup.

3 While the pears are poaching prepare the sauce. Put in a blender the thawed raspberries, ½ cup sugar, juice of 1 lemon, and orange liqueur. Purée the mixture. (If you have an extra 2 minutes, it's a nice touch to force the sauce through a strainer to remove the seeds.)

4 Lift the pears out of the syrup and let them stand on the sink board for about 5 minutes to drain well. Place the pears in a deep serving dish. Pour the sauce over them and chill well. Turn the pears occasionally if the sauce does not completely cover them.

TO SERVE

Serve the pears directly from the deep dish, 1 pear per person, liberally covered with the sauce. Pass optional whipped cream.

COOKING AHEAD

This dessert must be prepared at least 2 hours in advance, but could also be done the day before.

LOW-CHOLESTEROL VERSION

No changes in the recipe are necessary; omit the optional whipped cream.

Pear compote

This is a cousin to applesauce (which also is a splendid dessert when made at home) but is more delicate in flavor. Pass a large bowl of it and you will be pleased to see how much your guests prefer it to a rich cake at the end of a meal.

MAKES 4 CUPS; SERVES 6

WORKING TIME: *15 minutes*

COOKING TIME: *15 to 25 minutes*

CHILLING TIME: *2 hours*

INGREDIENTS

3   **pounds pears (7 or 8)**

1   **cup water**

½   **teaspoon cinnamon**

½   **teaspoon nutmeg, freshly grated**

     juice of 1 lemon

1   **cup sugar, depending on sweetness of fruit**

½   **teaspoon vanilla**

1   **tablespoon rum**

     Optional: powdered ginger

PREPARATION

1   Peel the pears with a swivel-bladed vegetable peeler; quarter them and cut out cores. Place the fruit in a heavy pot. Add the water, cinnamon, nutmeg, lemon juice and sugar. If the pears are sweet add ¼ cup less sugar. Cover and bring to a fast simmer on top of the stove; then reduce heat and simmer slowly, stirring often.

2   After 10 minutes of cooking, add the vanilla. When stirring, use a wooden spoon and mash the fruit a little.

3   The fruit will give off some liquid during the cooking, and if it seems too thin, uncover the pot and boil rapidly for about 10 minutes to reduce the liquid and thicken the compote. Usually this step is not necessary.

4   When the fruit is completely soft and reduced to a pulp, add the rum and mix well. Remove the pot from the heat and let the fruit cool, still covered.

5   Pass the fruit through a food mill and put it in a deep bowl. Chill well before serving.

TO SERVE

Spoon into individual saucers and sprinkle lightly with powdered ginger.

COOKING AHEAD

This chilled dessert can be made a day or two in advance; it also freezes well.

LOW-CHOLESTEROL VERSION

No changes in the recipe are necessary.

Crème aux poires

At first glance this light and refreshing pear cream may look like plain whipped cream. Only the hint of a deeper color suggests anything different. It's fun to watch faces light up as the pear flavor is discovered. Fortunately the pear season is a fairly long one, and I think you'll serve this dessert often.

SERVES 6

WORKING TIME: *16 minutes*

COOKING TIME: *10 to 20 minutes*

CHILLING TIME: *2 hours*

INGREDIENTS

1	**cup sugar**
½	**cup water**
1	**teaspoon vanilla**
2	**pounds Bartlett pears (4 to 5)**
1	**tablespoon kirsch or other fruit liqueur**
1	**cup heavy cream**

PREPARATION

1 Put the sugar, water, and vanilla in a large flat skillet and bring to a boil. Cover the skillet and simmer the syrup while preparing the pears.

2 Peel the pears, slice them in quarters, and cut out the center core and seeds. When all the pears are ready add them to the syrup. Cover and cook the pears for 10 to 20 minutes, depending on their ripeness. Turn them once or twice during the cooking. Cool the pears in the syrup.

3 Lift the pears out of the syrup and place them in a blender. Add 1 tablespoon of the cooking syrup plus the liqueur and purée the pears. Pour the purée into a mixing bowl and chill it very well.

4 No more than 3 hours before serving time, whip the cream until thick and carefully fold it into the purée. Chill the pear cream again.

TO SERVE

Spoon pear cream into deep individual bowls. Please do not garnish it. Serve with a teaspoon.

COOKING AHEAD

The pear purée can be made anytime, even the day before. The cream can be whipped several hours in advance, but it is best not to combine the two more than 3 hours before serving. Today's whipping cream will begin to separate and exude water after standing awhile.

LOW-CHOLESTEROL VERSION

Reduce the sugar used for poaching the pears to ½ cup. An Italian meringue is substituted for the cup of heavy cream. Put ½ cup plus 1 tablespoon of sugar in a small pot; pour ¼ cup of water over the sugar and place on high heat. While the syrup is cooking purée the pears and scrape them into a large mixing bowl. When the syrup almost reaches the soft-ball stage (238° on a candy thermometer) begin beating 4 egg whites with a pinch of cream of tartar. When the whites are firm and the syrup has reached 238°, pour the hot syrup into the beaten whites while continuing to beat them. After the syrup is incorporated, beat for 1 minute longer. Fold the meringue into the pear purée and chill well.

Banana cream

This is a good variation on the preceding pear cream recipe. The bananas give the dessert a fuller and more exotic flavor.

SERVES 6

WORKING TIME: *10 minutes*

COOKING TIME: *3 minutes*

CHILLING TIME: *2 to 4 hours*

INGREDIENTS

⅓   **cup lemon juice**

4   **bananas**

¾   **cup sugar**

1   **cup whipping cream**

PREPARATION

1   Pour the lemon juice into a blender. Peel the bananas and pull off any fibrous strings. Break the bananas into chunks and add them to the blender. Purée the bananas until smooth.

2   Pour the purée into a heavy pot and add sugar according to taste and the sweetness of the bananas. It is safer to begin with ½ cup and add more later if needed. Put the pot on medium heat and bring the purée just to the boiling point. Remove from heat at once. Scrape the purée into a medium-sized mixing bowl and chill.

3   About 2 hours before serving, whip the cream until very stiff and fold it into the purée. By whipping 1¼ cups of cream you can stretch the recipe to 7 or 8 servings, as well as cut the banana flavor a bit more.

TO SERVE

Spoon Banana Cream into deep individual bowls. Please do not garnish it. Serve with a teaspoon.

COOKING AHEAD

The banana purée can be made hours in advance or even the day before if kept tightly covered in the refrigerator. It is best not to mix the purée and whipping cream together more than 3 hours in advance because today's whipping cream exudes water after several hours.

LOW-CHOLESTEROL VERSION

As in the pear cream recipe, an Italian meringue is substituted for the heavy cream, but the procedure is a little different. Begin the recipe by combining ½ cup plus 1 tablespoon of sugar and ¼ cup of water in a small pot and put it on high heat to boil. Proceed with steps 1 and 2, but add no sugar to the banana purée; 1 tablespoon of polyunsaturated margarine may be added for more richness. When the syrup almost reaches the soft-ball stage (238° on a candy thermometer) begin beating 4 egg whites with a pinch of cream of tartar. When the whites are firm and the syrup reaches 238°, pour the hot syrup into the whites while continuing to beat them. Once the syrup is incorporated, beat for 1 minute more. Let the banana purée just come to the boil, remove it from the heat and pour it over the meringue. Fold the two together carefully and chill well.

Oranges confites

Candied Oranges can be bought in a jar—for a very pretty penny. The high price would lead one to believe that they are difficult to make. This recipe ought to set that straight. There is nothing complicated, pesky, or time-consuming about preparing this relatively inexpensive dessert. Oranges Confites (confit really means "preserved" in French) will keep in the refrigerator for at least two weeks. The long slow cooking thoroughly softens and sweetens the orange rind so it is as good to eat as the pulp. These cooked oranges can be kept on hand to chop or slice and add to vanilla ice cream or fruit cups. Peanut-buttered Bread (page 209) is a nice morsel to serve with this perfumed dessert.

SERVES 6

WORKING TIME: 9 minutes

COOKING TIME: 2 hours 15 minutes

CHILLING TIME: 3 hours

INGREDIENTS

1⅓   cups sugar

4   cups water

2   teaspoons vanilla

½   teaspoon cinnamon

6   seedless oranges

   juice of 1 lemon

   Optional: whipped cream flavored with brandy

PREPARATION

1   In a heavy pot that will hold the oranges snugly make a syrup of the sugar, water, vanilla, and cinnamon. Bring these ingredients to a boil, reduce the heat to medium, cover the pot, and simmer for 15 minutes.

2   Meanwhile, grate the skin of the oranges lightly to remove the least amount of rind possible. This scraping of the skin will allow the syrup to penetrate into the fruit. Instead of a grater, a "zester" can be used to make 6 to 8 regular long scored lines from top to bottom around the orange.

3   Add the oranges to the syrup. The oranges should be three-quarters covered by the syrup. Reduce the heat to low, cover the pot, and slowly cook the oranges for 2 hours. Turn them once or twice during the cooking.

4   Remove the pot from the heat, add the lemon juice, re-cover the pot, and let the oranges cool in the syrup. Chill.

TO SERVE

Place a candied orange on a saucer-shaped dish. Spoon over the orange 1 or 2 tablespoons of the syrup. Provide a fork and a spoon for eating. Pass separately the optional whipped cream and, if you like, Peanut-buttered Bread.

COOKING AHEAD

As noted above, Candied Oranges will keep for at least 2 weeks in the refrigerator.

LOW-CHOLESTEROL VERSION

No changes in the recipe are necessary.

Marrakesh oranges

Not only are these delicious oranges a complete dessert in themselves, but they also can be added inventively to a number of desserts. A few suggestions are listed below, but I'm sure many others will occur to you. Marrakesh Oranges give a textural contrast between the soft fruit and the cooked rind, which retains a bit of crunch. This is a good-looking and completely satisfying dessert for just a few minutes' work.

SERVES 6

WORKING TIME: 5 minutes

COOKING TIME: 30 minutes

CHILLING TIME: 3 hours

INGREDIENTS

2 **cups sugar**

3¼ **cups water**

½ **cup plus 2 tablespoons rum**

4 **seedless navel oranges**

Optional: candied violets, lilacs, or rose petals as garnish

PREPARATION

1 Put the sugar, water, and ½ cup rum in a pot, and bring them to a boil. Reduce the heat, cover the pot, and simmer the syrup for 10 minutes.

2 Meanwhile, cut off the thick ends of the oranges and discard. Cut the oranges into slices about ¼ inch thick. When the syrup is ready, add the oranges and any juice that may have collected from them. Cover and simmer for 20 minutes.

3 Remove the pot from the heat, add the remaining 2 tablespoons of rum, re-cover at once, and put aside to cool. Chill in the refrigerator for 2 hours.

TO SERVE

Arrange 4 or 5 orange slices on an individual plate and sprinkle with the optional candied flowers. (The orange slices can also be placed in a deep bowl—glass is particularly pretty— and sprinkled with the garnish.)

COOKING AHEAD

Marrakesh Oranges must be made at least 3 hours in advance. But since they will keep for a week or more, make them at your leisure.

LOW-CHOLESTEROL VERSION

No changes in the recipe are necessary.

Marrakesh-orange fruit plate

Though Marrakesh Oranges are good by themselves, they also add an exotic note to simple fruit combinations. The trio of fruits listed below makes an especially attractive pattern on the plate, and capitalizes on whatever fruits are in season.

SERVES 6

WORKING TIME: 4 minutes

INGREDIENTS

2 **oranges, cooked Marrakesh style**

2 **bananas**

Optional: orange liqueur

½ **cup grated coconut**

6 **large or 12 medium strawberries**

PREPARATION

1 Select 6 salad-size plates. Make a circle of the orange slices just inside the edge of the plate. Cut the bananas into ¼-inch slices and make 1 or 2 circles working toward the center, but leaving the center empty. The number of circles will depend on the size of the plates and how copious a dessert you want to make.

2 Sprinkle a tablespoon of the syrup from the oranges and the optional liqueur over the fruit. Sprinkle with coconut and place the strawberries in the center.

Angel food cake à la marrakesh

SERVES 8

WORKING TIME: 4 minutes

INGREDIENTS

½ large or 1 small angel food cake
2 oranges cooked Marrakesh style
   rum
   Optional: candied flowers for garnish

PREPARATION

1 While the oranges are cooking, carefully cut the cake horizontally into three slices. As soon as the oranges are cooked, pour about ¼ cup of the hot syrup and 1 tablespoon of rum over each slice of angel food cake. Put the slices back together in the cake's original shape and let stand. Re-cover the pot and let the oranges cool.

2 Coarsely chop half the orange slices. Separate the cake layers and spread the chopped orange on top of the two bottom layers. Re-form the cake into its original shape and arrange the remaining orange slices over the top layer. Decorate with the candied flowers.

COOKING AHEAD

Prepare the orange slices and refrigerate. A few hours before serving, reheat about 1 cup of the orange syrup and proceed as in step 1.

LOW-CHOLESTEROL VERSION

No changes in the recipe are necessary.

Sponge cake à la marrakesh

SERVES 8

WORKING TIME: 4 minutes

INGREDIENTS

1 sponge cake
2 oranges cooked Marrakesh style
   rum
   Optional: candied flowers, and whipped cream

PREPARATION

1 Follow the preceding directions for the angel food cake. Serve with whipped cream.

2 Individual servings can be prepared by placing a slice of sponge cake on a dessert plate and sprinkling it liberally with the hot syrup and rum. Arrange 2 or 3 cooled orange slices over the cake and garnish with candied flowers. Serve with whipped cream.

COOKING AHEAD

See directions for the angel food cake.

Coffee cream custard

The real reason French Crème Caramel is so popular is the caramel. Plain custard at the end of a meal can be too cloying and rich. It needs to be cut with some sparkling flavor. Here the same effect is achieved with coffee, which is much easier to sprinkle in than cooking up a caramel. Coffee Cream Custard has a nutty brown color and is a cool delight on the tongue.

Instead of passing the usual cookies with this special custard, try something novel. Cut pound or sponge cake into even slices and, just before serving, fry them in hot butter. The ice-cold custard with the warm, mellow cake makes a sparkling combination. Since it takes just a few minutes to do the frying, you will not be away from the table very long. I fry the cake while clearing the dishes for dessert. The cake can be kept in the freezer for this purpose. If sliced before it has completely thawed, it will cut more easily and evenly.

SERVES 6

WORKING TIME: *8 minutes*

BAKING TIME: *1¼ hours*

CHILLING TIME: *2 hours*

INGREDIENTS

2	**cups milk**
1	**cup water**
2	**tablespoons instant coffee**
3	**eggs**
3	**egg yolks**
½	**cup cream**
¾	**cup sugar**
1	**teaspoon vanilla**

PREPARATION

Preheat oven to 350°.

1 Select a heavy nonaluminum pot that will hold 1 quart. Pour the milk into the pot and slowly bring it to the boiling point. Meanwhile, boil 1 cup of water and pour it over the instant coffee. Stir the dissolved coffee into the milk.

2 While the milk is heating, put the eggs and yolks in a large mixing bowl and beat together thoroughly with a wire whisk. Then beat in the cream and sugar.

3 When the milk just reaches the boiling point, slowly pour it into the egg mixture, while beating with the whisk. Add vanilla and beat again.

4 Pour half the coffee-cream into a 10-inch pie dish or a 6-cup soufflé dish. Set the dish in a larger pan with enough water to reach halfway up the side of the dish. Place the pan in the oven. Pour in the rest of the coffee-cream, or enough to fill the dish to the top. Any leftover cream can be baked in individual custard cups. Reduce the heat to 325° and bake about 1¼ hours, or until a knife plunged into the center will come out clean and dry. Remove the custard dish from the pan of water and cool, then chill very well. It must be served icy cold.

TO SERVE

Place the baking dish on a larger dinner plate and pass at the table with two large spoons for serving.

COOKING AHEAD

Since coffee custard must be chilled, it is essential to prepare it in advance. It can even be baked the day before serving.

REMARKS

A pie dish is the more classic presentation, but it is wide and can present a problem when selecting a large pan to hold the water. A cookie pan with edges is my solution. Place the pie dish in it, and finally pour in the water.

Strawberry surprise for Carlo

Carlo is an appreciative young fan whose words of greeting invariably are "What new have you baked for me?" Desserts are always firmly in mind. Thanks to his incentive a new kind of custard emerged from the oven—a strawberry delight. The juice from frozen berries flavors the custard and the berries themselves are puréed to spread as a topping. Its handsome presentation completely disguises the reasonable cost. Since this was a November treat for Carlo, frozen berries had to be used. This is one way to serve them without any apologies.

SERVES 6 TO 8

WORKING TIME: 13 minutes

COOKING TIME: 1¼ to 1½ hours

CHILLING TIME: 3 hours

INGREDIENTS

1	16-ounce box frozen sliced strawberries, thawed
2¼	cups milk
6	tablespoons sugar
½	teaspoon vanilla
½	cup rice
1	cup heavy cream
1	tablespoon cornstarch
3	eggs
1	tablespoon orange liqueur
2	teaspoons butter
½	cup ground walnuts

PREPARATION

Preheat oven to 375 degrees.

1 Put a sieve over a small bowl, dump in the berries, and put aside to drain.

2 Pour 2 cups of milk in a heavy, non-aluminum pot. Add 2 tablespoons of sugar and the vanilla and bring to a slow simmer. Stir in the rice. When the milk returns to a slow simmer, cover the pot, reduce the heat to very low and cook for 20 minutes. Stir once or twice during the cooking. The milk should be completely absorbed. Fluff the cooked rice with a fork.

3 Meanwhile, measure the strawberry juice; there should be 1 cup, if not add milk. Pour the juice into a heavy non-aluminum pot and add the cream. (If the rice is cooked in advance, the same pot can be used.) Stir in 4 tablespoons of sugar and put on the fire. Bring the liquid almost to the boiling point. While heating the cream and the juice, put the cornstarch in a small mixing bowl and add the eggs; whisk until smooth. When the liquid is quite hot, slowly pour it over the eggs while whisking briskly. Add the orange liqueur and beat again.

4 Smear the butter in a 9-inch pie dish. Pat the rice into a smooth layer in the dish. Pour the custard sauce over the rice and place the pie dish in a pan containing about a half-inch of water.* Place the pan in the oven and reduce the heat to 325 degrees. Bake for ¾ hour.

5 Purée the drained berries in the blender. Spread them over the partially baked custard and sprinkle the ground nuts over the top. Return to the oven for 30 minutes. Test for doneness by jiggling the pie dish. If the center remains solid and doesn't jiggle, the custard has set. The usual knife-test cannot be used here because the moist berry purée prevents an accurate determination of dryness. Cool, then chill.

TO SERVE

Place the pie dish on a round platter and cut in wedges at the table. Lift out the portions with a spatula, making certain that the rice layer is included.

COOKING AHEAD

Note: An attractive effect can be created by smoothing the purée into a wide circle, leaving the center clear. The pale pink custard peeking through makes a pretty contrast.

Meringue des îles

An inexpensive way to make this offbeat dessert is to save egg whites from recipes calling for yolks only. Egg whites freeze perfectly. Just keep adding them to a container in the freezer, marking on a tag how many whites there are. When you have collected six, make Meringue des Iles and no one will guess that you haven't been extravagant. Do not use too large a baking dish since, even though the meringue puffs up impressively in the oven, it will shrink somewhat as it cools.

SERVES 6

WORKING TIME: *12 minutes*

BAKING TIME: *45 minutes to 1 hour*

INGREDIENTS

1½	**cups sugar**
½	**cup water**
6	**egg whites, room temperature**
¼	**teaspoon cream of tartar**
1	**teaspoon vanilla**
2	**tablespoons plus 2 teaspoons instant coffee**
2	**tablespoons cornstarch**
1	**teaspoon oil**
	Hot Chocolate Sauce (page 219)

PREPARATION

Preheat oven to 325°.

1 In a small pot boil the sugar and water to the soft-ball stage (238° on a candy thermometer). When the syrup reaches 100° on the thermometer, begin beating the egg whites with an electric beater. Sprinkle on the cream of tartar and beat the whites until very firm.

2 Pour the hot syrup over the beaten whites while continuing to beat at a fast speed. Turn the speed to high and beat for 2 minutes more. Add the vanilla and 2 tablespoons of instant coffee. Beat again at high speed until the flavorings are thoroughly blended in. Lightly fold in the cornstarch.

3 Lightly oil an 8-cup soufflé mold and scoop the meringue into it. Tap the dish on the counter a few times to settle the meringue into it. Smooth the top with a spatula and sprinkle 2 teaspoons of instant coffee over it.

4 Place the soufflé mold in a pan containing 1 inch of hot water. Place the pan in the oven and bake for 45 minutes to 1 hour, or until the meringue puffs and begins pulling away from the sides. Remove from the oven and cool. The meringue will shrink somewhat.

TO SERVE

Place the soufflé dish on a round dish and at table cut into the meringue with two spoons. Spoon the hot chocolate sauce over the meringue.

COOKING AHEAD

The meringue can be made easily in the morning for dinner. It is best not to make it a day before.

LOW-CHOLESTEROL VERSION

No changes in the recipe are necessary.

Honey mousse

Do you know someone with a terribly sweet tooth? Here is his kind of recipe. Honey Mousse comes from Central Europe where honey is a favorite flavoring for everything from tea to cakes to frothy concoctions like this. For those who prefer a less sweet dessert, just serve smaller portions of the mousse. It is delicious, and a little goes a long way.

SERVES 6 TO 8

WORKING TIME: *11 minutes*

COOKING TIME: *5 to 6 minutes*

CHILLING TIME: *2 hours*

5   eggs, separated

1   cup honey

1   teaspoon vanilla

   pinch cream of tartar

1   Separate the eggs, putting the yolks in a heavy pot and the whites in a mixing bowl. Add the honey and vanilla to the yolks and beat together with an electric beater for a few seconds. Put the pot on medium heat and cook the eggs and honey while continuing beating.

2   When the mixture begins to bubble, reduce the heat, but continue beating over the heat until the honey and yolks double in volume and thicken. This should take about 5 minutes. Scrape the cooked honey into a bowl and cool.

3   Add cream of tartar to the egg whites and beat them until quite firm. Fold ⅓ of the beaten whites into the honey until well blended. Lightly fold in the rest of the whites. Spoon the mousse into a large serving bowl or individual dessert dishes. Chill well.

Serve the chilled Honey Mousse with crisp, not-too-sweet cookies.

Honey Mousse can be made as much as ½ day in advance.

Baked strawberries

The better the berries, the better this warm dessert obviously will be. On the other hand, if the berries aren't top quality, they will be vastly improved by this mingling of good flavors.

SERVES 6

WORKING TIME: *9 minutes*

BAKING TIME: *20 minutes*

5   tablespoons butter

1   quart strawberries

2   tablespoons orange juice

2   tablespoons orange liqueur

1½   cups graham cracker crumbs

4   tablespoons brown sugar

   Optional: whipped cream flavored with orange liqueur

Preheat oven to 350°.

1   Smear 1 tablespoon of butter in a 2-quart baking dish or pie pan. Hull and rinse the berries and place them close together in the baking dish. Sprinkle orange juice and orange liqueur over them.

2   Sprinkle graham cracker crumbs and brown sugar over the berries; less crumbs and less sugar may be used, the amount will depend on size of dish. Smooth crumbs and sugar together lightly with the palms of your hands. Melt 4 tablespoons of butter and dribble on. Bake for 20 minutes.

Serve very warm, but not hot out of the oven. Pass with optional whipped cream.

Berries can be rinsed and hulled and placed in the buttered dish. The remaining ingredients, however, should be added just before the dessert is baked. This will take less than a minute. The baked strawberries can be held for 15 to 20 minutes before serving.

Substitute polyunsaturated margarine for the butter; no other changes in the recipe are necessary.

Chocolate soufflé

Many people consider chocolate soufflé the ultimate dessert. Some restaurants stake their reputation on it. At Lei Mouscardins, a chic fish restaurant that overlooks the sparkling St. Tropez harbor, the most popular house specialty is a delicious chocolate soufflé baked in the untraditional gratin dish.

Classically, the soufflé must be put together at the last minute, a forbidding chore for most home chefs. Now this grand finale can be presented with ease since it can wait in the mold several hours before going into the oven.

INGREDIENTS

1   tablespoon soft butter

¾   cup sugar

½   cup water

1   tablespoon instant coffee

6   ounces semisweet chocolate

6   eggs

½   cup cream

1   tablespoon Grand Marnier, or other orange liqueur

12   ounces cream cheese

Optional: additional 2 egg whites for a lighter soufflé

PREPARATION

Preheat oven to 375°.

1   Select a 6-cup soufflé dish or other mold and grease it liberally with the butter. Sprinkle in ¼ cup of the sugar and rotate the mold to coat it with the sugar. If any spot is left uncoated, butter it and sprinkle on a little more sugar. Shake out the excess.

2   Put the remaining ½-cup sugar, water, coffee, and chocolate into a small saucepan and melt together over low heat. Remove from heat and cool slightly.

3   Break the eggs into a blender and add the cream and Grand Marnier. Blend for about a half-minute or until the eggs and cream are thoroughly mixed. With the blender running, scrape in the melted chocolate and then the cream cheese, breaking the cheese into chunks as you add

it. When the batter is completely mixed, blend at high speed for a few seconds.

4   Pour the batter to the ¾ level of the prepared dish and place in the hot oven. Bake for about 50 to 60 minutes for a soufflé that is still moist in the center. You can test by gently shaking the dish. If the center is still soft, it will jiggle. An absolutely flat or slightly convex surface indicates that the soufflé has been cooked firm throughout. This means you will not have the soft center to use as a sauce over the baked portions.

COOKING AHEAD

As noted above, this soufflé can be prepared several hours in advance, placed in its mold, and kept in a cool spot. If the kitchen is very hot, put the soufflé in the refrigerator, but allow an extra 5 minutes for the baking.

Apricot sherbet

This refreshing apricot sherbet can be made in a shorter time than it would take to go to the corner grocery store and buy some. If a last-minute dinner is being put together, whip up this dessert first thing, put it in a metal container and by the end of the meal the sherbet will be ready.

SERVES 6

WORKING TIME: 4 minutes

FREEZING TIME: 2 to 3 hours

INGREDIENTS

1   1-pound-14-ounce can apricots

juice of 1 or 2 lemons

2   teaspoons kirsch or other fruit liqueur

PREPARATION

1   Select a deep mixing bowl because the liquid will splatter during the beating. Pour the apricots and their syrup into the bowl. Add the lemon juice and liqueur. If you don't have any liqueur, use the juice of 2 lemons.

2 Beat with an electric beater until the fruit is broken into small bits; this will take 2 to 3 minutes. If you find there is a lot of splattering, hold a lid, tilted, over the bowl, or put the bowl in the sink.

Note: Do not be tempted to use a blender to make this sherbet. The fruit will be puréed too smoothly and the sherbet will be very icy.

3 Pour the sherbet into a metal container for fast freezing, or any other container for normal freezing. After 1 hour in the freezer stir the sherbet to break up the ice crystals.

TO SERVE

Beat the sherbet with a wooden spoon and spoon it into individual dishes. Serve with cookies.

COOKING AHEAD

Obviously the sherbet must be made in advance. If it is held in the freezer for more than a day, let the sherbet stand at room temperature for about 30 minutes, then beat with a wooden spoon to break up the icy crystals.

LOW-CHOLESTEROL VERSION

No changes in the recipe are necessary.

Lemon sherbet

Lemon Sherbet is a wonderfully fresh dessert. Whether served alone or with Champagne Fruit Cup (page 185) it is universally appreciated the year round. Since only a few minutes are needed to prepare this recipe with ingredients costing well under a dollar, even the busiest of cooks should give up forever prepackaged factory-produced sherbets that get their flavor from chemicals rather than the pure fruit.

SERVES 6

WORKING TIME: *8 minutes*

COOKING TIME: *5 to 10 minutes*

FREEZING TIME: *3 to 4 hours*

INGREDIENTS

1½ **cups sugar**

3½ **cups water**

¾ **cup lemon juice (4 to 5 lemons)**

PREPARATION

1 Boil the sugar and water together in a small pot for 5 to 10 minutes (220° on a candy thermometer). Meanwhile squeeze the lemon juice and strain it into a mixing bowl.

2 Pour the juice into the sugar syrup and bring it back just to the boiling point. Remove the pot from the heat at once. Cool the mixture, then freeze for several hours or until the sherbet is mushy.

3 Beat the sherbet until it is light and fluffy, then return it to the freezer until it is firm. For a different presentation, freeze the sherbet in a loaf pan, soufflé dish, or other mold.

TO SERVE

Spoon the sherbet into individual dishes and pass with plain cookies. A sprig of mint makes a pretty garnish. If the sherbet has been frozen in a mold, fold a clean dish towel to the approximate size of the mold and place it on a chilled serving platter. (The towel is used to prevent the sherbet from sliding while it is being cut into slices.) With a hot knife cut the sherbet loose from the mold on all sides, then dip the bottom of the mold in hot water for a few seconds. Reverse the sherbet onto the towel and smooth the sides with a spatula.

COOKING AHEAD

Since this sherbet will not turn icy it can be made several days in advance and kept in the freezer.

LOW-CHOLESTEROL VERSION

No changes in the recipe are necessary.

Tropical sherbet

The recipe that I first saw for this sherbet rather snootily insisted on bananas from the Canary Islands and fresh pineapple from the Azores. I suppose they make a difference, but a dessert this good shouldn't wait for the rare occasions when such exotic fruits are available. The recipe has been adapted with supermarket shopping in mind. The end result still has the lush taste of the tropics.

SERVES 8

WORKING TIME: 10 minutes

FREEZING TIME: 3 hours

INGREDIENTS

juice of 2 lemons

½ **cup orange juice**

1 **20-ounce can pineapple chunks**

2 **pounds ripe bananas (5 or 6)**

1 **cup heavy cream**

1 **cup apricot jelly**

¼ **cup water**

1 **tablespoon kirsch or other fruit liqueur**

PREPARATION

1 Put the lemon and orange juices in a blender. Drain the pineapple chunks and add 1 cup of the syrup and the pineapple pieces to the other juices. Begin puréeing while peeling and adding chunks of bananas. Increase blender speed as necessary to make a very smooth purée.

2 Whip the cream until it is very thick but not stiff. Pour the fruit purée into the cream and fold it in well with a spatula or wooden spoon. Once the cream and purée are blended, beat for ½ minute with a wire whisk.

3 Pour the sherbet into an 8-cup mold (soufflé dish or bread loaf pan) and freeze.

4 Prepare the sauce by melting the apricot jelly, water, and kirsch together. Bring the mixture to one boil and remove from the heat. Cool, then chill.

TO SERVE

Remove the sherbet from the freezer ½ hour before serving. Unmold it onto a chilled platter or scoop the sherbet directly from the mold. Pass the chilled sauce separately.

COOKING AHEAD

Like all frozen desserts, sherbet must be made in advance, but not more than 2 days.

Granita al caffè

Here is a crisp, nonrich way to finish a meal. Coffee ice, in true Italian style, should be slightly icy, but only slightly so. The final beating of the granita breaks up the hard ice and turns the dessert into a frothy heap. Since it costs only a few pennies, it is a wise use of 7 minutes to make some ahead and keep it ready for any last-minute need for a dessert.

SERVES 4

WORKING TIME: 7 minutes

COOKING TIME: about 10 minutes

FREEZING TIME: 3 to 4 hours

INGREDIENTS

½ **cup sugar**

3 **cups water**

2 **tablespoons instant coffee**

1 **teaspoon brandy**

1 **teaspoon rum**

PREPARATION

1 Boil the sugar and 2½ cups of water in a small pot for about 10 minutes (210° on a candy thermometer).

2 Meanwhile boil ½ cup water while measuring the coffee and liquors into a mixing bowl. Pour the boiling water over the coffee and stir to dissolve the grains. Pour in the syrup and cool.

3 Put the bowl in a freezer for 3 to 4 hours. Before the granita is completely frozen, beat it to break up the ice crystals. This can be done once or twice.

4 Just before serving beat the *granita* with a wooden spoon until it is frothy. Work fast, beating for only a minute or so. Heap into individual bowls and serve at once.

COOKING AHEAD

Like all frozen desserts, *granita* must be prepared in advance.

LOW-CHOLESTEROL VERSION

No changes in the recipe are necessary.

Champagne snow

Whenever you have a fine champagne, by all means drink it, preferably with a close friend. If it's cheap, cook with it and nobody will know it's not Dom Perignon. Reasonably priced champagne does not necessarily mean bad champagne. But it can never approximate the fine vintage products that bubble out of the Champagne district around Epernay, France. There are several kinds of inexpensive champagnes. Some of the best are the vins mousseux (bubbly wines) that come from France but from outside the restricted Champagne area. They can be quite good, especially if they are brut (very, very dry). American champagnes are another even less expensive solution.

Why can't still white wine be substituted for champagne in cooking? It can, but the results won't be the same. There is an indefinable spark that comes only from the real stuff. You can still taste the champagne in this frozen dessert, which is not as firm as ice cream or sherbet. It is soft and fluffy, just like snow. It also melts quickly, providing the pleasure of drinking what you don't eat first.

SERVES 8

WORKING TIME: *6 minutes*

COOKING TIME: *approximately 4 minutes*

FREEZING TIME: *4 to 5 hours*

INGREDIENTS

1 **cup sugar**

1 **cup water**

¼ **teaspoon salt**

¾ **cup orange juice**

juice of 1 lemon

1 **bottle champagne, chilled**

1 **egg white, lightly beaten**

Optional decoration: crystallized flowers or chopped candied orange peel

PREPARATION

1 Boil the sugar, water, and salt together to the soft-ball stage (230° on a candy thermometer); this will take about 3 minutes. Add the orange and lemon juices and bring to a boil. Remove the pot from the heat and cool this syrup.

2 Pour the syrup into a large bowl, add half the bottle of champagne, and mix. Place the bowl in the freezer and freeze until mushy. Beat the frozen crystals until they turn almost liquid again; add the egg white and the remaining half-bottle of champagne. Return the bowl to the freezer.

3 Stir from time to time to prevent the snow from getting too icy. Freeze for several hours; the exact amount of time will depend on the efficiency of the freezer.

TO SERVE

Chill individual serving bowls, and at the last moment, spoon the Champagne Snow into each bowl and decorate with the flowers or orange peel.

COOKING AHEAD

Champagne Snow must be made at least 4 hours before serving. It can also be made a day in advance.

LOW-CHOLESTEROL VERSION

No changes in the recipe are necessary.

Frozen maple mousse

Taking maple syrup off the breakfast table and using its crisp flavor for dessert is a sure way to win compliments. This frozen mousse also is convenient for parties since it can be made days ahead. If half the recipe is made, the preparation time is 5 minutes less.

SERVES 10

WORKING TIME: *17 minutes*

FREEZING TIME: *3 to 4 hours*

INGREDIENTS

4	eggs, separated
1	cup pure maple syrup
1½	teaspoons maple flavoring
1	tablespoon dark rum, or to taste
1	cup whipping cream
	pinch of cream of tartar
1	teaspoon oil
¾	cup chopped or ground black walnuts, or English walnuts

PREPARATION

1   Put the egg yolks in a small heavy pot and beat them until light, then add the syrup. Put the pot on low heat and heat through just until the liquid is hot to the finger. Be careful not to overcook. Remove at once from the heat and stir in the maple flavoring and rum. Scrape this syrup into a large mixing bowl.

2   While the syrup is heating, beat the cream until firm. Then using the same beaters, beat the syrup until it is light and frothy. Fold the cream into the syrup.

3   Add the cream of tartar to the egg whites and beat until firm. Fold the beaten whites into the mixture, one half at a time.

4   Lightly oil a 9-cup mold (a soufflé dish looks nicest) and sprinkle nuts on the bottom. If you prefer not to reverse the mousse after freezing, simply sprinkle the nuts on top and serve directly from the mold. Spoon in the mousse and freeze.

TO SERVE

Cut around the mold with a hot knife and dip the bottom of the mold into hot water. Turn onto a serving dish.

COOKING AHEAD

Like all frozen desserts, this maple mousse must be prepared in advance.

Jamaican squares

Sugar and spice and a tot of rum give these delicious cookies their island character. They are crisp on the outside, chewy within, and never stay on the dish very long. Any Jamaican Squares that happen to be left over can be frozen for later enjoyment.

Although this recipe makes only 1 pan of cookies (about 36 pieces), you will find it goes a long way since they are quite rich. If you happen to be out of rum, substitute brandy; orange, cherry, or plum liqueur; or even orange, apple, or pineapple juice. Rum, though, is still the best.

MAKES ABOUT 36 COOKIES

WORKING TIME: *8 minutes*

BAKING TIME: *30 minutes*

INGREDIENTS

2   tablespoons butter

1   cup sugar

¾   cup flour

1   teaspoon baking powder

1   teaspoon cinnamon

½   teaspoon freshly grated nutmeg

¼   teaspoon ground cloves

1   cup chopped dry dates, coated with
       sugar

1   cup chopped walnuts or pecans

2   eggs

1   tablespoon rum

       powdered sugar

PREPARATION

Preheat oven to 350°.

1   Liberally butter and flour a 9-inch-square cake pan. In a bowl blend together the sugar, flour, baking powder, cinnamon, nutmeg, and cloves. Mix the dates and nuts into the flour. Beat the eggs with the rum and stir into the dry ingredients.

2   Spoon the batter into the cake pan and smooth the top with a spatula. Bake for 25 to 30 minutes, or until the top is lightly browned. Remove the pan from the oven and immediately sprinkle with powdered sugar. While the baked batter is still warm cut it into squares or rectangles.

COOKING AHEAD

Jamaican Squares can be made a day or two before serving. They also can be frozen.

LOW-CHOLESTEROL VERSION

Instead of the eggs use ½ cup liquid egg substitute or 2 egg whites, plus 1 tablespoon polyunsaturated oil. Grease the pan with polyunsaturated margarine.

Orange-mincemeat squares

Here is a filled cookie that doesn't require all the usual time-consuming steps. Moist, luscious mincemeat is simply spread between layers of batter. This makes a rich cookie, so I do not recommend cutting it into large squares—but make plenty.

Since I like to make these cookies the year round, I buy extra jars of mincemeat at holiday time. You may not have noticed, but most stores do not carry the item except for those few months of heavy demand. Inventory controls dictate that we eat mincemeat only in November and December, but I find these little cakes are equally popular with cooling summer drinks.

MAKES ABOUT 36 COOKIES

WORKING TIME: *12 minutes*

BAKING TIME: *35 minutes*

INGREDIENTS

1½ **cups flour**

1 **cup brown sugar, firmly packed**

¾ **teaspoon salt**

2½ **cups oatmeal**

⅓ **cup orange juice**

⅔ **cup butter or margarine, melted**

1½ **cups prepared mincemeat**

1 **teaspoon orange liqueur**

1 **teaspoon brandy**

PREPARATION

Preheat oven to 350°.

1 In a bowl mix together the flour, brown sugar, salt, and 2 cups of the rolled oats. Sprinkle on the orange juice and melted butter; stir with a fork until the mixture is thoroughly combined. It will be quite moist.

2 Grease an 8- or 9-inch square cake pan; pack half the batter in smoothly. Spread the mincemeat over the batter, sprinkle it with the liqueurs and smooth it with the back of a spoon.

3 Mix the remaining ½ cup of oats with the rest of the batter. Spread this over the top of the mincemeat in an even layer.

4 Place in the preheated oven and bake for 35 minutes. Cool in the pan, then cut into squares.

COOKING AHEAD

These cookies freeze perfectly; cut into squares before freezing.

LOW-CHOLESTEROL VERSION

Use polyunsaturated margarine; no other changes in the recipe are necessary.

Peanut-buttered bread

The peanut butter and jelly sandwich has long been a boon to harassed mothers. Lunchtime, snack-time, in-between times, that all-American standby has provided tasty, inexpensive, protein-rich eating. So why change it? Only to make it better. Here is a do-ahead recipe that will put prepared peanut-buttered bread in the freezer. No defrosting time is necessary. Jelly can still be spread on for a snack. It can also be turned into a quick dessert with ice cream or stewed fruit heaped on top. Summer salads are given an extra lift when served with this crunchy tidbit. All this, and still something easy enough for the kids to do themselves.

MAKES 40 TO 60 SNACKS, DEPENDING ON SIZE

WORKING TIME: *11 minutes*

OVEN TIME: *10 minutes*

COOLING TIME: *1 hour*

INGREDIENTS

1   **1-pound loaf day-old sliced white bread**

1   **12-ounce jar creamy peanut butter**

½   **cup peanut oil**

1   **teaspoon vanilla**

1   **tablespoon sugar**

1   **cup wheat germ**

PREPARATION

Preheat oven to 250°.

1   Remove all crusts from the bread. Cut the bread slices into any shape you like— triangles, strips, squares, or rectangles. Put the sliced bread on a baking sheet and place in the oven for 10 minutes, or just until dry to the touch.

2   Meanwhile put in a saucepan the peanut butter, oil, vanilla, and sugar. Heat slowly on a low fire.

3   Spread some of the wheat germ in a small dish. Holding a piece of bread on a fork, dip it into the melted peanut butter, hold the bread above the pot for a second or two to allow the excess sauce to drip off. Transfer the bread to the dish and coat all surfaces with wheat germ. Add wheat germ to dish as needed. Place the bread slices on waxed paper and let them dry for at least 1 hour.

COOKING AHEAD

Peanut-buttered Bread must be prepared at least 1 hour before serving. It can be eaten immediately, refrigerated, or frozen.

LOW-CHOLESTEROL VERSION

Substitute polyunsaturated oil for peanut oil.

Blueberry clafouti

Clafouti *is a funny name for a delicious homespun dessert — a kind of baked thick fruit pancake. It is most popular in the Limousin region of south central France where it is traditionally made with black cherries. To save time, blueberries have been substituted for cherries, thus eliminating the chore of pitting. Other fruits can also be used: fresh peaches, pears, apricots, or tart apples. Though clafouti (sometimes spelled with a final "s") is considered a family dessert, guests will enjoy it no less. It is best served hot or warm.*

SERVES 8

WORKING TIME: *10 minutes*

BAKING TIME: *approximately 35 minutes*

INGREDIENTS

3½	**tablespoons butter**
3	**cups blueberries**
4	**eggs**
1	**cup milk**
¼	**cup cream**
	pinch salt
¼	**teaspoon nutmeg**
1	**teaspoon lemon juice**
1	**tablespoon vanilla**
2	**tablespoons orange liqueur**
1¼	**cups flour**
½	**cup sugar**
	Optional: powdered sugar

PREPARATION

Preheat oven to 375°.

1 Slowly melt 3 tablespoons of butter while rinsing and picking over the berries. Smear ½ tablespoon of butter in a 6- or 7-cup pie dish or cake pan and pour in the berries. Smooth into a neat layer.

2 Put in the blender the eggs, melted butter, milk, cream, salt, nutmeg, lemon juice, vanilla, and liqueur; blend. Add the flour and sugar and blend again until thoroughly mixed. Pour this batter over the berries.

3 Put the baking dish in the oven and bake for about 30 minutes or until the batter rises and puffs a little and a knife plunged into the center comes out clean. Serve hot or warm. *Clafouti* will shrink back into the dish a little as it cools. If it is to be served cold, sprinkle with powdered sugar just before serving.

COOKING AHEAD

If you plan serving the *clafouti* hot or warm, prepare the berries in the buttered dish and mix the batter. Refrigerate the batter and pour over the berries just before baking. Add 5 minutes to the baking time.

LOW-CHOLESTEROL VERSION

Use these ingredients and follow the steps outlined above: 3 cups blueberries, 5½ tablespoons polyunsaturated margarine (5 tablespoons melted, ½ tablespoon to grease the pie dish), 5 egg whites, 1¼ cups polyunsaturated liquid dairy cream substitute, 2 teaspoons lemon juice, 1 tablespoon plus 1 teaspoon vanilla, 3 tablespoons orange liqueur, 1½ cups flour, and ½ cup sugar. If the top of the *clafouti* does not turn a light brown during the cooking because of the lack of egg yolks, slip the pie dish under the broiler for ½ minute.

Blueberried cake

When blueberries are in season, I think they should be served as often as possible. One could begin the day with them at breakfast and, after dinner, this blueberry dessert will prove a treat worth waiting for. It's quite economical, too, since almost any kind of leftover white or yellow cake can be used. If the cake has an icing, though, it should be scraped off. Lacking leftover cake, use plain white bread, plus some extra sugar in the recipe.

SERVES 6

WORKING TIME: *11 minutes*

BAKING TIME: *30 minutes*

INGREDIENTS

2	cups (1 pint) blueberries
2½	tablespoons butter
3	cups cubed cake (angel food, sponge, layer) or white bread, crusts removed
½	cup orange juice
1	teaspoon cinnamon
¼	teaspoon nutmeg
	For bread: ½ cup sugar
2	eggs, well beaten
½	cup brown sugar
1	teaspoon lemon juice
1	teaspoon orange liqueur
	Optional: orange-flavored whipped cream, or plain heavy cream

PREPARATION

Preheat oven to 400°.

1 Rinse the berries and pick off any stems. Leave berries in a sieve to drain well. Melt the butter in a saucepan.

2 Cut the cake (or bread) into ½-inch cubes and place them in a mixing bowl. Pour the orange juice and melted butter over the cake. Sprinkle on the cinnamon and nutmeg. (Add the sugar for bread.) Toss all together with your hands. Beat the eggs in a small cup and pour over the cake; then beat the batter well with a wooden spoon for a few seconds.

3 Scrape the batter into a pie dish and flatten the top with the back of a spoon. Place the blueberries on top in an even layer. Sprinkle with brown sugar, lemon juice, and orange liqueur and bake for 30 minutes.

TO SERVE

Serve warm or cool. Cut portions with a knife and, using a spatula, place on dessert plates. Pass optional whipped cream or heavy cream.

COOKING AHEAD

Blueberried Cake can be made several hours in advance, but it is better made the same day.

LOW-CHOLESTEROL VERSION

Substitute polyunsaturated margarine for the butter and ½ cup liquid egg substitute for the whole eggs. Do not pass the optional cream.

Cobbled peach bake

This summertime treat closely resembles the famous French clafouti. Both are based on fresh fruits baked in a thin batter, the difference being in the more custardlike consistency of the Gallic version. This homespun pie is just as delicious and is easy to do. It is best served warm while it is still nice and puffy. Once chilled, it collapses a little and is less attractive, but it could easily be covered with whipped cream, and then who would know the difference?

SERVES 10 TO 12

WORKING TIME: *13 minutes*

BAKING TIME: *40 to 45 minutes*

INGREDIENTS

1	**stick butter**
1¼	**cups flour**
¼	**teaspoon salt**
1	**cup sugar**
3	**teaspoons baking powder**
1	**cup milk**
½	**teaspoon vanilla**
2	**pounds ripe peaches (6 to 8)**
	Optional: 1 pint heavy cream, whipped

PREPARATION

Preheat oven to 375°.

1   Select a 9-x-13-inch pan and melt the butter in it; tilt the pan so the butter completely covers the bottom surface.

2   Measure all the dry ingredients into a bowl and stir the milk in slowly to keep the mixture smooth. Add the vanilla and pour the batter into the pan, directly over the butter. Spread the batter into an even layer.

3   Peel and slice the peaches and arrange the slices in rows on top of the batter. Place in the oven for 40 to 45 minutes or until the top is a deep golden brown.

TO SERVE

Serve warm, cutting into squares. If cream is passed with the peach bake, make sure the cream is quite cold.

COOKING AHEAD

As noted above, Cobbled Peach Bake is best served warm. If baked long in advance it can be covered with aluminum foil and reheated in a 350° oven for 10 minutes. If served cold, pass with whipped cream.

LOW-CHOLESTEROL VERSION

Substitute polyunsaturated margarine for the butter, and skimmed milk for whole milk; increase the vanilla to 1 teaspoon. Do not pass the optional whipped cream.

Apple cake mousse

This is as light and delicate a cake as anyone could hope to make in only 15 minutes. It requires no icing, which is a boon to cake lovers who are shying away from rich toppings. Although all the ingredients are simple, the refined, featherlight texture and luscious flavor of the cake belie its humble beginnings. Apple Cake Mousse looks best if baked in a springform pan, so it can show off its three distinct layers when uncorseted from the pan.

SERVES 10

WORKING TIME: *15 minutes*

BAKING TIME: *45 to 50 minutes*

INGREDIENTS

6   **tablespoons butter**
2   **cups graham cracker crumbs**
1   **teaspoon cinnamon**
3   **eggs, separated**
1   **tablespoon cornstarch**
1   **14-ounce can sweetened condensed milk**
3   **tablespoons lemon juice**
2   **cups (16 ounces) applesauce**
    pinch cream of tartar

PREPARATION

Preheat oven to 350°.

1   While melting 3 tablespoons of butter in a saucepan, pour the graham cracker crumbs into a mixing bowl and stir in the cinnamon. Pour the melted butter over the crumbs and stir until all the butter has been absorbed.

2   With 1 tablespoon of butter, heavily grease an 8-inch springform pan or a deep 10-inch layer cake pan. Pat in half the crumbs.

3   Separate the eggs, placing the yolks in one mixing bowl and the whites in another. Beat the cornstarch into the yolks, then stir in the condensed milk and lemon juice. Beat the batter until smooth. Finally, beat in the applesauce.

4   Add the cream of tartar to the egg whites and beat them until stiff. Fold half the beaten whites into the batter, then the remaining half. Pour the batter carefully into the pan, so as not to disturb the layer of crumbs. Smooth the top of the batter. Sprinkle the remaining crumbs over the top in a smooth layer; pat gently. Melt the remaining 2 tablespoons of butter and dribble over the crumbs.

5   Bake in the preheated oven for 45 to 50 minutes, or until a crack begins developing on top of the cake.

TO SERVE

If a springform pan was used, remove the ring that forms the sides and place the cake on a platter. If the cake was baked in a regular cake pan, cut and serve directly from the pan. Use a serrated cake or bread knife and cut in a gentle sawing motion.

COOKING AHEAD

Apple Cake Mousse can be made a day ahead but not before.

LOW-CHOLESTEROL VERSION

Substitute polyunsaturated margarine for the butter and increase the quantity to 5 tablespoons. Increase graham cracker crumbs to 2½ cups and place more than half the crumbs in the bottom of the cake pan. Use the following ingredients for the batter: ¾ cup flour, ¾ cup sugar, one 13-ounce can evaporated skimmed milk, 1 teaspoon vanilla, 2 cups (16 ounces) applesauce, 3 tablespoons lemon juice, pinch cream of tartar, 3 egg whites. Pour the flour into a mixing bowl, stir in the sugar and mix together thoroughly. Slowly pour in the milk, stirring to keep smooth. Add the lemon juice, vanilla, and the applesauce. Proceed as in step 4 above.

Honey cake

Just about everyone likes the flavor of honey, and in this luscious cake that flavor comes through emphatically. The oven time may seem a little long, but it is necessary to bake the cake completely. Occasionally, I like to underbake it by about 10 minutes so that the interior still has a moist texture. This is a rather rich cake that can be cut into thin slices to pass with fruit or ice cream desserts. I also feel that it's better not to ice the cake, letting the honey flavor shine by itself.

SERVES 12

WORKING TIME: *8 minutes*

COOLING TIME: *15 minutes*

BAKING TIME: *1 ½ hours*

INGREDIENTS

1	**cup honey**
10	**tablespoons butter (1 stick plus 2 tablespoons)**
3	**eggs**
2¼	**cups flour**
	pinch baking soda
	butter to grease pan
	aluminum foil

PREPARATION

Preheat oven to 350°.

1   Melt the honey and butter in a pot over low heat. Pour into a mixing bowl and set aside to cool.

2   Using an electric beater or whisk, beat the honey mixture a little, then add the eggs, one at a time, beating well between each addition.

3   Measure the flour and baking soda into a sifter and sift into the honey, ⅓ at a time. Beat well between each addition of flour, and when all is incorporated, beat well for 1 minute.

4   Grease and flour an 8-inch springform or regular cake pan. Pour in the batter, scraping all of it in. Place aluminum foil over the top of the cake pan and bake for 1 hour.

5   Remove the foil and bake for another 20 to 30 minutes or until the top is nicely browned and the cake pulls away from the sides of the pan. A toothpick plunged into the center should come out dry. Another test is to watch the ring of soft, slightly sunken batter in the center. As the cake bakes toward the center the moist area will disappear.

6   Cool for 10 minutes in the pan, then remove to a cake grill.

COOKING AHEAD

Honey Cake keeps very well, as long as 10 days in the refrigerator.

LOW-CHOLESTEROL VERSION

For the butter, substitute 12 tablespoons polyunsaturated margarine (1½ sticks); for the eggs, ¾ cup liquid egg substitute. Add 1 teaspoon vanilla to the cooled honey and butter.

Oatmeal ambrosia cake

This is a moist cake that comes gilded with its own coconut topping. No other icing is necessary. I've used it as a non-traditional birthday cake with great success.

SERVES 10

WORKING TIME: *14 minutes*

STANDING TIME: *20 minutes*

BAKING TIME: *40 to 45 minutes*

INGREDIENTS

1¼ cups boiling water

9 tablespoons butter (1 stick plus 1 tablespoon)

1 cup raw quick-cooking oatmeal

2 beaten eggs

1 cup white sugar

1 cup dark brown sugar

½ teaspoon salt

1 teaspoon baking soda

1 teaspoon baking powder

½ teaspoon nutmeg

1 teaspoon cinnamon

1½ cups flour

Topping

6 tablespoons butter (room temperature)

½ cup sugar

½ teaspoon vanilla

½ cup heavy cream

1 3½-ounce can Angel Flake Coconut

PREPARATION

Preheat oven to 375°.

1 Bring the water to a boil. Put 1 stick of butter and the oats in a mixing bowl and pour the boiling water over them. Stir for a few seconds and put the bowl aside for 20 minutes. Meanwhile grease an 8-by-12-inch cake pan with 1 tablespoon butter.

2 Add to the oatmeal the beaten eggs, white and brown sugars, salt, baking soda, baking powder, nutmeg, and cinnamon. Mix these ingredients together thoroughly and add the flour. Beat again and pour the batter into the prepared cake pan.

3 Bake for 40 to 45 minutes or until a toothpick plunged into the center comes out clean.

4 While the cake is baking, prepare the topping. In a small bowl cream together the butter and sugar. Beat in the vanilla and cream. Finally stir in the coconut.

5 Spread the topping on the cake as soon as it is removed from the oven. Put the cake under a preheated broiler for 1 or 2 minutes, or just until the butter melts and the coconut browns a bit.

COOKING AHEAD

This cake keeps well because of its moistness. Cover well.

LOW-CHOLESTEROL VERSION

In the cake batter use polyunsaturated margarine and ½ cup frozen egg substitute for the 2 eggs. Instead of the coconut topping make a pattern of Marrakesh Orange Slices (page 196) or spread with the Chocolate Icing (page 219), which is made with cocoa.

Tarte alhambra

This is a sweet dessert, the kind that especially appeals to people in hot Spanish-speaking countries, hence its name. However, a sweet tooth is not a prerequisite for enjoyment of its ambrosial medley of flavors and textures. It will be a popular dessert in any climate.

SERVES 8

WORKING TIME: *11 minutes*

COOKING TIME: *10 to 15 minutes*

COOLING TIME: *about 1 hour*

CHILLING TIME: *2 or more hours*

INGREDIENTS

2¼	**cups sugar**
1¼	**cups water**
2	**pounds peaches (6 to 8)**
2	**tablespoons dry white wine**
2	**tablespoons honey**
¼	**teaspoon cinnamon**
1	**tablespoon butter**
7	**tablespoons apple, quince, or apricot jelly (not jam)**
1	**cup ground pecans or walnuts, or a combination**
4-5	**½-inch slices of cake—sponge, angel food, white**
2	**tablespoons kirsch or other fruit liqueur**

PREPARATION

1 In a covered skillet boil the sugar and water together for about 10 minutes to make a light syrup. Rinse the peaches and add to the syrup, re-cover, and simmer for 10 to 15 minutes, or until the peaches are almost soft. The timing will depend on the ripeness of the fruit. Remove from fire and cool the peaches in the syrup.

2 Meanwhile, melt together in a small pot the wine, honey, cinnamon, butter, and 2 tablespoons of jelly. Put the nuts in a mixing bowl and pour this hot syrup over them. Stir until the nuts have absorbed all the syrup. (Do not wash the pot.)

3 Fit the cake slices in the bottom of a 9-inch pie plate, or any serving dish about 1½ inches deep. The bottom must be completely covered by the cake but the neatness of the slices does not matter at all. Press cake slightly with the palms of your hands. Spread the nuts over the cake in a smooth layer.

4 Lift the peaches out of the syrup and slip off their skins. Cut the peaches in half and place over the nuts, rounded side up.

5 Place 5 tablespoons of jelly and the liqueur in the previously used syrup pot and bring to a boil. Remove from the fire immediately, cool slightly, and dribble this syrup over the peaches. Chill well.

TO SERVE

Present the dessert in its dish. Cut wedges at the table and lift onto individual plates, making certain the spatula reaches beneath the cake.

COOKING AHEAD

Since the tarte must be chilled it can be made long before serving. It should not, however, be kept for a full day.

LOW-CHOLESTEROL VERSION

Substitute polyunsaturated margarine for the butter. No other changes in the recipe are necessary.

REMARKS

This syrup can be frozen and reused later when poaching any fruit.

Six-minute chocolate cake

This delicious, moist chocolate cake is so unorthodox that I've heard it referred to as crazy cake. Crazy like a fox. It is put together in a flash. There is not a single mixing bowl to wash since the cake is mixed right in the baking pan. Another crafty point is its low cost. No eggs, butter, cream, or expensive nuts and seasonings are called for. What is more, with no substitutions whatsoever, it also happens to be perfect for low-cholesterol diets. The addition of vinegar may, indeed, seem crazy, but it sharpens the flavor and makes it extra chocolaty.

SERVES 8 TO 10

WORKING TIME: 6 minutes

BAKING TIME: 25 minutes

INGREDIENTS

1	**cup sugar**
1½	**cups flour**
⅓	**cup cocoa**
1	**teaspoon baking soda**
½	**teaspoon salt**
2	**teaspoons vanilla**
½	**cup oil**
1	**cup cold water**
2	**tablespoons vinegar**

powdered sugar or Chocolate Icing (page 219)

PREPARATION

Preheat oven to 375°.

1 Select an 8 x 8 x 2-inch cake pan or a 9-inch round cake pan. Measure all the ingredients, except the vinegar, into the pan. Stir them well with a fork or wire whisk until they are thoroughly blended.

2 Add the vinegar and stir quickly to thoroughly blend in the vinegar, and immediately place in the hot oven. There must be no delay in baking after the vinegar is added.

3 Bake the cake for 20 to 25 minutes or until the center is slightly puffed and the sides begin to pull away from the pan. Cool. Sprinkle the top with powdered sugar before serving or spread with chocolate icing.

COOKING AHEAD

Six-minute Chocolate Cake is better if allowed to mellow for a day.

LOW-CHOLESTEROL VERSION

Use polyunsaturated oil; no substitutions are necessary.

Texas sheet cake

Here is an old-time favorite with a rich-ness that belies its easy preparation. This is a large cake that will beautifully an-swer the need for dessert at a party or even serve as a birthday cake for some-one with a chocolate sweet tooth. Texas Sheet Cake freezes perfectly and can even be eaten without defrosting, much like an ice-cream cake. Why Texas? Be-cause it's big, a really big cake.

SERVES 20

CAKE:

WORKING TIME: 10 minutes
BAKING TIME: 20 minutes

ICING:

WORKING TIME: 8 minutes
COOKING TIME: 4 minutes

INGREDIENTS

2   **sticks plus 2 tablespoons butter**
1   **cup water**
4   **tablespoons cocoa**
2   **cups granulated sugar**
2   **cups flour**
1   **teaspoon baking soda**
½   **cup sour cream**
2   **eggs, beaten**

PREPARATION

Preheat oven to 375°.

1   Select a heavy pot measuring 6 to 8 inches across the top. (This size will save work later when making the icing.) Put the 2 sticks of butter, water, and cocoa in the pot and bring to a boil.

2   Meanwhile use the remaining 2 table-spoons of butter to grease a cookie pan with edges approximately 16 x 11 inches. Measure into a mixing bowl the sugar, flour, and soda. Stir the dry ingredients a little.

3   When the mixture in the pot comes to a boil, immediately pour it into the dry ingre-dients. (Do not wash the pot.) Beat the batter well for about ½ minute. Stir in the sour cream, and finally beat in the eggs.

4   Pour the batter into the greased pan and spread into a smooth layer. Bake for about 20 minutes or until a toothpick plunged into the center comes out clean.

Note: The cake should be iced while it is still very warm; so have the icing ingredients assembled and ready to boil.

COOKING AHEAD

Texas Sheet Cake is moist and keeps very well. It can easily be made a day or two before serving. It also freezes well.

LOW-CHOLESTEROL VERSION

Use polyunsaturated margarine; increase flour quantity to 2¼ cups; add 1 teaspoon vanilla to the batter; substitute low-fat yogurt for the sour cream; use 3 egg whites, or ½ cup liquid egg substitute, instead of 2 whole eggs.

Chocolate icing

This icing makes Texas Sheet Cake wickedly chocolaty—pure ambrosia for chocolate lovers. However, the topping is so good and easy to do that it should also garnish white and yellow cakes. The icing itself should be warm and spread on the cake while it is still warm, so have the ingredients assembled and ready to boil. Recipe makes enough icing for 1 large sheet cake or icing and filling for a 9-inch double-layer cake.

WORKING TIME: 8 minutes

COOKING TIME: 4 minutes

INGREDIENTS

1   stick margarine (not butter)
6   tablespoons milk
4   tablespoons cocoa
1   teaspoon vanilla
1   pound confectioners' sugar
    Optional: 1 cup chopped walnuts or pecan

1   In a heavy pot measuring 6 to 8 inches across the top, melt together the margarine, milk, and cocoa. When it comes to a boil, add the vanilla.

2   Using an electric beater, beat the icing while pouring in the confectioners' sugar. When all the sugar has been incorporated, beat for a few seconds at high speed. Stir in the optional nuts.

3   Using a rubber spatula, spread the icing on the hot cake as soon as it is removed from the oven.

LOW-CHOLESTEROL VERSION

Use polyunsaturated margarine; no substitutions are necessary.

Sauce chocolat

This rich chocolate sauce was specifically designed to go with Meringue des Iles (page 200), but it also does wonders for vanilla or coffee ice cream, slices of fried sponge cake, and Poires Belle Hélène (poached pears with vanilla ice cream).

MAKES 2½ CUPS SAUCE

WORKING TIME: 3 minutes

COOKING TIME: 1 minute

INGREDIENTS

⅓   cup sugar
1   cup milk
3   tablespoons cocoa
4   tablespoons butter
1   teaspoon vanilla
2   tablespoons rum
1   tablespoon orange liqueur

PREPARATION

1   Put all the ingredients in a blender and blend for 1 minute. Pour the sauce into a small saucepan and bring it to a slow simmer. Simmer for 1 minute.

COOKING AHEAD

Chocolate sauce can be refrigerated for several days and reheated at serving time.

LOW-CHOLESTEROL VERSION

Substitute evaporated skimmed milk for the whole milk and 5 tablespoons of polyunsaturated margarine for the 4 tablespoons of butter. Add an extra ½ teaspoon of vanilla.

Piecrusts

Good piecrust does not come out of a box nor from the frozen food counter. It is made at home from scratch. Most cooks have their favorite recipes for piecrust, but I am giving three here for three different reasons. The French Sweet Pastry Dough is made in the traditional manner, which takes a good bit of time both to make and roll out. I include this particular recipe because it is very rich and extremely good —whenever you feel like splurging the time and the calories on it.

The other two recipes are made in an unorthodox way. They are not rolled out, but pressed into the pie dish and one even is made right in the dish. These two low-cholesterol doughs are more healthful and faster to make than conventional ones. Nevertheless, very few recipes in this book call for piecrust, because I have found that many weight-conscious people are avoiding it these days. Piecrust basically is a vehicle that carries other foods and, more and more, is being left on the plate.

French sweet pastry dough

This is the ultimate piecrust. It is rich, fragile, and delicious. It must have been specifically devised for open fruit tarts.

1 10-TO-11-INCH SHELL

WORKING TIME: 15 minutes

CHILLING TIME: 1 hour

INGREDIENTS

2   cups flour
½   teaspoon salt
⅓   cup sugar
8   tablespoons butter, room temperature
1   egg yolk
¼   teaspoon vanilla
¼   cup cold water

PREPARATION

1 Put the flour in a deep bowl, make a well in the center, and put in the salt, sugar, butter, egg yolk, vanilla, and 1 tablespoon of water. Mix with your fingertips, slowly incorporating the flour, working all together until it resembles coarse meal. Sprinkle on 2 more tablespoons of the water and assemble the pastry with your fingertips. This should be enough water, if not, sprinkle on a bit more. Add water sparingly, just enough to form the dough into a ball.

2 Put the dough on a floured pastry board and with the heel of your hand, push small sections of the dough away from you, pushing it about 6 inches. Reassemble the dough and repeat the process. This thoroughly blends the fat and flour together. Re-form the dough into a smooth ball, cover with waxed paper, and refrigerate for at least an hour. It can be kept 1 or 2 days in the refrigerator, but in that case, wrap the waxed paper in plastic. Because of the egg yolk in the dough, it should be frozen if it is to be kept longer than 2 days.

3 Flour well the pastry board, rolling pin, and the dough itself. The dough is rich and will break easily. Roll the dough to the size of the pie dish. Wrap the rolled dough loosely around the rolling pin to transfer it to a lightly greased tart pan. Trim and flute the edges.

4 To bake a blind shell: prick the bottom of the crust with a sharp knife. Place parchment paper or lightweight foil on the dough and weight it with either uncooked beans, a slightly smaller pie pan, or a soufflé dish. This will prevent the pastry from buckling. Place in a 400° oven for 2 or 3 minutes, or until the dough seems to whiten a little. Reduce the heat to 375° and bake for about 15 minutes or until the crust is nicely browned.

Low-cholesterol rolled pie-crust

This piecrust recipe can be prebaked as a pie shell since it is rolled. It needs no chilling, as the previous recipe does, so it can be stirred together and be ready at a moment's notice.

8- OR 9-INCH DOUBLE CRUST

WORKING TIME:

4 minutes for single crust
6 minutes for double crust

INGREDIENTS

2 **cups flour**
1½ **teaspoons salt**
¼ **cup cold skimmed milk**
½ **cup polyunsaturated oil**

PREPARATION

1 Sift the flour and salt into a mixing bowl. Pour the milk and oil into a cup, but do not stir. Add the liquid all at once to the flour and stir lightly with a fork. Form the dough into a ball, divide in half, and flatten each portion slightly.

2 Dampen the working surface and place on it a 12-inch square of waxed paper. (The water keeps the paper from slipping.) Put one portion of the pastry on the waxed paper and cover with another 12-inch square of waxed paper. Roll the pastry. When the dough reaches the edges of the paper it is the right thickness for the piecrust.

3 Peel off the top sheet of paper, fit the dough, paper side up, into the pie plate. Peel off the other sheet of paper. Fill the pie and repeat with the other portion of dough, fitting it over the filling. Trim and flute the edges.

Low-cholesterol stir-and-bake piecrust

This pastry will not have the smooth texture or yellowish color that most do. In fact, it will appear slightly lumpy and somewhat gray. Never mind, it all bakes out beautifully.

1 9-INCH PIECRUST

WORKING TIME: *6 minutes*

CHILLING TIME: *30 minutes*

INGREDIENTS

2 **cups flour**
1 **teaspoon salt**
1½ **teaspoons sugar**
½ **cup polyunsaturated oil**
¼ **cup water**

PREPARATION

1 Place a sifter in a pie pan and sift the dry ingredients directly into the pan.

2 Mix the oil and water in a small bowl and slowly pour over the dry ingredients, stirring with a fork as you do. When all the flour has been dampened, beat it a few seconds with the fork.

3 Press the pastry to line the bottom and sides of the pan. Chill for at least 30 minutes, then push the firm dough further up the sides and make a fluted top by pinching the dough between thumbs and index fingers. The crust can be chilled again, or baked immediately.

SAUCES

The sauces in this section are not meant to be used only with specific recipes that they accompany in this book. They are good enough to perk up any number of dishes, both fresh and leftover. The sauces described with various dishes throughout the book are equally flexible. The Champagne Sauce that garnishes broiled oysters would do wonders (hot or cold) for many fish and vegetable dishes, such as crab, sole, asparagus, or broccoli. Leftover vegetable marinades should be saved and used to dress up salads and other cold vegetables. The Hot Curry Sauce served with cold tomatoes adds an exotic touch to poached eggs. The Cucumber Sauce spooned over poached salmon would be equally appreciated with other fish or even grilled ham steak. Be adventurous with these sauces. The few minutes it takes to stir them together will reward you with a whole new dimension when added to food. No sauce out of a bottle can promise that, no matter how much it costs.

Quick tomato coulis

In an earlier cookbook I gave the recipe for the best tomato sauce I know, Coulis de Tomates. Every August, when fresh tomatoes are at their best, I spend long hours making this thick Provençal tomato sauce and freezing it in small containers. Inevitably, the coulis is all used up long before the next August. Since a superior sauce cannot be made with inferior supermarket tomatoes, I experimented with canned Italian plum tomatoes. The result, I think, comes awfully close to the flavor and consistency of the traditional coulis. This easier version seems to have a natural affinity for egg dishes. Try it also with meat loaf; mixed with string beans; on fried ham, veal, beef, chicken, or pork; yes, even on spaghetti.

MAKES 2 CUPS SAUCE

WORKING TIME: 8 minutes

COOKING TIME: 30 minutes

INGREDIENTS

- **1   2-pound 3-ounce can Italian plum tomatoes**
- **2   tablespoons pure olive oil**
- **½   cup chopped onions**
- **2   garlic cloves, mashed**
- **1   small piece orange rind, about 1 by 1½ inches**
- **1   bay leaf**
- **½   teaspoon fennel seeds**
- **½   teaspoon basil**
- **½   teaspoon coriander**
- **piece of fresh celery, about 6 inches long**
- **pinch saffron**
- **1   teaspoon salt**
- **pepper**
- **2   tablespoons tomato paste**
- **¼   cup dry white wine**

PREPARATION

1   Drain the tomatoes, reserving the juice to use in stews and soups but discarding the basil leaf. Chop the tomato pulp coarsely and put in a small sauce pot.

2   Add all the remaining ingredients, cover, and simmer for 30 minutes. Discard the bay leaf, orange rind, and celery.

COOKING AHEAD

The sauce can be used at once or stored in the refrigerator for 3 or 4 days. It also freezes perfectly.

LOW-CHOLESTEROL VERSION

Use polyunsaturated oil instead of olive oil; add 2 bay leaves instead of 1 and increase basil to 1 teaspoon.

Blender mayonnaise

The busy cook and the not-so-busy cook usually buy prepared mayonnaise to save time. Another reason is that homemade mayonnaise has an undeserved reputation of being temperamental. Visions of oil separating from egg yolks have long deterred otherwise adventurous cooks. There is no mystery about making successful mayonnaise. If all ingredients are at room temperature, failure is just about impossible. Now that a blender can do the work for you there is no reason not to enjoy the mellow flavor of economical, freshly made mayonnaise. This recipe gives added stabilizing insurance with a little trick at the end.

MAKES ABOUT 1¼ CUPS SAUCE

WORKING TIME: 4 minutes

INGREDIENTS

1   **whole egg**

½   **teaspoon prepared mustard**

½   **teaspoon salt**

⅛   **teaspoon white pepper**

1   **cup oil**

1   **tablespoon lemon juice or vinegar (or a combination)**

PREPARATION

1   Have all ingredients at room temperature. This is critical. Put the egg, mustard, salt, and pepper in a blender and run at low speed for ½ minute. While the blender is running, slowly add the oil in a thin stream. Increase the speed of the blender as the mayonnaise thickens.

2   Put the vinegar or lemon juice in a metal spoon and hold it over a flame or hot electric grid to heat the liquid almost to the boiling point. Add the hot vinegar to the mayonnaise and blend again at high speed until it is mixed into the mayonnaise. Taste for seasonings and correct if necessary, again blending after any addition. Scrape into a container with a tight-fitting cover and refrigerate.

COOKING AHEAD

Made according to the above directions, mayonnaise will keep for at least a week.

LOW-CHOLESTEROL VERSION

By using polyunsaturated oil in the above recipe, this mayonnaise is a completely acceptable dressing for low-cholesterol diets. Blender mayonnaise uses a whole egg instead of the 2 egg yolks specified in most other methods. The large quantity of beneficial polyunsaturated oil that is forced into the egg dilutes the effect of the yolk. Furthermore, mayonnaise is used in such small quantities per serving that the actual amount of egg yolk eaten is negligible.

Basil mayonnaise

By adding a few judiciously chosen herbs to mayonnaise you can create a new dressing for cold dishes and salads. This one is especially good with fish, but also can turn cold leftover vegetables into an imaginative luncheon salad.

MAKES 1¼ CUPS SAUCE

WORKING TIME: 5 minutes

INGREDIENTS

2	tablespoons oil
1	teaspoon basil
½	teaspoon tarragon
½	teaspoon Worcestershire sauce
	juice ½ lemon
1	cup mayonnaise (see preceding recipe)

PREPARATION

1 Place all the ingredients, except the mayonnaise, in the blender and purée to a smooth paste.

2 Spoon the mayonnaise into a small bowl, then add the herb paste, beating with a wire whisk. If possible, let the sauce rest for 1 hour so flavors will blend completely.

COOKING AHEAD

Herb mayonnaise will keep for days in the refrigerator.

LOW-CHOLESTEROL VERSION

Use polyunsaturated oil; if following a very strict diet, use a low-cholesterol mayonnaise.

Sauce moutarde

This is a mellow mustard sauce that still has some snap to it. It is delicious served hot or cold.

MAKES ¾ CUP SAUCE

WORKING TIME: 2 minutes

COOKING TIME: 3 minutes

INGREDIENTS

1	teaspoon salt
2	tablespoons sugar
⅛	teaspoon pepper
2	teaspoons dry mustard
1	teaspoon cornstarch
1	egg
½	cup water
¼	cup vinegar

PREPARATION

1 In a small pot combine all the dry ingredients. Beat the egg and stir it into the ingredients in the pot; then stir in the water and vinegar.

2 Cook over medium heat, stirring often, until the sauce thickens; this will take about 3 minutes.

COOKING AHEAD

This mustard sauce will keep for a week or more in the refrigerator.

LOW-CHOLESTEROL VERSION

Substitute ½ cup liquid egg substitute for the whole egg.

Salsa verde

In Italy this sauce traditionally is served with hot Bolliti Misti (mixed boiled meats). It can also add its spicy touch to Pot-au-Feu (p.108). You'll find that Salsa Verde is an inspired way to liven up cold meats as well. I've used it on cold boiled potatoes, too. Don't laugh until you try it.

MAKES ABOUT ⅓ CUP

WORKING TIME: *7 minutes*

INGREDIENTS

¼   cup olive oil

    juice of 1 lemon

1   chopped shallot, or 2 scallions

1   garlic clove, sliced

4   anchovy fillets, chopped

2   tablespoons drained capers

½   teaspoon tarragon

¼   cup parsley leaves

PREPARATION

1   Put all ingredients in a blender and process until smooth. This is not a timid sauce, so only a little should be used at a time.

COOKING AHEAD

This sauce keeps very well in the refrigerator. It could easily be made a week before serving.

LOW-CHOLESTEROL VERSION

Substitute polyunsaturated oil for olive oil; no other changes in the recipe are necessary.

Toasted oregano

This is not a sauce, but a flavoring. When toasted, oregano develops a spicy and nutty taste. Toasted oregano should not be used indiscriminately, but sprinkled in discreet amounts to heighten prepared dishes. Try it especially on chicken, pork, grilled tomatoes, broccoli, and potatoes. Make a generous amount of it at a time and keep a tightly covered jar of the cooked herb handy next to the salt and pepper.

WORKING TIME: *1 to 2 minutes*

COOKING TIME: *1 to 2 minutes*

INGREDIENT

dried oregano

PREPARATION

1   Pour the oregano into a small skillet and put it over medium heat. Shake the skillet and stir the dried herb to prevent it from scorching. If burnt the oregano will develop a bitter taste. Crush the toasted oregano to a powder between your fingers.

HORS D'OEUVRES

Admittedly this is not a long chapter, even though many cookbooks provide a lavish array of hors d'oeuvres recipes. But I don't believe in hors d'oeuvres very much, and that is why I've spent little time in working out special recipes. At one time I used to put in as much time preparing the predinner snacks as I did on the meal itself. But guests ate so many snacks that their appetites were curbed long before they reached the dining room.

Now I serve mostly light things with cocktails —raw vegetable strips, nuts, thin pretzels, sometimes a dip. I'm also partial to the thin crisp Japanese crackers that now are available just about everywhere.

For those who like more substantial fare at the cocktail hour, recipes can be borrowed from other chapters in this book. Some good possibilities include Wine-marinated Mushrooms, Eggplant Caviar, and Italian Artichokes. Swiss Fondue makes a warming and convivial accompaniment to drinks, but since it is rich, I suggest it for cocktail parties and not before dinner. Then there are Marinated Oysters or small slices of Chicken and Ham Pâté on thin toast. They're all in the book for people who don't feel as I do that food with predinner drinks should be fairly Spartan.

Pimento spread

Since this Pimento Spread will keep for about a week in the refrigerator, it's a handy item to have ready to spread on crackers or melba toasts for last-minute cocktail snacks. It can also be used to liven many vegetables: stir a few table-spoons of the spread into hot cooked peas or lima beans.

MAKES 1 CUP OF SPREAD

WORKING TIME: *2 minutes*

INGREDIENTS

3   **ounces chopped pimento with juice**

1   **tablespoon cream**

½   **teaspoon Worcestershire sauce**

   dash Tabasco

   salt and pepper

4   **ounces cream cheese**

PREPARATION

1   Put into a blender the chopped pimento with the juice and the cream. Blend to purée the pimento. Add the Worcestershire sauce, Tabasco, salt, and pepper. Blend again.

2   Keep the blender running while adding chunks of the cream cheese until it is all blended in. Give a final spurt of high speed. Scrape the spread from the blender into a con-tainer, cover tightly, and refrigerate until needed.

TO SERVE

Spread on melba rounds or other plain crack-ers. Will make about 50 cocktail snacks.

COOKING AHEAD

Pimento Spread can be made long before it is needed, as much as a week, and kept refrigerated.

Pimento sandwich snacks

MAKES 36

WORKING TIME: *9 minutes*

INGREDIENTS

16   **slices thin-sliced white bread, untoasted**

1   **cup Pimento Spread**

   Optional: chopped parsley

PREPARATION

1   Arrange the bread in stacks of 4 slices each. Cut away the crusts from the bread. Spread 3 slices of bread with the Pimento Spread and stack. Cover with the last slice of plain bread. Wipe away any spread that may have oozed out between the slices. If there is time, wrap the bread stacks tightly in plastic wrap and refrigerate for about 1 hour. Chilling helps make the bread slice neatly.

TO SERVE

Remove the plastic wrap and cut each stack of bread into squares or rectangles, no more than 1 inch wide. A good size is arrived at by cut-ting the bread into thirds, first lengthwise, then crosswise. Optional garnish: Dip one side of each sandwich snack into the chopped parsley.

Blue cheese mold

If a cocktail snack is going to hold its own against all the talk and drinks, it should have a pretty strong personality. Not so strong as to stun the palate before dinner, but enough to tantalize the taste buds. Judiciously used, blue cheese can do just that. Cream cheese adds a civilizing note and smoothness to the granular, powerfully flavored cheese. The resulting pale green color creates a pretty platter image. In every respect this is an estimable cocktail food that, at other times, can be served as an unusual first course at the table.

SERVES 16 AS APPETIZER; 6 AS FIRST COURSE

WORKING TIME: 8 minutes

CHILLING TIME: 3 hours

INGREDIENTS

1	**tablespoon gelatin**
¼	**cup cold water**
½	**cup heavy cream**
1	**teaspoon brandy**
½	**teaspoon Worcestershire sauce**
	salt and pepper
6	**ounces blue cheese**
6	**ounces cream cheese**
2	**tablespoons chopped chives or scallion greens**

PREPARATION

1 Sprinkle the gelatin on the water in a small pot and let it stand a few minutes to soften. Put on heat to dissolve the gelatin. When the liquid turns clear, remove from heat and cool slightly.

2 In a blender put the gelatin liquid, cream, brandy, Worcestershire sauce, pepper, and just a pinch of salt. (The blue cheese is already quite salty.) Blend for a few seconds.

3 Add half the blue cheese and blend. Repeat with the other half. Then add the cream cheese in two parts, blending between each addition. Stir in the chives.

4 Pour into a 3-cup mold of any shape—oblong, round, or ring. Chill for at least 3 hours or until the mixture is firmly set.

TO SERVE

Cut around edges with a hot knife, then dip bottom of the mold in hot water for a few seconds. Unmold onto a bed of crisp lettuce. Pass with melba toast or crackers. As first course, decorate the mold with sliced pimento-stuffed olives and slice it at the table. Pass thin toast or melba toast.

COOKING AHEAD

The Blue Cheese Mold can be made 2 or 3 days in advance and unmolded several hours before being served if kept refrigerated.

Cheese mousse

The lavish flavor of this mousse completely belies its 4-minute preparation time. It can be a beautiful beginning to a meal, jelled in individual ramekins and unmolded on a piece of crisp lettuce. A few black olives alongside the creamy mousse make a nice contrast in color and texture. This recipe can also be used to upgrade the cocktail hour—jell in a small loaf or round dish, unmold, and serve with crackers. Don't overdo the garlic; it doesn't get cooked and its flavor can be quite pronounced if the garlic is used with a heavy hand. It should be there in the taste, but just as a hint.

SERVES 18 AS HORS D'OEUVRES;

8 AS FIRST COURSE

WORKING TIME: 4 minutes

COOLING TIME: 15 minutes

CHILLING TIME: 3 hours

INGREDIENTS

1½   **cups beef broth**

2   **tablespoons gelatin**

1   **garlic clove, sliced**

¼   **teaspoon curry**

    salt and pepper

12   **ounces cream cheese**

PREPARATION

1   Pour broth into a small pot, sprinkle on the gelatin, and let stand a few minutes to soften gelatin. Put on heat and bring almost to a boil, stirring a few times to dissolve the gelatin completely. Remove from fire and let cool.

2   Pour cooled broth into a blender. Add the garlic, curry, salt, and pepper. Blend for ½ minute.

3   Add about a third of the cream cheese at a time while the blender is running. When all the cheese is incorporated, give mixture one final burst of high speed.

4   Pour into a 3-cup mold or into 8 individual ramekins or custard cups. Refrigerate for about 3 hours or until mousse is set.

TO SERVE

Cut around edges with a hot knife, then dip bottom of mold in hot water for a few seconds. Unmold onto lettuce and decorate with a few black olives. Pass toast or crackers with mousse.

COOKING AHEAD

Obviously this mousse must be prepared a few hours in advance, but I have found it is better still if made at least a day ahead. The flavors marry better. And it lasts a week or more.

LOW CHOLESTEROL VERSION

To cut down on cholesterol and fat content in this recipe, substitute low-fat cream cheese (Neufchâtel) which has 30 percent less fat than regular cream cheese.

Hot mushroom canapés

The dome-shaped mushroom is one of the most versatile vegetables we have. We eat them raw in salads, stuff them, mince them, sauté them, bake them, even deep fry them. But there is always at least one more way to enjoy them: Make a purée of the pale morsels to use on tiny toast rounds for the cocktail hour. The delicate purée is also interesting for an unusual first course at dinner. In this case a whole slice of toast would be used. The plate could be garnished with a broiled slice of tomato for color contrast. It pays to make an ample quantity, since the purée freezes perfectly. Though I feel these canapés are best served hot, many friends like them just as much cold.

MAKES 1½ CUPS PURÉE,
ABOUT 72 CANAPÉS, OR 12 TOAST SLICES
WORKING TIME: *8 minutes*
COOKING TIME: *5 minutes*

INGREDIENTS

½   **pound mushrooms**
8   **tablespoons butter (1 stick)**
    good pinch nutmeg
    salt and pepper
1   **tablespoon lemon juice**
6   **tablespoons grated Parmesan cheese**

PREPARATION

1   Rinse the mushrooms under running water while melting 4 tablespoons of butter in a skillet. Add the mushrooms to the skillet. Sprinkle them with nutmeg, salt, pepper, and lemon juice. Cover and simmer for 5 minutes.

2   Spoon the cooked mushrooms and juice into a blender. Put the remaining 4 tablespoons of butter in the skillet to melt. Add the melted butter to the mushrooms in the blender. Purée.

3   Add the cheese and purée again. Scrape into a covered container and chill for at least 1 hour.

TO SERVE

Spread on toast (1 teaspoon for canapé size, 2 tablespoons for first-course size) and broil in oven for about 2 minutes or until the mushroom purée bubbles.

COOKING AHEAD

Mushroom purée can be made several days before needed and kept refrigerated. It also freezes perfectly. The toast, however, should not be spread with the purée more than an hour before being broiled. If it stands too long, the toast will become limp.

Tuna spread

A can of tuna on the shelf can be one of the handiest items in the kitchen. It will save (and stretch) everything from gratin and creamed dishes to casseroles and croquettes. Here it is presented for the cocktail hour. The spread comes snugly contained in a small bowl or crock, sparingly decorated and surrounded by crackers. It could also serve as a luncheon dish, along with a salad of mixed cooked vegetables. The same idea, scaled down in quantity, would be a light way to begin an evening meal.

SERVES 12 AS HORS D'OEUVRES; 6 AS FIRST COURSE
WORKING TIME: *12 minutes*
CHILLING TIME: *3 hours*

INGREDIENTS

1   **6½-ounce can tuna packed in oil**
1   **cup sour cream**
    juice ½ lemon
¼   **teaspoon soy sauce**
½   **teaspoon brandy**
    few drops Tabasco
    salt and pepper
2   **teaspoons chopped capers**
1   **tablespoon chopped parsley**
3   **tablespoons butter, melted**
    Optional Garnish: 1 pimento-stuffed
    green olive and a parsley sprig

1 Open the tuna can, leaving the lid attached at one point. Hold the can upside down over the sink, pressing the lid against the tuna to extract as much oil as possible. Leave the can on the counter, still upside down, to continue draining.

2 Put the sour cream in a mixing bowl. Add the lemon juice, soy sauce, brandy, Tabasco, salt, and pepper. Beat with a wire whisk until light and fluffy.

3 Place a rotary food mill over the mixing bowl and force the tuna through the food mill. Add the capers, chopped parsley, and melted butter. Stir.

4 Scoop the spread into a 2-cup crock or mold. Cover and chill for at least 3 hours. Overnight is better.

TO SERVE

Leave the tuna spread in the mold. For the optional decoration, slice the stuffed green olive into 5 or 6 slices, arrange in a shallow circle on the tuna with a parsley sprig in the center. Place the crock on a dish and surround with crackers or melba toast.

COOKING AHEAD

As noted in step 4, the spread is better if made in advance. It even can be made a day or two before serving. Decorate when ready to serve.

LOW-CHOLESTEROL VERSION

Substitute low-fat plain yogurt for the sour cream and ¼ cup polyunsaturated margarine for 3 tablespoons butter. Increase the soy sauce to ½ teaspoon and the capers to 1 tablespoon.

Honeyed walnuts

Pass these honeyed walnuts when pouring port or sherry —an irresistible combination. With after-dinner coffee they also are much more of a novelty than the usual mints.

MAKES 3 CUPS

SERVES APPROXIMATELY 12

WORKING TIME: *6 minutes*

BOILING TIME: *approximately 5 minutes*

COOLING TIME: *1 hour*

INGREDIENTS

1½ **cups sugar**

½ **teaspoon salt**

¼ **cup honey**

½ **cup water**

1 **teaspoon vanilla**

3 **cups walnut halves**

PREPARATION

1 In a 2-quart saucepan boil together the sugar, salt, honey, and water to a firm-soft stage (250° on a candy thermometer). This takes approximately 5 minutes. Have ready a wooden, lucite, or marble slab, or place a sheet of waxed paper on a counter top or baking sheet.

2 As soon as syrup is ready, remove from heat, add the vanilla and nuts. Mix all together thoroughly, but quickly. Turn onto the waxed paper. With a spatula smooth the nuts into one layer. Cool for at least 1 hour.

3 Break coated nuts apart, or cut them apart with a knife. Keep nuts loosely covered, but not in an airtight container.

COOKING AHEAD

Honeyed Walnuts will stay crisp for weeks if kept loosely covered.

LOW-CHOLESTEROL VERSION

No changes in the recipe are necessary.

INDEX

Kidney Bean Purée, 176; in menu, 6

103; in menu, 6
Pâté, Mixed, in Aspic, 131
with Tuna Sauce, 104; in menu, 6
wines with, 6, 86, 102
vegetables, 137–77
soups, 15–17, 20–26
wines with, 4, 5, 10, 28
See also herbs; salads, and individual
vegetables
Virginia's Chinese Mushrooms, 50; in menu, 7
Vitello Tonnato, 104; in menu, 6
Volaille, Mousse de Foies de, 96
Volaille, Terrine de Foies de, 95

Walnuts, Honeyed, 235
Waterford Cucumbers, 146
Wilted Salad, 46; in menu, 9, 10
Wine-Marinated Mushrooms, 45
wines, 2–8
with brunch, 4
with cheese, 4–6, 8, 11, 28, 52
with desserts, 184
with dinners, 5–11
with eggs, 4–6, 28
with entrées, 28
with fish, 4–6, 8, 9, 11, 62
with lunch, 4–5, 52
with meat, 5–11, 102
with poultry, 6–9, 11, 86
with seafood, 5–7, 9, 10, 28, 62
serving temperatures, 3
with soups, 24
with supper, 4–5
with vegetables, 4, 5, 10, 28

Zucchini
Marinated, 42–43; in menu, 7, 11
Quick-Fry, 174–75
Sauté, 174